DATE DUE

DEMCO 38-296

THE 2000 ANNUAL: Volume 1 Training

(The Thirty-Fourth Annual)

Jossey-Bass
Pfeiffer

THE 2000 ANNUAL: Volume 1 Training

(The Thirty-Fourth Annual)

Edited by Elaine Biech

Jossey-Bass
Pfeiffer

San Francisco

Published by

Jossey-Bass
Pfeiffer

350 Sansome Street, 5th Floor
San Francisco, California 94104-1342
(415) 433-1740; Fax (415) 433-0499
(800) 274-4434; Fax (800) 569-0443

www.pfeiffer.com

Acquiring Editor: Matthew Holt
Director of Development: Kathleen Dolan Davies
Editor: Rebecca Taff
Senior Production Editor: Dawn Kilgore
Senior Manufacturing Supervisor: Becky Carreño

Printing 10   9   8   7   6   5   4   3   2   1

PREFACE

Welcome to the *2000 Annual: Volume 1, Training*. This year represents the twenty-ninth year the *Annuals* have been published, the sixth that they have been published as a set of two: Volume 1, Training and Volume 2, Consulting. The materials in the training volume focus on skill building and knowledge enhancement, as well as on the professional development of trainers. The materials in the consulting volume focus on intervention techniques and organizational systems, as well as on the professional development of consultants. The performance-improvement technologist, whose role is one of combined trainer and consultant, will find valuable resources in both volumes.

As we begin our trek into the 21st Century and all that it promises for us, it is natural to look back to see where the profession has been as well as forward to where it is going. The two volumes this year are representative of both. We all remember fifteen years ago or so when some leaders in our profession were predicting the end of the training profession. It was thought that most learning would occur via the computer and that imprecise measures of the ROI of training would be discouraging to organizations. To the contrary, computers seem to have increased the need for training. In addition, the need for training professionals has grown as companies everywhere recognize the value of training. Yes, training has changed. The performance-improvement technologist has been added to the list of professions, more companies are outsourcing their training, the profession has expanded to the executive suite, we are using web-based training, the "learning organization" has been added to our jargon, and many other things have developed. Training is alive and well.

The same can be said of the consulting field. The number of consultants is growing by 20 percent each year. Certainly traditional consultants abound, including management development consultants and organizational development consultants. In addition, many consultants specialize in areas that did not exist ten years ago. We have web-page design consultants, diversity consultants, environmental consultants, executive coaches, and those who focus on spirituality in the workplace. It's been said that all of us will spend a portion of our careers as consultants—even if for just a short time.

Whether you are a trainer or a consultant, or a bit of both, the *2000 Annuals* will be your companions as you begin your HRD journey into the new century. Experiential learning activities in these volumes range from the basic topic of learning transfer to the high-tech topic of computer communication. Instruments measure a wide variety of issues important to individuals, teams, and organizations: attitudes toward sexual harassment, aptitude for mentoring, performance of teams, and an organization's ability to adapt to the future. Articles address age-old topics such as decision making and strategic planning and also address cutting-edge topics such as spirituality in the workplace and web-based training. You will also be challenged to use improvisational theater games as a training technique and aligning teams with the organization's values as a consulting process.

Both volumes provide a broad spectrum of material. We have tried to balance the basics you've come to us for in the past with the mind-stretching cutting-edge ideas you'll need in the future.

One aspect of the *Annuals* that will never change is the way in which they continue to contribute toward your professional competence. You will find experiential learning activities, instruments, and articles that you may use to develop workshops and seminars for many or use for mentoring and coaching one-on-one. We want you to use everything you find in the *Annuals,* and we want to make it easy for you to use them. All of the materials in the *Annuals* are yours to duplicate for educational and training purposes. You may also adapt and modify the materials to meet your audience's needs. Please ensure that the credit statement found on the copyright page is included on all copies you make. If the materials are to be reproduced in publications for sale or are intended for large-scale distribution (more than one hundred copies in twelve months), *prior written permission is required.* Reproduction of material that is copyrighted by another source (as indicated in a footnote) requires written permission from the designated copyright holder. Please call us if you have questions. We believe our liberal copyright policy makes it easier for you to do your job.

All this is possible due to professionals in the HRD field like you. It is our contributing authors—your colleagues—who, through their work as trainers, consultants, facilitators, educators, and performance-improvement technologists, have experimented with and perfected new material in real-life settings with actual participants and clients. They have contributed activities, techniques, models, instruments, theories, and methods that they have developed and used to meet real-world needs. This is your reassurance that the activities produce results, the instruments measure what they claim to measure, and the articles have given value to others prior to publication.

We would like to invite you to submit materials to be considered for publication in the *Annuals.* At your request we will provide a copy of the guidelines for preparing your material. We are interested in receiving experiential learning activities (based on the five stages of the experiential learning cycle: experiencing, publishing, processing, generalizing, and applying); inventories, questionnaires, and surveys; and presentation and discussion resources (articles that include theory related to practical application). Contact the Jossey-Bass/Pfeiffer Editorial Department at the address listed on the copyright page and we will send you our guidelines for contributors. In addition, we welcome your comments, ideas, and questions. You may contact me through Jossey-Bass, or e-mail me directly at *ebbiech@aol.com*.

Thank you to the dedicated people at Jossey-Bass/Pfeiffer who produced the 2000 *Annuals:* Arlette Ballew, Laurel Bergman, Jamie Corcoran, Kathleen Dolan Davies, Matthew Holt, Ocean Howell, Jan Hunter, Dawn Kilgore, Carol Nolde, Susan Rachmeler, and Rebecca Taff. Thanks also to Beth Drake of ebb associates inc, whose patience and persistence ensures that we make all the impossible deadlines. And, most importantly, thank you to our authors, who represent the rich variety in the fields of training and consulting. In-house practitioners, consultants, and academically-based professionals have shared the best of their work so that other professionals may benefit. Your generosity contributes to professional development for many of us.

Elaine Biech
Editor
August 1999

About Jossey-Bass/Pfeiffer

Jossey-Bass/Pfeiffer is actively engaged in publishing insightful human resource development (HRD) materials. The organization has earned an international reputation as the leading source of practical resources that are immediately useful to today's consultants, trainers, facilitators, and managers in a variety of industries. All materials are designed by practicing professionals who are continually experimenting with new techniques. Thus, readers and users benefit from the fresh and thoughtful approach that underlies Jossey-Bass/Pfeiffer's experientially based materials, books, workbooks, instruments, and other learning resources and programs. This broad range of products is designed to help human resource practitioners increase individual, group, and organizational effectiveness and provide a variety of training and intervention technologies, as well as background in the field.

CONTENTS

---

*See Experiential Learning Activities Categories, p. 6, for an explanation of the numbering system.

**Topic is "cutting edge."

GENERAL INTRODUCTION
TO THE 2000 ANNUAL

The 2000 Annual: Volume 1, Training is the thirty-fourth volume in the *Annual* series, a collection of practical and useful materials for professionals in the broad area described as human resource development (HRD). The materials are written by and for professionals, including trainers, organization-development and organizational-effectiveness consultants, performance-improvement technologists, educators, instructional designers, and others.

Each *Annual* has three main sections: *experiential learning activities; inventories, questionnaires, and surveys;* and *presentation and discussion resources.* Each published submission is classified in one of the following categories: Individual Development, Communication, Problem Solving, Groups, Teams, Consulting and Facilitating, Leadership, and Organizations. Within each category, pieces are further classified into logical subcategories, which are identified in the introductions to the three sections.

The last category, Organizations, first appeared in the 1999 *Annual.* This addition reflects the changing nature of the field, as professionals take on more and more responsibilities in their organizations or as consulting professionals to organizations. The more widely accepted role of performance-improvement technologist brings with it more broadly defined responsibilities, often more "organizational" in nature. In addition, after four years of publishing a separate consulting volume, the need to incorporate the broader Organization category in the *Annual* series became self-evident. We encourage you to broaden your perspective to include this category as you consider submitting material for future *Annuals.*

A new subcategory, "Technology," was also added last year. Much has changed for the HRD professional in recent years, and technology has led much of that change. Given the important role technology plays, we will continue to publish material that relates technology to the HRD field and how the HRD professional can use technology as a tool.

Another addition, beginning in 1999, is the identification of "cutting edge" topics. This designation highlights topics that present information, concepts, tools, or perspectives that may be recent additions to the profession or that have not previously appeared in the *Annual.*

The series continues to provide an opportunity for HRD professionals who wish to share their experiences, their viewpoints, and their processes with their colleagues. To that end, Jossey-Bass/Pfeiffer publishes guidelines for potential authors. These guidelines are available from the Pfeiffer Editorial Department at Jossey-Bass Inc., Publishers, in San Francisco, California.

Materials are selected for the *Annuals* based on the quality of the ideas, applicability to real-world concerns, relevance to current HRD issues, clarity of presentation, and ability to enhance our readers' professional development. In addition, we choose experiential learning activities that will create a high degree of enthusiasm among the participants and add enjoyment to the learning process. As in the past several years, the contents of each *Annual* span a wide range of subject matter, reflecting the range of interests of our readers.

Our contributor list includes a wide selection of experts in the field: in-house practitioners, consultants, and academically-based professionals. A list of contributors to the *Annual* can be found at the end of the volume, including their names, affiliations, addresses, telephone numbers, facsimile numbers, and e-mail addresses. Readers will find this list useful if they wish to locate the authors of specific pieces for feedback, comments, or questions. Further information is presented in a brief biographical sketch of each contributor that appears at the conclusion of each article. We publish this information to encourage "networking," which continues to be a valuable mainstay in the field of human resource development.

We are pleased with the high quality of material that is submitted for publication each year and often regret that we have page limitations. In addition, just as we cannot publish every manuscript we receive, you may find that not all published works are equally useful to you. Therefore, we encourage and invite ideas, materials, and suggestions that will help us to make subsequent *Annuals* as useful as possible to all of our readers.

Introduction
to the Experiential Learning Activities Section

Experiential learning activities ensure that lasting learning occurs. They should be selected with a specific learning objective in mind. These objectives are based on the participants' needs and the facilitator's skills. Although the experiential learning activities presented here all vary in goals, group size, time required, and process[1], they all incorporate one important element: questions that ensure learning has occurred. This discussion, led by the facilitator, assists participants to process the activity, to internalize the learning, and to relate it to their day-to-day situations. It is this element that creates the unique experience and learning opportunity that only an experiential learning activity can bring to the group process.

Readers have used the *Annuals'* experiential learning activities for years to enhance their training and consulting events. Each learning experience is complete and includes all lecturettes, handout content, and other written material necessary to facilitate the activity. In addition many include variations of the design that the facilitator might find useful. If the activity does not fit perfectly with your objective, within your time frame, or to your group size, we encourage you to adapt the activity by adding your own variations. You will find additional experiential learning activities listed in the "Experiential Learning Activities Categories" chart that immediately follows this introduction.

The 2000 Annual: Volume 1, Training includes fourteen activities, in the following categories:

---

[1]It would be redundant to print here a caveat for the use of experiential learning activities, but HRD professionals who are not experienced in the use of this training technology are strongly urged to read the "Introduction" to the *Reference Guide to Handbooks and Annuals* (1999 Edition). This article presents the theory behind the experiential-learning cycle and explains the necessity of adequately completing each phase of the cycle to allow effective learning to occur.

Leadership: Interviewing/Appraisal

654. Communication Games: Eliminating Unproductive Behavior During Performance Reviews by Don Morrison

Leadership: Motivation

655. Millennium Mobile: Learning Four Functions of Management by Erica Nagel Allgood and Terry Carlyle

Leadership: Styles

656. Leadership Style: Learning to Take Risks by Lois B. Hart

Locate other activities in these and other categories in the "Experiential Learning Activities Categories" chart that follows, or the comprehensive *Reference Guide to Handbooks and Annuals*. This book, which is updated regularly, indexes all of the *Annuals* and all of the *Handbooks of Structured Experiences* that we have published to date. With each revision, the *Reference Guide* becomes a complete, up-to-date, and easy-to-use resource for selecting appropriate materials from all of the *Annuals* and *Handbooks*.

EXPERIENTIAL LEARNING ACTIVITIES CATEGORIES

	Vol.	Page
INDIVIDUAL DEVELOPMENT		
Sensory Awareness		
Feelings & Defenses (56)	III	31
Lemons (71)	III	94
Growth & Name Fantasy (85)	'72	59
Group Exploration (119)	IV	92
Relaxation & Perceptual Awareness (136)	'74	84
T'ai Chi Chuan (199)	VI	10
Roles Impact Feelings (214)	VI	102
Projections (300)	VIII	30
Mastering the Deadline Demon (593)	'98–1	9
Learning Shifts (643)	'00–1	11
Secret Sponsors (657)	'00–2	11
Self-Disclosure		
Johari Window (13)	I	65
Graphics (20)	I	88
Personal Journal (74)	III	109
Make Your Own Bag (90)	'73	13
Growth Cards (109)	IV	30
Expressing Anger (122)	IV	104
Stretching (123)	IV	107
Forced-Choice Identity (129)	'74	20
Boasting (181)	'76	49
The Other You (182)	'76	51
Praise (306)	VIII	61
Introjection (321)	'82	29
Personality Traits (349)	IX	158
Understanding the Need for Approval (438)	'88	21
The Golden Egg Award (448)	'88	89
Adventures at Work (521)	'95–1	9
That's Me (522)	'95–1	17
Knowledge Is Power (631)	'99–2	13
Spirituality at Work (658)	'00–2	15
Sex Roles		
Polarization (62)	III	57
Sex-Role Stereotyping (95)	'73	26
Sex-Role Attributes (184)	'76	63
Who Gets Hired? (215)	VI	106
Sexual Assessment (226)	'78	36
Alpha II (248)	VII	19

	Vol.	Page
Sexual Values (249)	VII	24
Sex-Role Attitudes (258)	VII	85
Sexual Values in Organizations (268)	VII	146
Sexual Attraction (272)	'80	26
Sexism in Advertisements (305)	VIII	58
The Promotion (362)	IX	152
Raising Elizabeth (415)	'86	21
The Problem with Men/Women Is . . . (437)	'88	9
The Girl and the Sailor (450)	'89	17
Tina Carlan (466)	'90	45
Diversity		
Status-Interaction Study (41)	II	85
Peer Perceptions (58)	III	41
Discrimination (63)	III	62
Traditional American Values (94)	'73	23
Growth Group Values (113)	IV	45
The In-Group (124)	IV	112
Leadership Characteristics (127)	'74	13
Group Composition (172)	V	139
Headbands (203)	VI	25
Sherlock (213)	VI	92
Negotiating Differences (217)	VI	114
Young/Old Woman (227)	'78	40
Pygmalion (229)	'78	51
Race from Outer Space (239)	'79	38
Prejudice (247)	VII	15
Physical Characteristics (262)	VII	108
Whom To Choose (267)	VII	141
Data Survey (292)	'81	57
Lifeline (298)	VIII	21
Four Cultures (338)	'83	72
All Iowans Are Naive (344)	IX	14
AIRSOPAC (364)	IX	172
Doctor, Lawyer, Indian Chief (427)	'87	21
Life Raft (462)	'90	17
Zenoland (492)	'92	69
First Impressions (509)	'94	9
Parole Board (510)	'94	17

	Vol.	Page
Fourteen Dimensions (557)	'96–2	9
Adoption (569)	'97–1	9
Globalization (570)	'97–1	19
Generational Pyramids (571)	'97–1	33
People with Disabilities (594)	'98–1	15
Expanding the Scope of Diversity Programs (617)	'99–1	13
Tortuga Place and Your Place (644)	'00–1	15
Unearned Privilege (659)	'00–2	25
Life/Career Planning		
Life Planning (46)	II	101
Banners (233)	'79	9
Wants Bombardment (261)	VII	105
Career Renewal (332)	'83	27
Life Assessment and Planning (378)	'85	15
Work-Needs Assessment (393)	X	31
The Ego-Radius Model (394)	X	41
Dropping Out (414)	'86	15
Roles (416)	'86	27
Creating Ideal Personal Futures (439)	'88	31
Pie in the Sky (461)	'90	9
What's in It for Me? (463)	'90	21
Affirmations (473)	'91	9
Supporting Cast (486)	'92	15
Career Visioning (498)	'93	13
The Hand You're Dealt (523)	'95–1	23
Living Our Values (548)	'96–1	25
Career Roads (549)	'96–1	35
Collaborating for Success (572)	'97–1	45
High Jump (573)	'97–1	57
Issues, Trends, and Goals (595)	'98–1	21
Bouncing Back (596)	'98–1	35
Work Activities (597)	'98–1	43
From Good Intentions to Results (645)	'00–1	27

643. Learning Shifts: Seeing the Impact of Learning on the Whole Self

Goals

- To introduce the concept of individual roles and the complexity of the whole self.

- To develop awareness of the impact learning has on individuals' whole being.

- To develop awareness that learning shifts beliefs, assumptions, language, and behaviors.

Group Size

Five to twenty-five participants.

Time Required

Approximately one hour.

Materials

- An assortment of compressed (instant pop-up) sponge sheets (available at craft stores) cut into random and odd shapes (six shapes for each participant). Approximately twelve pieces can be cut from a 3" x 4½" square.

- An 8" paper plate for each participant.

- A pen for each participant.

- A four-ounce paper cup with three to four teaspoons of water in it for each participant.

- A sheet of paper for each participant.

Physical Setting

A table or desktop surface for each participant.

Process

1. Prior to the session, place a paper plate, pen, paper cup with water, and sheet of paper at each seat.

2. Explain the goals of the activity. Generally, this activity is intended to enrich the participants' understanding and awareness of the impact of learning on the whole self. (Five minutes.)

3. Announce to the participants: "Think of a single, significant learning event or experience that you have had. This event or experience may have occurred at school, home, or work. For the purpose of this activity, 'significant' means an event or experience that caused a shift in your beliefs, attitudes, or behavior. Write your event or experience on the sheet of paper for your own use. You will refer to this throughout the remainder of this activity." (Five minutes.)

4. When everyone has finished, say to the participants: "One way of thinking about our whole self is through the various roles we have in our lives, such as student, spouse, friend, parent, professional, and so forth. Identify the six major roles you have in your life, and write them on your sheet of paper for your own use." (Five minutes.)

5. After everyone has finished, show participants the various shapes of sponge material. Inform them that "Each piece represents one of the major roles you have in your life." Pass around the pieces and instruct participants to take a number of pieces to equal the number of roles on their pieces of paper. Tell them that size and shape do not matter and that they can choose randomly.

6. When everyone has the right number of sponge pieces, tell them to write one of their roles on each piece and to place their pieces on their plates so that they can clearly see the roles. Tell them to butt the edges of their pieces together, touching as many edges as possible without overlapping them. Gaps that are created by natural contours of the shapes are okay, but each piece should touch another piece. (Five minutes.)

7. Let them look at their shapes for awhile. Explain that this collection is one way of viewing their various roles of the whole "self." It is one perspective of their individual nature. Say to the participants: "Refer back to the significant experience or event you wrote on your piece of paper. Now, look at your roles and determine which role motivated you the most to participate in the experience or event. Write the letter 'X' on that piece." (Five minutes.)

8. Tell the participants: "The water in the cup represents the learning event or experience. Now, let's look at how you have integrated or used that learning. Look at all your roles. Which of those have been influenced by the experience or event? This influence can be in terms of your behavior, attitude, beliefs, words, or whatever you wish. Pour water (the learning experience or event) on those roles that have been influenced. Vary the amount by what you believe is the level of influence the event or experience has had on a particular role. You may choose to use all or part of the water. The remaining water represents the unused aspects or nonproductive parts of the experience or event." (Ten minutes.)

9. To process the activity, ask participants to look at the subtle and dramatic changes that occurred to their whole "self," their structure. The following questions are helpful in initiating group dialogue:

■ How many of your roles were influenced by your experience or event?

■ As compared to other roles, to what extent was the role that motivated you (the one marked with an "X") influenced?

■ What occurred to your individual structure as you began to integrate the experience or event (water)?

■ Given that the water represented the learning experience or event, what is the impact to the structure of your self?

■ What other observations and thoughts can you offer about this experience?

(Ten to twenty minutes.)

Variations

■ With twelve or more participants, divide participants into three or four subgroups to process the activity and report their insights and findings to the rest of the group.

■ This exercise is also appropriate in academic settings in which learning theory and practice are explored.

References

Csikszentmihalhyi, M. (1993). *A psychology for the third millennium: The evolving self.* New York: HarperCollins.

Knowles, M. (1990). *The adult learner: A neglected species* (4th ed.). Houston, TX: Gulf.

Rogers, C., & Freiberg, H.J. (1994). *Freedom to learn* (3rd ed.). New York: Macmillan.

Senge, P. (1990). *The fifth discipline.* New York: Doubleday Currency.

Tough, A. (1971). *The adult's learning projects: A fresh approach to theory and practice in adult learning.* Toronto, Ontario, Canada: Ontario Institute of Studies in Education.

Vaill, P.B. (1996). *Learning as a way of being: Strategies for survival in a world of permanent white water.* San Francisco, CA: Jossey-Bass.

Submitted by Judith A. Free.

Judith A. Free is an organization development/quality specialist for the U.S. Navy. She provides consultation and facilitation in the areas of strategic planning, networked leadership teams, organization design, corporate communication, group development, quality management, process analysis, and labor/management partnership. She is a certified U.S. Navy Total Quality Leadership instructor and Myers-Briggs Type Indicator administrator. She holds a B.S. in business/management and is a June 1999 candidate for a master of science in organization development from Johns Hopkins University in Baltimore, Maryland.

644. TORTUGA PLACE AND YOUR PLACE: UNDERSTANDING DIVERSITY

Goals

- To give participants a framework for understanding diversity in the workplace.
- To help participants recognize the potential impact of different sources of diversity.
- To enable participants to identify various sources of diversity in their own organizations.
- To provide an opportunity to examine the impacts of diversity on different levels of an organization.

Group Size

Up to thirty participants.

Time Required

One to one and one-half hours.

Materials

- The Tortuga Place and Your Place Lecturette for the facilitator. (Copies may be provided to all participants as a handout, if desired.)
- A transparency of Tortuga Place and Your Place Diversity Is . . .
- One copy of the Tortuga Place and Your Place Handout for each participant.
- Tortuga Place and Your Place Matrices I and II for each participant.
- An overhead projector and screen (optional).
- A flip chart and felt-tipped markers.

Physical Setting

A room large enough to allow subgroups to complete assignments without disturbing one another.

Process

1. Introduce the topic of diversity and explain the need for individuals to understand how it can impact the workplace. Display the transparency and, if desired, give copies of the lecturette to participants as handouts.

2. Give the lecturette. Make it clear that each individual has diverse identities and that there are sources of diversity that may not ordinarily come to mind. Answer any questions and list the main points on a flip chart. (Ten minutes.)

3. Have participants form subgroups of five or six, give everyone a copy of the Tortuga Place and Your Place Handout and allow time for them to read the case. (Ten minutes.)

4. Distribute Matrix I to each participant, and ask each subgroup to work together to identify sources of diversity that exist at one of the operating levels (internal or external) of the Tortuga organization. For example, assign one group the island population, one the labor force, one the owners' association, and so forth. If there are more groups than levels, subdivide the levels or assign the same level to more than one group. All groups should identify sources of diversity as they relate to demographic, psychological and cultural, and geographic issues. Provide one simple example from the case for each of the three types of issues (e.g., age difference and educational level for demographic issues, personality traits for psychological issues, and residency status for geographic issues). (Ten to fifteen minutes.)

5. Have subgroups select any cell of the matrix they have just completed and discuss the possible impact of the sources of diversity on the performance of the manager in the case study. Have each subgroup present its results briefly for the total group. You may wish to summarize the results on the flip chart. Explain that the matrix is a tool that can be used for understanding the impact of diversity on their own workplaces.

6. Give everyone a blank copy of Matrix II and lead a discussion about the operating levels of the participants' organization(s) and how they are different from Tortuga Place. Ask the participants whether the three areas of diversity discussed earlier apply to their organization(s) and whether

a fourth or fifth are appropriate. (If participants are from different organizations, rearrange the group into appropriate subgroups for this discussion.) (Twenty-five minutes.)

7. Have participants form small groups to fill in the second matrix by identifying the diversity factors associated with the various levels of their own organization(s).

8. Bring everyone together to discuss the following questions:

- How do various diversity factors impact your organization's mission?

- How do the diversity factors you identified impact various levels of your organization?

- How do these diversity factors impact the employees in your organization?

- What management skills are needed to manage diversity factors for the well-being of the organization and its members?

(Fifteen minutes.)

Variations

- Use the case only, rather than discussing the participants' organization(s).

- Use the case as a model for comparison with the participants' own organization(s).

- If there is time, ask each subgroup to fill in the matrix for each of the operating sectors.

- Modify the matrix to address operating sectors relevant to participants' organization(s) and/or organizational levels.

Submitted by C. Louise Sellaro, Anne M. McMahon, and Betty Jo Licata.

C. Louise Sellaro consults in the areas of management information services, human development, business management, and health care systems. She is co-author of several teaching cases and has published articles in The International Journal of Commerce and Management, Journal of Health and Human Resources, International Journal of Management, The Health Care Supervisor, *and* The Journal of Systems Management.

Anne M. McMahon *is the diversity information provider for Youngstown State University in Youngstown, Ohio. She currently organizes the Partnership for Workplace Diversity program with Youngstown area employers and is a member of the university's diversity team, funded by a grant from the Association of American Colleges and Universities. She serves as diversity advocate of the Western Reserve Chapter of the Society for Human Resource Management. In addition to diversity, she specializes in micro and macro organizational processes and has published in several interdisciplinary journals.*

Betty Jo Licata *has conducted numerous training workshops for health care institutions, manufacturing organizations, and colleges and universities. She has published articles in* Training & Development, The Journal of Management, *and* The Journal of Psychology. *She is also an education advocate for the Western Reserve Chapter of the Society of Human Resource Management. Her primary teaching and research interests are in the field of human resource management.*

Tortuga Place and Your Place Lecturette

Diversity refers to the vast array of differences among individuals to which a group assigns social meaning and value. Although race, gender, and cultural heritage are commonly discussed diversity factors, other factors such as disability, family structure, and sexual orientation carry value and meaning as well.

Each individual has multiple identities that influence the perspectives he or she has about the workplace. In addition, the organization itself creates more diversity through mergers, market shifts, and work design. Various organizational segments generate new perspectives that vary by individual and work assignment. Because it is beneficial to an organization to have access to a variety of perspectives, it is good business to foster activities that protect and expand the diversity available within the organization and to encourage the expression of different perspectives about market issues and work processes. Diversity must be seen as a resource that contributes to the success of an organization. At the same time, the organization becomes a place in which each individual's identities are valued and developed.

The United States has often been described as a "melting pot" in which immigrants become assimilated into one American culture influenced by many different heritages. The appropriateness of the melting pot idea has often been questioned, and it is an idea whose usefulness is fading as we enter the next century. In today's workplace, inclusion of difference is a matter of accommodations and appreciation, not assimilation. It is predicted that 45 percent of all new additions to the U.S. workforce in the next few years will be nonwhite, and half of these will be immigrants. Two-thirds of the new workers will be women. These new workers will represent different types of family patterns and carry values associated with identities held in other arenas of their lives. They will add value to the organizations to which they belong.

Diversity factors are influential not only in the employment base of an organization, but within its markets as well, as the marketplace for products and services becomes increasingly segmented. Good competitive business practices require us to address these multiple markets and changing niches.

The case study we will use, Tortuga Place, is an example of how various sources and types of diversity impact all levels of an organization.

Tortuga Place and Your Place Diversity Is. . .

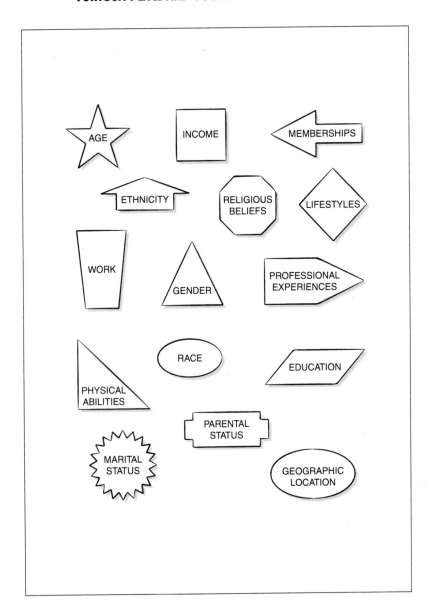

The 2000 Annual: Volume 1, Training/© 2000 Jossey-Bass/Pfeiffer

TORTUGA PLACE AND YOUR PLACE HANDOUT

San Cyprian is an island located in the Caribbean about an hour by air from the tip of Florida. It is home to approximately 26,000 Cyprians whose origins reflect a broad range of cultural and racial backgrounds. Many people from other countries also live there full-time, which increases the size of the resident population. In addition, there is a large temporary labor force and many tourists visit year-round, which can increase the island's population at any one time to over 75,000.

Economic Development

San Cyprian is a dependent territory of Great Britain, and the government is anxious to continue expanding tourism, now the largest industry on the island. Because there are more service jobs open than there are natives to fill them, green cards are widely issued to individuals (often functionally illiterate) who come from neighboring islands, as well as from many other countries. Many of those who hold green cards are supporting families who still live elsewhere in their original homelands.

An escalation of business activities on the island is bringing a wide variety of international businesspeople, who influence the island by bringing their own traditions and expectations. Today, the island has become an international cross section of people who arrive to vacation, to develop businesses, or to work in service positions. This mix of cultures has created a challenging environment for many islanders.

Island people tend to be family-oriented, warm, caring individuals. Because the service jobs are low-paying, many work two full-time jobs. Because there are so many service positions available, education does not have a high priority for native islanders. This has contributed to a situation of "overemployment" for portions of the service sector. It also makes it difficult to obtain workers for other, less desirable sectors of the developing economic base, especially general laborers. Economic and cultural differences are evident in how any type of work or social endeavor is approached. For example, because most laborers can easily find work, they may be inclined to show up late for work or not come to work at all.

Tortuga Place

Within one year of coming to the island on assignment with other members of a U.S.-based management consulting firm, Jennifer Wescott met and married a citizen of San Cyprian. While looking for island-based employment, she discovered that managerial positions appropriate to her qualifications were scarce. The island government's protectionist policy stated that even those married to native-born citizens were not allowed to take jobs for which any native was qualified. Fortunately, within six months after her marriage, Jennifer applied for and was hired as manager of Tortuga Place, a condominium association.

The Executive Committee

A five-member Executive Committee represents the condominium owners at Tortuga Place on matters of importance. These individuals have varying degrees of business expertise, ranging from a person with very little to the CEO of a multimillion-dollar manufacturing firm. The committee's responsibilities include policy development and advising the manager. Because they are widely separated geographically during most of the year, the committee members' duties are often interpreted and executed on an ad hoc basis. Little documentation of policies and procedures exists. This situation often leads to heated confrontations at the committee's annual meeting, a precursor to the general membership meeting at which all condominium association members deliberate about association actions taken by the manager during the previous months.

Jennifer was experienced in using many different supervisory styles, but dealing with the chairman of the Executive Committee presents a challenge. He can be paternalistic, sadistic, or really nice, in random sequence, which often leads to stressful interactions between him and Jennifer during Executive Committee meetings or during daily management of the complex.

One discouraging, yet typical, encounter occurred when the chairman of the Executive Committee planted himself in Jennifer's office and began a litany of complaints about sand and water that had been thrown onto the front porches by a nor'wester the previous day. Jennifer had scheduled additional clean-up, but scheduling any type of clean-up is nearly impossible on San Cyprian, as the crews come around when the spirit moves them and not before.

Condo Owners

The facility consists of eighteen luxurious, individually owned units, each large enough to easily accommodate six people. Ten units are used as vacation residences and are occupied only part-time by the owners and their guests. Eight units are occupied by the owners only a few weeks out of the year, then rented on a daily basis to individuals who come to the island on a temporary basis. The people who stay in the condos come from many parts of the globe, including Germany, England, Holland, Spain, Brazil, Venezuela, Canada, Norway, the United States, and Japan. The maximum amount of time per year spent by an owner in any of the condos is about four weeks. The owners range in age from their mid-20s to their 80s.

Jennifer sees some of the condo association's problems as originating with the two basic types of condo ownership plans. Owners of rental units have different objectives for ownership and are charged differently for certain budget expenditures than are owners of units that are not rented out. She also sees that many differences are related to the owners' work attitudes, values, and needs, which are integrally tied to how people use their assets and what they expect from the condo's operations and the condo association.

TORTUGA PLACE AND YOUR PLACE MATRIX I

Directions: Fill out the boxes below to show the various diverse factions at work within the Tortuga Place organization.

Sources of Diversity

Operating Sectors of the Organization	Demographic	Psychological and Cultural	Geographic
External Organizational Environment			
Internal Organizational Environment (Owner's Association)			
Internal Organizational Environment (Administration)			
Internal Organizational Environment (Labor)			

Tortuga Organization

Tortuga Place and Your Place Matrix II

Directions: Fill out the matrix below with the types and sources of diversity within your own organization. Identify as many as you can.

Sources of Diversity

Operating Sectors of the Organization	Demographic	Psychological and Cultural	Geographic	Other
External Organizational Environment I				
External Organizational Environment II				
Internal Organizational Environment I				
Internal Organizational Environment II				
Internal Organizational Environment III				

Your Organization

645. From Good Intentions to Results: Avoiding Procrastination

Goals

- To encourage follow-through after a learning experience or a meeting.

- To enhance the participants' understanding of the dynamics of procrastination.

- To encourage the participants to generate ways to overcome their own procrastination.

Group Size

Three to twenty pairs of participants.

Time Required

One to one and a half hours, depending on the level of discussion and sharing desired.

Materials

- One copy of the From Good Intentions to Results Theory Sheet for each participant.

- Two copies of the From Good Intentions to Results Work Sheet for each participant (one to use during the activity and one to keep for future use).

- One copy of the From Good Intentions to Results Readiness-Evaluation Sheet for each participant.

- A pencil for each participant.

- A timer with a sound to indicate the end of time allotted for each phase of the activity (optional).

Physical Setting

A room with enough space for the pairs to spread out and work without disturbing one another. If tables or desks are not available, provide a clipboard or other portable writing surface for each participant.

Process

1. Distribute copies of the From Good Intentions to Results Theory Sheet and ask the participants to read this handout. (Five minutes.)

2. After all participants have read the theory sheet, lead a discussion on the participants' reactions to the content. (Five to ten minutes.)

3. Distribute copies of the From Good Intentions to Results Work Sheet and pencils, clarifying that each participant is to use one copy during the activity and save the other for use with future events requiring follow-through. Briefly explain the process of the activity, stating that the participants will be choosing "accountability buddies" or partners to complete the task. Emphasize that the participants must choose partners on the basis of ability and willingness to work together, both during and after the activity. Elicit and answer questions.

4. Ask each participant to choose a partner. State that each participant will complete the work sheet by telling the partner his or her responses while the partner records these responses. (Explain that this approach allows the person sharing to concentrate on responses, rather than on filling in the form.)

5. Ask the partners to complete the "What?" section of the work sheet by determining what they will do as a result of having spent time and energy during this session. Each participant, with the assistance of the partner, is to select one good intention and then provide as much detail as possible for the partner to record. (Five minutes.)

6. Instruct the partners to complete the "Why?" section next. Each participant, again working with the partner, is to cite as many reasons as possible for taking this action while the partner records these reasons. Explain that the more good reasons people have to act, the greater their motivation. (Five to ten minutes.)

7. Have the partners complete the "How?" section. Each participant is to brainstorm all the possible ways the particular goal could be accomplished while the partner writes down these options. Explain that if a roadblock is

encountered later, participants will be able to refer to this section of their work sheets for backup plans. (Five to ten minutes.)

8. Instruct the partners to complete the "Why Not?" section. Each participant is to complete each sentence with the first thing that comes to mind while the partner jots down responses. (Five minutes.)

9. Ask the partners to complete the "What Changes Do I Need to Make?" section. Each participant is to identify what he or she needs to do to get off the fence and increase the likelihood of results; the partner records responses. (Five to ten minutes.)

10. Distribute copies of the From Good Intentions to Results Readiness-Evaluation Sheet. Have the partners work individually to complete the "Ready" and "Aim" sections. Before they begin, review the instructions and explain the formula, one factor at a time.

> SD means *sufficient dissatisfaction* with the present situation. The higher one's dissatisfaction, the more he or she is motivated to change that situation. For example, a 10 would indicate not being able to stand the situation any longer.
>
> CV stands for a *clear vision* of how much better the situation will be once action has been taken and the desired results achieved. The higher the number in this factor, the more one is being pulled toward a more desirable situation by the power of vision.
>
> KH means *know-how*. In order to take action, one has to know strategies that will lead to success. The higher the score for this factor, the greater one's willingness to take the first steps.
>
> BIS indicates *belief in self*. The most important component of the equation is one's belief in his or her ability to act and achieve successful results. A high number in this factor indicates a great deal of self-confidence and the feeling that "When I make up my mind to do it, I will get the results I desire."
>
> The scoring is based on a maximum of 300 points: $(10 + 10 + 10) \times 10 = 300$. Generally, scores under 150 points mean that one is not ready to succeed, but is only ready to put forth effort in trying. The interpretation of individual factors with number evaluations under 5 indicate areas in which one needs to work to build greater readiness.

11. Have the partners share their results in the "Ready" section and then discuss the contents of the "Aim" section and what they plan to do to increase their readiness for action. Encourage the partners to help each other add to their small task lists. (Five to ten minutes.)

12. Ask the partners to spend a few minutes making arrangements to follow up with one another (at a specific date and time) in person, over the phone, or through e-mail to check on progress, encourage each other, and share ideas for solving problems and removing obstacles. (Five minutes.)

13. To increase the participants' benefit from this activity, lead a ten-to-fifteen minute total-group discussion at the end. Base the discussion on the following questions:

- What have you learned about procrastination in general? About your own habits with regard to procrastination?

- What have you learned about ways to overcome procrastination?

- How can you use these ideas in the future when you find yourself not taking some desired action?

(Fifteen minutes.)

Variations

- Use the process described in this activity as a problem-solving tool to uncover the real reasons why certain actions are not being taken and what changes need to be made to increase the chances of positive results.

- Encourage managers to use this activity as a coaching tool with performance appraisals; employees can be invited to take a realistic look at the conditions under which they will be able to do their best work.

Reference

Nightingale, E. *Insight* tape series. 800-525-9000.

Submitted by Robert Younglove.

Robert Younglove, M.A., M.Ed., *is the president and co-founder of PATH Associates, a Baltimore-based consulting firm, and is affiliated with The Johns Hopkins University. He is a professional speaker, author, and workshop facilitator. Mr. Younglove combines his education in behavioral psychology with his experience as a counselor of troubled youth to motivate people to take positive actions to become happier, healthier, and more successful. He also works with the topics of building self-esteem in children, finding the ideal career, and developing healthier habits.*

FROM GOOD INTENTIONS TO RESULTS THEORY SHEET

Organizations expect a return on investment (ROI) of the time and money spent on a training session, a problem-solving effort, or a meeting. It is not enough for us as participants to listen and learn; we also must act to obtain improved results. After all, it is not what we *know*, but what we *do* with what we know, that makes a difference in our lives. This principle is summarized in the following quote from Sydney J. Harris: "It is not an act of intellect that makes people change themselves for the better, but an act of will. For intelligence without courage is as static as courage without intelligence is rash. It is intelligence with courage that results in the necessary act of the will we need in order to bring about constructive change in ourselves" (Nightingale).

Although all of us know that this is true, often we procrastinate. Procrastinating is like straddling a picket fence. On one side of the fence is the decision to do a task, and on the other is the decision not to do it. Indecision keeps the procrastinator uncomfortably perched on the fence, thinking "I should, I ought to, but I don't want to." The solution sounds simple: Just choose one alternative or the other and get off the fence. It is not always so easy, however, to take the action required.

One approach to overcoming procrastination calls for increasing motivation. The principle involved is that if you identify the reasons why a task has not been done or probably will not be done (lack of time, money, will-power, or reward, for example) and share them with others, you can decrease your own resistance and increase the likelihood that you will act. This approach, which also involves an element of figuring out when conditions will be favorable, is a process of examining yourself. Therefore, it requires honesty on your part as well as a climate of trust for sharing.

Reference

Nightingale, E. *Insight* audiotape series. 800-525-9000.

FROM GOOD INTENTIONS TO RESULTS WORK SHEET

What? (My Good Intentions)

State your intentions; be specific and complete. I want to:

Why? (Reasons for Following Through/Benefits)

List all the reasons for following through on your intentions.

How? (Various Ways to Follow Through)

Brainstorm and list all the possible ways to make it happen.

Why Not? (Why I Haven't Followed Through)

Complete each of the following sentences with the first thing that comes to mind

1. The real reason I haven't followed through is:

2. I would if only:

3. It's difficult for me to act because:

4. The one thing holding me back is:

5. It would be easier for me if:

What Changes Do I Need to Make? (What Would Need to Be Different for Me to Act)

To be successful I need to:

1.

2.

3.

FROM GOOD INTENTIONS TO RESULTS READINESS-EVALUATION SHEET

Sometimes a person's good intentions are not turned into positive results because the timing is wrong. The original idea was, or perhaps still is, a good idea, but for various reasons the person is not ready to implement it at this time. By completing this sheet, you can learn whether you are ready to act and figure out how to increase your readiness if necessary.

Ready (Conditions Necessary for You to Be Motivated to Take Action Now)

Directions: To determine your readiness for action, give yourself a score from 1 to 10 (1 = very low readiness; 10 = very high readiness) on each of the following factors. Then follow the formula below to compute your action score (your choice and commitment to act now).

My Score (1 to 10)

SD (Sufficient dissatisfaction with the way things are now): _____

CV (Clear vision of how I want things to be in the future): _____

KH (Know-how to get started): _____

BIS (Belief in self; confidence in my ability): _____

Action Score: (SD + CV + KH) x BIS = A (Action)

(_____ + _____ + _____) × _____ = _____

Aim (Actions That Will Lead to Success)

What factors need to be increased to improve your chances of taking action? Think about the big tasks that you need to complete; then break each task into little, easy-to-do steps that you could take quickly (making a phone call, writing a paragraph, setting an appointment, and so on). Use the space below to list as many of those small steps as you can.

Fire (Commitment to Act on One of the Above Tasks Each Day)

"Fire off" one action from the above list each day. Use the space below to list the three you will do first.

646. COLORING BOOK: GIVING OBJECTIVE FEEDBACK

Goals

- To demonstrate the impact of critical or vague feedback.

- To practice ways to make objective statements.

- To develop participants' awareness of effective behaviors to practice when giving feedback.

Group Size

Nine to twenty-four participants, divided into triads.

Time Required

One hour and twenty minutes.

Materials

- One child's coloring book or sticker book and assorted crayons or markers for each triad. (Books that are humorous work best for this activity.) Glitter pens, stars, stickers, and various decorative art items may be added as desired.

- One copy of the Coloring Book Feelings Response Work Sheet for each triad.

- One copy of the Coloring Book Sample Response Work Sheet for each triad.

- One copy of the Coloring Book Answer Sheet for each triad.

- Newsprint and an easel for each triad.

- Felt-tipped markers in at least two different colors for each triad.

- Masking tape.

Physical Setting

A room large enough for each triad to sit comfortably at a separate table.

Process

1. Explain to the group that they are going to begin with a warm-up activity to get their creativity flowing. Have them divide into groups of three, using any method you wish. Provide one coloring book or sticker book and other supplies to each triad. (Five minutes.)

2. Announce to the group: "Each triad is to work together on a creative project. Determine your own organizational approach and design and complete any three or four pages you select from your book. There are no specific restrictions on this project, other than that all group members must be involved. You have an assortment of tools to accomplish this goal. Be creative and have fun." (Ten minutes.)

3. Call time and direct the triads to pass their books to another triad. Give each group a flip chart and markers and announce to the group: "Take a few minutes to critique the book you have received. Select a member of your group to act as recorder to write down your comments about each of the completed pages on the flip chart. Also designate a spokesperson who will be sharing this information with the entire group later. (Ten minutes.)

4. When the triads have finished with their critiques, have each, in turn, report the comments they have written on newsprint to the entire group. (Fifteen minutes.)

5. Give each triad a copy of the Coloring Book Feelings Response Work Sheet and ask them to respond to the questions, then to write their answers on newsprint. (Twenty minutes.)

6. When the triads have finished, give them each a copy of the Coloring Book Sample Response Work Sheet and ask them to complete them as a triad. Tell them to indicate whether the descriptions of employee performance given on the work sheet are objective or subjective and to note the tone—positive or negative—for each statement. (Five minutes.)

7. Give each triad a copy of the Coloring Book Answer Sheet and ask them to briefly review it in their groups. Then lead a discussion with the entire group, soliciting answers and comments from participants about how to give objective, specific feedback. (Five minutes.)

8. Now ask the triads to go back and review the critiques that they completed on the creative work of another triad. Say to the group: "After examining your feedback to determine whether it was specific and objective and whether it was framed in positive tones, rewrite your critiques using specific and objective terms. Use the same newsprint handout, but write with a different color." (Ten minutes.)

9. Query participants by asking: "What lessons from this activity might be applied to mentoring or supervising others in the workplace?" Record their ideas on a flip chart, allowing participants to share ideas freely. To generate further discussion, ask: "Can you think of some informal opportunities to provide feedback to co-workers, even if you are not officially mentoring or supervising the person?" Have the group share some examples. (Five minutes.)

Variations

- Ask everyone to fill out the Coloring Book Sample Response Work Sheet individually. Bring the group together and debrief the activity.

- If time is short, post the questions on newsprint yourself and lead a total group discussion of the work sheets.

Submitted by Joanne R. Zukowski.

Joanne R. Zukowski is the director of the Regional Development Center at The University of North Carolina at Pembroke. With more than fifteen years in training and development, Ms. Zukowski has designed and delivered numerous programs for organizations in both the public and private sector. In addition to a traditional management portfolio, her current work involves leadership development, marketing, and strategic planning. She is active in ASTD and has chaired ASTD's National Management and Assessment Committee.

COLORING BOOK FEELINGS RESPONSE WORK SHEET

Directions: Read the questions below and respond based on what you experienced during this activity.

1. How did you feel at the beginning of this activity?

2. What aspects of the creative project were most interesting to you?

   Did your triad mates allow you to perform in this area?

3. How did you feel when you exchanged coloring books with another triad?

4. Did your feeling change during their oral critique of your book?

5. Was there a noticeable point when this process moved from "fun" to "serious"?

   What effect did that have on you or on your triad?

6. How could the critique of your book have been done more positively and have been less judgmental?

COLORING BOOK SAMPLE RESPONSE WORK SHEET

Directions: Read the descriptions below of employee performance. Put an "O" next to each one that represents an objective statement of performance. Put an "S" next to each one that is subjective.

———— 1. Alicia's average production rate this week was a disappointing twenty-three per day.

———— 2. Dotty did her usual outstanding job in dealing with six major overdue accounts this month.

———— 3. Mac's insistence on measuring widgets his way makes him one of our slower producers.

———— 4. Sheila types eighty words per minute, but she makes too many mistakes.

———— 5. Max filled twenty-eight orders in the morning and only sixteen in the afternoon.

Coloring Book Answer Sheet

__O__ 1. The word "disappointing" is subjective, although the basic description is factual and thus objective.

__S__ 2. "Her usual outstanding job" is vague and subjective and so is "deal with." "Six accounts" is specific, but the description is still subjective.

__S__ 3. "Slower" is vague and so is "measuring widgets his way." Is Mac's "insistence" the problem or does he need retraining? This is not specific enough and is not objective.

__S__ 4. How much is "too many"?

__O__ 5. Completely factual.

647. MEDIATED MESSAGE EXCHANGE: EXPLORING THE IMPLICATIONS OF DISTANCE COMMUNICATION IN THE WORKPLACE

Goals

- To investigate the impact of computer-mediated distance communication on dialogue between two people.

- To allow individuals to reflect on ways that limitations and/or benefits of computer-mediated communication can shape their personal communication and their treatment of those with whom they communicate.

- To simulate the process of e-mail communication in a workshop setting to enable individuals to consider the implications this technology has for their own work.

- To consider the impact of industry trends toward distance working.

Group Size

Any size, but this activity is ideal for ten to twelve participants.

Time Required

Approximately forty-five to sixty minutes.

Materials

- One copy of the Mediated Message Exchange Background Sheet for each participant.

- One envelope containing the Mediated Message Exchange E-Mail Memo for each participant. (Two sets should be prepared in advance, numbered sequentially according to how many members are in the group. For twelve participants in two groups of six, you will have two sets of envelopes numbered from one to six.)

- At least four plain white envelopes per participant.

- Pens for all participants.

- At least four sheets of plain white paper for each participant.

- A stopwatch.

Physical Setting

Two small rooms or a large open space with a partition to divide the room so that when participants are separated into two groups neither group can see the other. If neither option is possible, a separation can be accomplished by participants sitting back-to-back in chairs, with a gap between the lines of chairs.

Process

1. Frame the activity as a simulation of a distance work situation involving e-mail. Give everyone a copy of the Mediated Message Exchange Background Sheet and give them time to read it. Then summarize the situation in the following way:

   "Thanks for coming to this meeting. You have been selected by your company, Star Enterprises, as a member of a virtual work group. The group has been assigned a special project: restructuring the company. You will be required to work closely with your assigned partners, but due to the organizational changes taking place and the timely nature of this project, you will be able to communicate with your partners only via e-mail.

   You have already been assigned a partner, and when you return to your work station you will receive an e-mail message that will briefly explain the project and your role in it. In brief, you and your partner must present a short task report at a general meeting scheduled later today. This means you will have about twenty minutes to work together on this report, beginning when you receive your first message. You must begin by immediately reading your message, contacting your partner, and working on your assignment."

2. Inform the group that you will answer no questions once the activity starts. Ask if there are any questions at this time; if there are any, simply clarify the information you have already given.

3. Divide the group into two smaller groups and place each in a designated work space, either in separate rooms or behind partitions if possible. Number the people in each group separately and then assign partners according to the like number in the other group. Do not give people the name or any "real world" clues about their partners. If there is an odd number of participants, ask for a volunteer to help you in the role of a courier.

4. After everyone is settled, give each person an envelope corresponding with his or her number and containing a copy of the Mediated Message Exchange E-Mail Memo describing the project and the specific task.

5. Give everyone a few minutes to read their e-mail memos.

6. Choose one group to respond immediately to the e-mail message. Hand out writing paper, pens, and envelopes to everyone in that group. Tell them they have four minutes to write messages to their partners. Explain that, when they are finished, they should place their e-mail messages into plain envelopes, write their numbers on the envelopes, and send them to their partners via "courier." (Five minutes.)

7. Collect the envelopes and distribute them to the appropriate people in the second group. Give that group four minutes to read and respond to their messages, using either the sheets of paper they received or new sheets. Tell them to place their responses in envelopes, write their numbers on the outside, and send the envelopes back to their partners via the "courier." Again, collect all the envelopes and distribute them in the other group. (Five minutes.)

8. Repeat the process at least four times within the time constraints. It is important to keep track of time and adhere strictly to the exchange time. This helps to emphasize the constraints of electronic communication (quick and brief) and ensures that individuals are able to exchange several messages within the total time limit.

9. Notify the groups when they are exchanging their last messages.

10. After the last e-mail exchange, ask everyone to take a few minutes to evaluate his or her own communication. Ask participants to write down their answers to the following questions:

- How would you rate your ability to communicate with your partner during this exercise?

- Were you able to work on the task effectively? Why or why not?

- Did you form any opinions about your partner during the exchange of messages? If so, what were they?

- What can be learned from your experiences?

(Ten minutes.)

11. Bring the group together. Allow each pair to meet. Have the partners share their observations with one another for a few minutes. Then bring the entire group together and lead them in processing the activity. Allow each pair to share its observations with the total group; then pose the following questions:

- How did you feel as you went through this activity?

- What factors affected your communications with your partners?

- Was it difficult to communicate? Why or why not?

- Did you notice anything about your communication with your partner as the activity progressed?

- If you were to do this activity again, what would you do differently?

- How do distance and means impact one's ability to communicate?

- If this had been an actual work situation, what would the benefits have been from communicating in this manner? The disadvantages? The consequences?

- Are you currently involved in any work situations in which you have to use e-mail or other forms of technology to communicate with others at a distance?

- What did you learn from this activity that you could apply to those situations?

(Twenty minutes.)

Variations

- Each subgroup can be divided into pairs who together decide on the content of the messages and then exchange them with like pairs in the other subgroup. Then they can be introduced to one another and allowed to discuss the task for five minutes.

- The group can be divided into three subgroups. Individuals can then complete this same task in sets of threes, being required to communicate with two other trios. (This method require another individual to help with the courier task.)

- Allow the individuals to come together after fifteen minutes and spend five to ten minutes to complete their task "in real time." Then ask them to compare their long-distance versus face-to-face interactions.

- The entire group can be given the same task, or each pair can be assigned a different one. The activity can be structured to be relevant to a specific group of workers or to a particular organization.

Submitted by Heidi A. Campbell.

Heidi A. Campbell is a Ph.D. candidate at the University of Edinburgh-Scotland in computer-mediated communications and practical theology, researching virtual communities and how online communication impacts interaction within a face-to-face setting. She has worked as an experiential educator and has ten years' experience as a freelance writer, with work appearing in publications such as Personnel Journal *and the 1997 and 1998* Annuals. *She has also presented research papers at the Michigan Academy (U.S.A.) and the British Sociological Association (U.K.) conferences.*

MEDIATED MESSAGE EXCHANGE BACKGROUND SHEET

We live in a world in which communication is becoming increasingly mediated through various forms of technology. It is common for individuals, alone or collaboratively, to conduct their work at a distance from the workplace using computer-mediated communication (CMC). Individuals frequently utilize various electronic mail and computer software to transmit and receive information based on text, images, and even sound over great distances with relative ease and efficiency. Within many organizations, face-to-face communication is often not possible, although the same levels of quality and clarity of communication are expected among its workers. Thus CMC is used to bridge the gap.

According to Barry Wellman (1997): "Many workers are involved in multiple work teams, rather than solidary groups, and they are as apt to work with colleagues across the country as with those in the next seat. The computerized flow of information drives their work, not the office clerk handing out the day's 'snail mail.'"

When direct contact is eliminated, there are unknown consequences. Because computer-meditated communication is void of face-to-face contact, many wonder at the implications for the workplace. Does mediated communication lead to a depersonalizing form of communication, second-best to face-to-face interaction? However, the human element is not altogether lacking in computer-mediated communication. After all, it is humans who produce and shape the communication. Yet the tools they use do influence this process. Workers can see themselves as interacting with text, rather than with other individuals. Workers and management must consider how the newer forms of communication may impact not only the process, but also the end products of their work.

Reference

Wellman, B. (1997). An electronic group is a social network. In S. Kielser (Ed.), *Cultures of the Internet.* Mahwah, NJ: Lawrence Erlbaum.

MEDIATED MESSAGE EXCHANGE E-MAIL MEMO

Date sent: Mon, 1 Feb 00 10:54:00-0800
From: Star Enterprises <headquarters@star.com>
Organization: Star Enterprises
To: Partner groups <workgroup@star.com>
Subject: Work group assignments

Star Enterprises recently hired an independent consultant who proposed that we switch to smaller satellite offices, connected electronically via e-mail and the Internet, rather than expanding our current headquarters to meet our increasing business demands. This move would mean a considerable cost savings.
The consultant also recommended that employees be allowed to telecommute, that is, work from home connected to satellite offices via the company computer network. Work done in the offices would then be broken into smaller, more individually focused tasks. In order to remain competitive, Star Enterprises has decided that it must follow these recommendations. The changes that must be made will undoubtedly affect all employees.

You have been selected to serve on a special team that will plan this restructuring and have been assigned a work partner from another department. Your goals as a partnership are to evaluate how these changes would affect the workplace.

Your first task is to produce a short report on how these potential changes could impact your job in particular and the company as a whole. You and your partner are to present a report—summarizing the ideas you both have—at this afternoon's general company meeting, so you must work quickly. Remember that your suggestions may influence the direction of the entire organization, so your focused effort and clear input are extremely important.

The nature of your current assignment via e-mail is also intended as an experiment to see how the proposed changes might affect communication between and relationships among workers.

After reading this e-mail, contact your partner (unless your partner has been chosen to contact you first). Then immediately proceed with your task.

Thank you for your efforts on behalf of Star Enterprises.
Hal Edwards, General Manager.

648. TELEPHONE CONFERENCE: PREPARING FOR BEST RESULTS

Goals

- To learn and practice ways to achieve best results from a telephone conference.

- To experience a telephone conference with and without participating in a prior forming activity.

Group Size

From twelve to twenty participants.

Time Required

Forty-five minutes to one hour.

Materials

- Copies of the Telephone Conference Getting Acquainted Sheet for each person.

- Copies of the Telephone Conference Instruction Sheet for each person.

- Copies of the Telephone Conference Tips Handout for each participant.

- Two speaker phones connected by an actual phone link.

Physical Setting

Two rooms. One room should be large enough to hold the entire group; the other room should be large enough for half of the group. Either room should be large enough to allow all participants to sit around a conference table with a working speaker phone in the center.

Process

1. Prior to the beginning of the session, set up the speaker phones in both rooms and be sure they can be used easily.

2. While in the larger room, put participants in groups of twos or fours. Hand out the Telephone Conference Getting Acquainted Sheet to all participants and ask them to complete them in their small groups. (Ten minutes.)

3. When everyone is finished, divide the large group in two by having participants count off by 2's. Be sure that participants who interacted in the first activity are separated as much as possible. (To do this, have them count off while they are still in their small groups.)

4. Tell participants they will be holding a teleconference meeting. Give everyone copies of the Telephone Conference Instruction Sheet and go over them with everyone. Then ask one group to remain in the large room and escort the other group to the second room. Help the groups connect via speaker phone and ensure that the equipment is working effectively. Instruct the participants to begin the activity and remind them they will have twenty minutes. (Twenty minutes.)

5. After twenty minutes, bring the groups back together again. Discuss the following questions:

   - How did you begin your meeting?

   - What ground rules did you use during your meeting?

   - How did these ground rules help you accomplish your goals?

   - What did you notice when communicating with those in the other room?

   - What differences were there between your small-group meetings and the teleconferencing meeting? Why were the meetings different, besides being face-to-face.

   - Did you notice any difference in your level of comfort or connection when communicating with those who had participated in your earlier group activity? Why was that?

   - How might this experience be the same as or different from telephone conferences you experience in your work environment?

   - What might you do differently in the future to improve your own telephone conferences?

- What could you do to make a telephone conference meeting seem more personal?

(Fifteen to twenty minutes.)

6. Wrap up the discussion and give participants copies of the Telephone Conference Tips Handout to use in the future. Encourage them to add any new tips they have heard during the discussion.

Variations

- Give participants more explicit instructions, such as, "Introduce yourselves, choose a time keeper and recorder," prior to the telephone conference meeting.

- Use the Getting Acquainted Sheet and the Instruction Sheet during an actual telephone conference to help participants form relationships and set ground rules for the meeting on the spot.

Submitted by Debra Reed.

Debra Reed is an independent consultant with twenty-five years' experience in the area of corporate human resource development. She facilitates focus groups, conducts needs assessments, develops and conducts workshops, and assists numerous organizational structures. Ms. Reed has a master's degree in geographically dispersed work groups.

Telephone Conference Getting Acquainted Sheet

Instructions: As a small group, share your answers to all the items in Section A and at least one in Section B. You will have ten to fifteen minutes to complete this activity.

Section A

■ What is your name?

■ Where do you work?

■ Briefly describe your job.

Section B

■ Discuss with other members of your group something you enjoy doing outside of work.

■ Describe your favorite vacation spot.

■ Tell something about a hobby you enjoy and why.

■ Give some information about your family.

■ Describe a favorite work project you have participated in and tell why you enjoyed it.

■ Share something about your favorite movie, book, or song.

TELEPHONE CONFERENCE INSTRUCTION SHEET

Instructions: As one large group, your job during this twenty-minute telephone conference meeting is to prioritize a list of ground rules for successful telephone meetings, from the most to least important. Feel free to add your own ground rules to the list below before prioritizing them as a group.

Telephone Conference Ground Rules

- State your name each time you speak until everyone can recognize your voice.
- Be sure everyone has a copy of the agenda before the meeting begins.
- Determine to whom, how, and when to distribute meeting minutes.
- Acknowledge others before stating your own points.
- Balance participation among individuals.
- Express feelings verbally.
- Do not attempt to do other work while participating in a teleconference meeting.
- No sidebar conversations please.
- Begin the meeting by acknowledging everyone present at both sites.
- Select a meeting leader or facilitator, time keeper, and recorder.

TELEPHONE CONFERENCE TIPS HANDOUT

- Become acquainted with people through means such as the getting-acquainted questions you practiced earlier in small groups.

- Spend a few minutes in personal conversation at the beginning of a telephone conference.

- Exchange pictures with those at the other site if teleconferencing will be an ongoing method for conducting business.

- Keep photos of those on the other end of the telephone line in plain view to remind yourself of those with whom you are conversing.

- Establish and follow your own set of ground rules for effective telephone conferencing.

649. Diametrically Opposed: Persuading Others

Goals

- To heighten awareness that complex issues may present diametrically opposed opportunities.
- To provide a way for participants to create a plan for change.
- To develop persuasion skills.

Group Size

Any number in groups of five to eight participants.

Time Required

Seventy-five minutes.

Materials

- Copies of the Diametrically Opposed Overheads 1 and 2 for the facilitator.
- One copy of the Diametrically Opposed Handout for each participant.
- An overhead projector.
- Paper and pencils for participants.
- A flip chart and felt-tipped markers.

Physical Setting

A room that has tables at which groups of seven or eight can work together.

Process

1. Explain to the group that life today is filled with oxymorons and paradoxes. For example:

   - We are expected to "do more with less."

   - We have more time-saving devices than ever before, and yet we seem to have less time.

   - Some experts tell us that we need radical transformations of business structures; other experts tell us that we need to take a slow, incremental, kaizen-like approach to improvement.

   - We pride ourselves on being a nation of "lone rangers," and yet we are expected to work cooperatively on teams.

2. Elicit other examples from the group. (Five minutes.)

3. Discuss the difficulty of making sense out of the contradictory information that comes our way each day. Eggs, for example, are declared high in cholesterol one day and pronounced perfectly safe a year later. Then say: "I am going to show you two quotations now. Decide which of the two is more aligned with your way of thinking. Neither is right or wrong. The statements simply express two different ways of looking at situations."

4. Show Overheads 1 and 2. Ask participants to decide which philosophy more closely matches their own. (Five minutes.)

5. Ask them to form small groups, joining with others whose philosophies match their own. Hand out paper and pencils.

6. Continue by giving the following instructions:

   "You are now working with people who feel as you do about effective positive change—in our lives, in our workplaces, in our society. You will have fifteen minutes to come up with *one* idea—a grand plan for those of you who chose the first quotation and a smaller plan for those of you who opted for the second quotation. Your plan should involve changing some topics we've discussed in this session. You may think about an improvement plan as far as customers or work processes or internal communication is concerned. Or, you may think about an improvement plan for the environment. It may be a plan for learning more or earning more—the choices are infinite."

   (Fifteen minutes.)

7. Distribute the Diametrically Opposed Handout and have group members discuss their answers in relation to the plans they have formulated in

their groups. Tell them they will have ten minutes to consider the most persuasive way to present their plans to others so that others will be willing to support them. (Ten minutes.)

8. Ask for a volunteer spokesperson from one group to present that group's plan. Instruct the remaining groups to listen carefully. They are to evaluate the plan itself and also evaluate the extent to which they were persuaded to participate.

9. Once the first plan has been presented, give the other groups a few minutes to discuss it among themselves and then ask the groups to take turns giving feedback about it. Continue in this manner until all plans have been presented and feedback has been solicited on each. (Ten minutes.)

10. Lead a concluding discussion by asking:

   - How likely is it that the plan you presented will be implemented? Why or why not?

   - What must happen for change to occur?

   - How are planning and change related?

   - What role does persuasion play in implantation?

   - What are you likely to do differently as a result of this exercise?

   (Twenty minutes.)

11. Wrap up by observing that great ideas are often born in training rooms, where participants are free from everyday demands and can consider them in detail. Note that, unfortunately, many of the great ideas that are born in training rooms also die there. Encourage participants to make a difference—to take some of the plans they have devised and to actually implement them. Remind them that it is relatively easy to make a plan, but much harder to make a difference.

Variations

- Allow an additional ten to fifteen minutes for the feedback stage. Ask the groups delivering the feedback to structure their comments in such a way that the receiving group will be more likely to incorporate the suggestions for improvement.

- While the feedback groups are planning what to say and how to say it, the group that made the original presentation can discuss ways the presentation could have been improved.

Submitted by Marlene Caroselli.

Marlene Caroselli, Ph.D., has authored thirty-five books. She also writes for the National Business Employment Weekly, *the* ICSA Journal, *and Stephen Covey's publications. A popular trainer and keynote speaker, she travels extensively and writes intensively. Her expertise lies in the areas of communication, creativity, and management.* Principled Persuasion: Influencing with Integrity, Selling with Standards *is her most recent book.*

"Make no small plans,

for they have no power

to stir the soul."

—Anonymous

"We can do no great things,

only small things

with great love."

—Mother Teresa

Diametrically Opposed Handout

Peter Drucker, the father of modern management science, has observed that exceptional leaders know how to ask questions. Whenever we attempt to lead the thoughts of others, whenever we attempt to persuade them to see our points of view or join with our plans of action, we should be asking questions of ourselves first so we will be prepared with answers for others. Here are some questions to consider as you plan your persuasion efforts.

- What outcome do I intend to achieve?

- What influencing techniques have worked for me in the past?

- What is likely to work under the current circumstances?

- How is this plan superior to others that are similar?

- What benefits will accrue and to whom if this idea is implemented?

- What precedents could I cite to encourage adoption of this plan?

- To what extent will this plan consume me? In other words, will I have time to see it through to completion?

- How much support would I have for this plan among my peers? Back on the job?

- What homework would I have to do?

- What is there to lose? For me? For others?

- What is there to win? For me? For others?

- What might be a penalty associated with success?

- What might be a reward associated with failure?

- Hearing this plan, would someone who does not know me/us see the value or ethical principles behind it?

- How does this plan advance the organizational mission?

- How would it impact the bottom line?

- What does it make faster, cheaper, more efficient?

- How could it be replicated in other places?

- What objections am I likely to hear?

- How will I overcome them?

- How much resistance will this plan generate? From what quarters?

- Who might serve as a mentor on this project?

- Have I considered widening the audience that will hear this message? What are the pros and cons of doing so?

- Who might benefit indirectly from this plan?

- What emotional intelligence issues should be considered?

650. Piccadilly Manor: Improving Decision Making in a Political Milieu

Goals

- To study conditions under which rational and nonrational decisions are often made.

- To examine the use of rational and nonrational decision-making concepts when resources are limited, political stakes are high, and group goals are diverse.

- To develop skills for reaching consensus in a diverse group.

Group Size

Up to thirty-six participants in groups of eight or nine.

Time Required

Approximately two hours.

Materials

- Copies of the Piccadilly Manor Rational and Nonrational Decision Making Handout for all participants.

- Copies of the Piccadilly Manor Background Sheet for all participants.

- Copies of the Piccadilly Manor Case Study and Roles Sheet for all participants.

- Copies of the Piccadilly Manor Observer Sheet for all observers.

- A flip chart and felt-tipped markers for each small group.

- Masking tape distributed for use by each of the small groups.

- Pencils or pens and writing paper for participants.

Physical Setting

A room large enough for participants to move into small group discussions easily. Hard surfaces for writing.

Process

1. Explain that making decisions is a crucial skill for group leaders and that, in general, group decisions may be rational or nonrational. Say that the purpose of this activity is to enable group members to examine the conditions that favor making rational decisions. (Five minutes.)

2. Give all participants copies of the Piccadilly Manor Rational and Nonrational Decision Making Handout and summarize the key points by writing them on the flip chart as participants follow along. Note that participants will be asked to discern how the different models are represented in a case study and then they will take part in a group decision-making exercise. (Ten minutes.)

3. Divide the participants into small groups of eight or nine and give each participant a copy of the Piccadilly Manor Background Sheet and a copy of the Case Study and Roles Sheet. Each group should have six role players and at least two observers.

4. Ask participants to read the Background Sheet, study the Case Study and Roles Sheet individually, determine the decision-making styles being used, and then to decide as a group who will play what role and who will act as observers. (Fifteen minutes.)

5. Hand out paper and pens or pencils and ask participants to write down some key points about their roles so they can stay in character. (Five minutes.)

6. Give observers in each group copies of the Piccadilly Manor Observer Sheet. Then tell the participants playing Mayor Jackson in each small group to begin the discussion and to act as the facilitator and recorder during the discussion, jotting down ideas for resolving the management problem and alternative funding sources on the flip chart. (Twenty minutes.)

7. After announcing the end of the discussion period, tell the "mayors" to facilitate a discussion to reach a consensus on solutions. Ask the mayors to write a summary of the decisions made on the flip chart for later reporting to the large group. Say that each mayor must be prepared to state the criteria on which the group's decisions were made, the reasons

for the choices, and the decision-making model(s) that were predominate. Tell mayors to post their charts on the wall. (Twenty minutes.)

8. Announce that time is up and ask the mayors to read and explain their groups' decisions to the large group. (Fifteen minutes.)

9. Ask participants to reflect on the decision-making process in their groups and note whether and how the diversity of interests helped or hindered creativity. Have observers report what they saw in each group. (Ten minutes.)

10. Lead a discussion on these questions:

   ■ What type of decision-making model did members of your group use? What conditions affected the type of model used?

   ■ How did members create options for solving the administrative problems?

   ■ What criteria did your group use to evaluate the suggestions of group members? How did they establish these criteria?

   ■ How did differences among the interests and goals of group members affect the process of decision making?

   ■ How did the differences among members affect your group being able to come up with novel solutions?

   ■ How were political differences resolved?

   ■ How satisfied were members of your group with the solutions chosen?

   (Twenty minutes.)

Submitted by A. Carol Rusaw.

A. Carol Rusaw is an assistant professor at the University of Southwestern Louisiana, where she teaches consulting, training, and group behavior. She has written eight journal articles and a book, Transforming the Character of Public Organizations: Techniques for Change Agents. *She holds a B.A. in English, an M.A. in education, an MPA, an M.A. in religious studies, and an Ed.D. in adult education and human resource development.*

PICCADILLY MANOR
RATIONAL AND NONRATIONAL DECISION MAKING HANDOUT

Helping a group to make a decision is difficult for leaders, not only because of constraints of time and other resources, but also because of the difficulty of finding ways to meet different needs and interests. Often, leaders must reconcile different points of view, even among people from a homogeneous work environment. In addition, the "best" decision that leaders could make in terms of efficient and effective use of resources may not be accepted by the group. Leaders must examine all the possible decisions and how they may affect others.

In general, decision-making processes in a group can take two forms: rational and nonrational.

Rational Decision Making

Rational decision making involves defining, sorting, and prioritizing alternatives and then selecting one that maximizes outputs. Coalitions of group members often use rational methods, but the aim is to promote their own interests rather than the multiple interests of others. A dominant subgroup often has an abundance of resources, talents, and power strategies to enable its own interests to be met.

Rational decision making succeeds when people can agree on goals, objectives, and desired outcomes and when they have discretion in obtaining and allocating resources. Rational decision making follows a step-by-step process for reaching a "best" decision. Aldag (1991) describes them as:

1. *Investigate the problem.* Using rational decision-making methods, groups conduct an in-depth investigation into the issue confronting them. Typically, groups spend much time defining the problem. This is a difficult stage because what may attract a person's attention and may appear to be the core of a "problem" may be only a symptom of a larger problem.

   To illustrate, a noticeable increase in employee turnover may suggest a problem with employee dissatisfaction, inadequate salary and benefits, or structural problems that interfere with satisfactory performance, such as duplicate functions. It is important to examine the problem from different points of view and investigate how it might be linked with other areas.

2. *Identify decision objectives.* This step involves seeing what the situation will be like once the problem has been solved: What is the ideal state to be

achieved (i.e., fewer turnovers)? It requires determining what *must* be done versus what *should* be done.

3. *Diagnose causes.* Rational decision making involves investigating possible symptoms, contributors, and linkages to other problems.

4. *Develop alternatives.* Rational decision making uses creative problem-solving techniques, such as brainstorming, to generate as many alternatives as possible.

5. *Evaluate alternatives and select the best one.* In assessing alternatives, people use two important criteria: (a) How realistic the alternative is in terms of goals and resources of the organization, based on the information available and on their own imperfect judgment, and (b) how well the alternative will solve the problem, given the essential conditions and what would be ideal for optimal effects or results.

6. *Implement and follow up.* To put the best alternative into action requires the group to establish a structure and process. The leader sets up critical milestones, obtains necessary resources, such as staff and budgets, and sets up ways to track progress.

Deterrents to Rational Decision Making

1. *Uncertainty and risk.* Uncertainty may exist when external conditions are beyond the leader's control and when the leader lacks adequate access to information.

2. *Cognitive and perceptual limitations.* Perceptual and cognitive processes such as reliance on short-term memory, limited computational abilities, unarticulated doubts about outcomes, and stress may interfere with effective decision making.

3. *Turf wars.* A primary difficulty with rational decisions that dominant coalitions within groups make is that the solution selected often satisfies only that particular coalition. Dissatisfaction with the decision may give rise to competing groups; "turf wars" are frequent consequences.

Nonrational Decision Making

Nonrational decision making, on the other hand, is focused on the immediate interests of all group members, who examine a limited range of alternatives that seem to resolve a problem or issue, find common grounds for creating alternatives, and select a decision that each group member can accept. Nonrational methods use resources that are available and use bargaining and negotiating as tools for reaching consensus. Nonrational decision making integrates multiple viewpoints and results in decisions that the majority of participants can accept in principle. Nonrational decisions work best when situations involve uncertainty, disagreement among people, and use of scarce resources.

Three common nonrational models have been described as:

The "Muddling Through" Model

Lindblom (1959) suggests that because of the number of constraints within it, the rational model of decision making is indeed limited. He believes that it does not adequately describe what actually occurs. Instead, he offers the model of incremental decision making, which is based on limited, successive comparisons to existing policies.

This model has five central assumptions:

1. The decision calls for only small changes to existing conditions or policies. No new structures are formed.

2. The decision is noncomprehensive. It considers only the range of limited choices available to the decision maker at that particular moment.

3. The decision takes into consideration choices made in sequence over time, never one decision made once and for all.

4. The decision considers outcomes that are sufficient, but not optimal because of limited resources.

5. The decision does consider the pluralist nature of groups.

Satisficing and Garbage Can Approaches

Two variations of Lindblom's incremental approach are Simon's (1947) "satisficing" approach and March and Olsen's (1984) "garbage can" method of decision making. Simon maintains that individuals will make decisions that meet bare minimal criteria or that "satisfice" conditions. Decisions that "satisfice" or use "bounded" rationality frequently are put into effect when cost and time constraints prevent optimizing.

March and Olsen's "garbage can" model is appropriately called "organized anarchy" because both the problem definition and the solution emerge from unstructured group deliberations. When crises or periods of ambiguity arise, individuals are uncertain about what constitutes the problem because goals are unclear, group membership changes often, and the technologies are poorly understood or change rapidly. In the garbage can methodology, people may find bits and pieces of solutions and put them together. The exact nature of a problem or issue comes out of their collective knowledge and discussion.

Conclusion

Group decisions may entail using well-thought-out processes or using processes that do not seem to follow any systematic design. The "logic" groups use depends on several conditions, such as clear premises for making a decision, the degree of group member agreement and support of goals, discretionary use of available resources, how much situations change, and possible impacts of decisions on group members. When leaders have commitment of the group to attaining shared goals; abundant knowledge; technological, financial, and staff resources; and control over how people and resources attain agreed-on goals, they may follow rational processes to set and achieve goals. However, the greater the group diversity; degree of conflict; scarcity of time, money, and technical knowledge; and volatility of outcomes, the more the leader may rely on incremental decision processes.

Whether they use rational or nonrational models, however, leaders must cultivate group member participation. By remaining open to the ideas of others and incorporating their viewpoints in setting and reaching objectives, leaders can facilitate decisions that are both sound and acceptable to others.

References

Aldag, R.J. (1991). *Management* (2nd ed.). Cincinnati, OH: Southwestern.

Lindblom, C. (1959). The science of "muddling through." *Public Administration Review, 19*(1), 77–99.

March, J.G., & Olsen, J.P. (1984). The new institutionalism: Organizational factors in political life. *American Political Science Review, 78,* 734–749.

Simon, H.A. (1947). *Administrative behavior: A study of decision-making process in administrative organization.* New York: Macmillan.

PICCADILLY MANOR BACKGROUND SHEET

During the last fifty years, the federal government has created nearly two million public housing units for low income people. Although most newer units offer well-constructed homes and provide adequate property management services, most of the units over twenty-five years old were built in the inner cities and suffer from poor maintenance. As home dwellers moved to the suburbs in the 1950s and thereafter, many simply abandoned their homes. As the number of abandoned properties increased, decay took hold. Over time, the older units received fewer funds for upkeep.

Those still living in older units tend to be elderly; many of them are also disabled. Their average yearly income is less than $7,000 per year. The majority receive public assistance, which often fails to provide adequate health care, job training, remedial education, or recreation programs. Local community agencies or other local, state, or federal agencies provide additional, but limited, funds.

City governments oversee most inner city housing units through an independent, appointed board. Following federal grant guidelines, city councils develop an annual budget and delegate administration of the project to this independent board. The board determines tenant eligibility, participation in services, and rental rates. The board's director, who is usually appointed by a mayor, is responsible for the overall administrative operations. The city council makes all major decisions affecting the housing project.

The board creates a housing authority to provide day-to-day administration of the housing facilities. Typical responsibilities include maintenance and custodial work; purchasing and inventory; finance and accounting; processing tenant applications; personnel and training; security; and social services.

Housing authority employees range from unskilled to professional and legal personnel, depending on the extent of services they provide. Most of the housing authorities have personnel management systems that are not subject to civil service structures and benefits. Often, there is little protection for employees, morale is low, and performance is marginal. Many housing authorities both use unionized employees and contract with residents to oversee functional operations.

The control of a housing project is determined by "cooperation agreements" between the housing authority and HUD (Housing and Urban Development). The cooperation agreements affect both revenue available and services provided. Under the terms of the agreements, the municipal government waives normal real estate taxes but requires a payment in lieu of taxes equal to 10 percent of the rent received. This is less than the amount of taxes that would normally be paid. The cooperation agreement also commits the local jurisdiction to provide usual services and utilities, such as fire and police protection. However, in some areas, safety personnel are reluctant to enter housing projects. The absence of direct city government complicates this issue and worsens the isolation in which housing projects exist.

The public housing manager is subject to constant scrutiny, particularly because fiscal problems are often linked with inefficient management; demands for services usually outstrip available financial resources. Federal subsidies do not fill the gap between actual operating costs and rental income. In addition, federal block grants for housing have declined steadily over the last twenty years.

PICCADILLY MANOR CASE STUDY AND ROLES SHEET

Background

Piccadilly Manor is a public housing complex that sits in the middle of Springvale, a Northeastern city of 800,000. Nearly 60 percent of the 40-year-old complex of 700, three-story units are empty. Of the 280 occupied units, 174 (or about 62 percent) are occupied by single tenants aged 65 and over. The remaining tenants are single parents and their children. Nearly all residents receive public assistance, usually less than $7,000 per year.

Funding

Springvale and the U.S. Department of Housing and Urban Development (HUD) have signed a cooperation agreement that outlines the amount of federal funding allocated for specified public housing services based on formulas that match, dollar for dollar, the amounts raised with local funding, including tenant rent. For this fiscal year, HUD has allocated $7,000,000 for Piccadilly Manor. Funds are to be used to subsidize rent as well as to repair or maintain the structures. No funds have been allocated for renovation.

The $7,000,000 is a significant drop from the $12,000,000 peak funded in the early 1980s. In fact, for nearly two decades, federal subsidies have deteriorated. Because of the decline in funding, the Springvale City Council has decided against expensive upgrades to the units, postponed scheduled maintenance, and asked residents to help with the grounds upkeep. Springvale pays these residents minimal wages from other general assistance fund sources. To offset the expenses, moreover, Springvale has waived residents' normal real estate taxes, but required dwellers to pay the city 10 percent of the rent subsidy in lieu of taxes.

According to the cooperation agreement, Springvale must provide the usual municipal services and utilities, such as fire and police protection. In addition to finding a way to pay these expenses in the face of dwindling revenue, the city has encountered problems with city fire and police personnel. Because of the high crime rate in Piccadilly Manor, public safety employees are reluctant to answer resident calls. Their slowness to respond makes residents feel even more isolated from mainstream Springvale residents and more vulnerable to fires and to crime.

Piccadilly Manor Administration

Mayor and City Council

Primary responsibilities for running Piccadilly Manor are shared by a nine-member city council and an at-large mayor. To find alternative ways of funding Piccadilly Manor has been a primary goal of the council for the last four years. Various ideas have been explored, such as forming alliances with businesses, civic groups, and nonprofit organizations with interests in Piccadilly Manor. But the council terms are only two years long, which makes running for re-election a top priority for both council members and the mayor. This has prevented any serious long-range planning. Five of the nine current council members were elected at the same time last November.

Housing Authority Board

When Springvale built Piccadilly Manor in the early 1950s, the city council appointed a Housing Authority Board to oversee administration of government funds and to provide efficient day-to-day maintenance and security services. The Housing Authority Board determines tenant eligibility, participation, and rental rates. The board's current director, Kelly Wilson, was appointed by Mayor Jackson and reports to the city council.

The board also employs technical and professional civil-service personnel to carry out specialized services, such as maintenance and custodial work; purchasing and inventory; finance and accounting; processing of tenant applications; personnel and training; security; and social services. Although technical and professional employees are hired under Springvale's civil-service laws, the majority of Piccadilly Manor employees are residents who receive minimum wage public assistance funds. The technical and professional workers often argue with the employee-residents over work roles and responsibilities; "turf battles" have divided the two groups and have produced widespread poor morale and marginal performance. Moreover, employee-residents decry the fact that they have virtually no benefits and can be terminated without notice. They resent the benefits the city employees' union provides to the technical and professional employees.

Resident Complaints and Funding Issues

Resident complaints have escalated over the last two years. The most recent was an angry letter to the mayor and city council describing many residential frustrations. In the letter, Piccadilly Manor residents complained of rats in the buildings, improperly wired electrical systems, leaking toilets, drug dealers pitching gun battles on the streets, and inadequate public transportation services to suburban shopping centers, medical offices, and vocational training facilities.

Dealing with Complaints

It is now January and the new city council members have begun their terms. The highest priority items on their agenda are the angry resident letter and the continuing frustration of finding adequate funds for improving the administration of Piccadilly Manor. The mayor has convened a task-force meeting, which has been declared as a beginning step in dealing with the issues. The task force consists of Mayor Jackson; one incumbent and two new council members; Kelly Wilson, director of the Housing Authority Board; and two Piccadilly Manor residents. Jackson hopes the task force will find creative ways to address the administrative crises by thinking "out of the box." Frustrated with past strategies that, for various reasons, never bore fruit, Jackson wants to "re-invent" the way Piccadilly Manor is managed. By bringing residents together with those who can steer decisions through to actions, Jackson is confident the new council will take creative action.

Task Force Membership

The task force comprises the following members:

Mayor Terry Jackson

The mayor would like to accommodate the variety of interests on the board. Because Jackson will begin campaigning for re-election later this year, it is important to cultivate the support of both residents and interest groups associated with housing. The mayor believes that this can be achieved by offering several financial incentives, such as tax breaks to businesses and nonprofit organizations. The mayor is eager to show voters that the Manor's financial management is sound and has improved the well-being of residents.

Council Member Taylor Jones

Jones is a newly elected liberal who believes that the housing project should be moved from the inner city to the suburbs. The reasoning is that tax receipts will be higher there, services will be more abundant, and the quality of life will be improved for the residents, especially for families with school-aged children. Jones proposes financing the move through a variety of means, such as grants, nonprofit funds, and grass-roots fund-raisers. Jones was friends in college with a person who is the head of a popular rock group and has asked the person to donate the proceeds from a concert to help a relocation funding.

Council Member Tracy Smith

Smith, a returning member of the council, is a pessimist who thinks that moving tenants to the suburbs will solve nothing. In fact, Smith is sure it will create more problems and that suburban property values will tumble, crime rates will increase, and "white flight" will escalate. Smith believes that existing housing is generally structurally sound, based on recent studies, and that tenants are opposed to moving. Smith believes that some upgrading of the Manor is necessary, but cannot count on major sources of revenue. Smith thinks that what money does come in may be best diverted to self-help programs in which tenants learn to manage their units' upkeep, security, and services.

Council Member Cam Brown

Brown, a local business owner and first-time council member, strongly believes that inefficient management should be eliminated. The solution, Brown thinks, is to contract out essential services at a cost lower than is spent for civil service employees currently. In this scenario, the council would be responsible for direct oversight of contracted work and would pinpoint and correct deficiencies quickly, easily, and efficiently. Brown does not believe the council should invest more money in the existing system because that system does not work.

Worker-Resident Pat Davis

Davis is a Piccadilly Manor tenant and worker-resident who has been active in obtaining support for public housing from several neighborhood, legal, medical, religious, and charitable nonprofit organizations. Davis is rumored to have had ties with militant groups in the late 1960s and has a style that is direct and confrontational. Davis believes that other council members are insensitive to the needs of housing tenants and are perpetuating racial, ethnic, and economic bias by refusing to commit additional resources to tenant management.

Tenant Chris Gomez

Gomez, like Davis, is a Piccadilly Manor resident. Gomez voices the frustrations of many other tenants: lack of consistent and adequate plumbing and heating, poor medical and protective services, and escalating rent. Gomez also favors additional council financial and social service aid, but is less militant than Davis. Gomez would like to have tenants trained in community organizing and leadership skills, as well as in maintenance. Gomez believes that a strong community can take care of itself and is committed to creating awareness and support for mutual help from within.

Housing Authority Board Director Kelly Wilson

Before adjourning last May, the Springvale City Council appointed Wilson to replace Corky Corcoran, who was implicated in an article in the Springvale *Times* in a real estate scandal involving use of federal housing funds. Corcoran resigned and took a job as finance director in another city. Wilson, a former political science professor and director of a nonprofit, self-help organization, is knowledgeable about administrative reform and is eager to lead the board in providing first-rate services. Wilson wants to expunge the political influences in the board and promote more participation from a mix of citizens, residents, and civic and community leaders who would help in determining policy.

PICCADILLY MANOR OBSERVER SHEET

Directions: You are to observe the role play and then give members of the group your feedback and invite reactions from them. Some questions to keep in mind during the role plays are:

1. What were some differences in points of view that emerged among players? How did participants manage these differences?

2. How did different task force members facilitate creative problem solving? What words or behaviors encouraged this? What words or behaviors discouraged creativity?

3. How did member interaction set the stage for the type of decision model (rational or nonrational) that the task force adopted?

4. What were some criteria task force members used in making their decisions? What values were revealed during the decision-making process?

651. Alpha "Bets":
Introducing Organizational Issues

Goals

- To develop cohesion among participants through use of a challenging icebreaker.
- To heighten awareness of organizational issues.
- To initiate dialogue regarding the relationship between the present training session and organizational issues.

Group Size

Five groups of at least two members each.

Time Required

Twenty minutes.

Materials

- Alpha "Bets" Handouts 1, 2, 3, 4, and 5. (There should be equal numbers of each handout; the total number of handouts should equal the number of participants.)
- One Alpha "Bets" Answer Key for the facilitator.
- A flip chart and felt-tipped markers.

Physical Setting

A room that is large enough to permit small groups to work together without disturbing one another.

Process

1. Begin by noting that the session will touch on a number of issues that are important to organizations and to the individuals who work for them. Explain that they will be doing word searches to start. Give an example of the word "m-i-s-s-i-o-n." Write "___ ___ S S ___ ___ ___" on the flip chart, say that "every organization should have one," and let them solve the puzzle. (Five minutes.)

2. Continue by saying: "I've compiled a list of twenty-five words that represent other organizational issues. All of the words are also alphabetically challenged and are missing some letters, but I'm betting that you will be able to identify at least one of the words from a list of five I will give you."

3. Divide the participants into five groups of roughly equal size.

4. Distribute Alpha "Bets" Handout 1 to participants in Group 1; Alpha "Bets" Handout 2 to participants in Group 2; and so on.

5. Tell everyone that each group has five minutes to identify at least one word on its list. Say that it may look impossible at first, but the task is easier because the words all relate to important business topics and that they may choose any of the five words. (Five minutes.)

6. Call on spokespeople from each group to share their results. On the flip chart, write their answers or supply the answers if they were unable to come up with any.

7. Fill in the answers for the entire list, then ask each group to choose one word from the complete list (a different word from each group) and explain how it relates to the training they are about to receive. (Ten minutes.)

8. Make notes for yourself as they are sharing their views. Then use some of their comments to officially introduce yourself, the course, and the course objectives.

Variations

- Combine the five handouts into one and distribute it to each participant at the beginning of the session. Announce that the person who figures out the most words will receive a prize. Award an inexpensive crossword puzzle book to the winner.

- Ask groups to select the top five priorities for the training session from the list. Then invite a member of senior management, who has been given the list in advance, to share those he or she has chosen as the top priorities for the session. Lead a discussion of any discrepancies that exist.

Submitted by Marlene Caroselli.

Marlene Caroselli, Ph.D., has authored thirty-five books. She also writes for the National Business Employment Weekly, *the* ICSA Journal, *and Stephen Covey's publications. A popular trainer and keynote speaker, she travels extensively and writes intensively. Her expertise lies in the areas of communication, creativity, and management.* Principled Persuasion: Influencing with Integrity, Selling with Standards *is her most recent book.*

Alpha "Bets" Handout 1

Directions: Identify the words below that are related to your organization and the topic of today's training by supplying the missing letters.

1. A __ __ __ E __ E __ E __ __

2. B __ R R __ __ __ __

3. C __ M M __ __ __ __ __

4. D E __ E __ A __ __ __ __

5. E __ __ __ __ E __ __ E __ __

Alpha "Bets" Handout 2

Directions: Identify the words below that are related to your organization and the topic of today's training by supplying the missing letters.

6. F __ __ __ __ Y

7. G __ __ __ S

8. H E __ __ __ __ __ __ __ E

9. I __ __ O __ __ __ __ __ O __

10. J __ __ S __ __ __ S __ __ __ __ __ __ __ __

ALPHA "BETS" HANDOUT 3

Directions: Identify the words below that are related to your organization and the topic of today's training by supplying the missing letters.

11. K __ __ __ __ E __ __ E

12. L E __ __ E __ __ __ __ __ __

13. M __ __ I __ __ __ I __ __

14. N E E __ S __ __ __ __ __ S __ S

15. O __ __ I M I __ __ __ I __ __

ALPHA "BETS" HANDOUT 4

Directions: Identify the words below that are related to your organization and the topic of today's training by supplying the missing letters.

16. P __ __ __ __ __ T __ __ __ T __

17. Q __ __ __ __ __ Y

18. R E __ __ __ __ __ E __

19. S __ __ __ S S

20. T __ __ __ __ O __ O __ __

Alpha "Bets" Handout 5

Directions: Identify the words below that are related to your organization and the topic of today's training by supplying the missing letters.

21. U __ D __ __ __ __ __ __ D __ __ __

22. V __ __ U __ __

23. W __ __ __ E

24. X-__ E __ E __ __ __ __ __ __

25. Y 2 __ __ __ __ B __ __ __

Alpha "Bets" Answer Key

1. Achievement
2. Barriers
3. Community
4. Delegation
5. Empowerment
6. Family
7. Goals
8. Healthcare
9. Information

10. Job Satisfaction
11. Knowledge
12. Leadership
13. Motivation
14. Needs Analysis
15. Optimization
16. Productivity
17. Quality
18. Resources

19. Stress
20. Technology
21. Understanding
22. Values
23. Waste
24. X-Generation
25. Y2K Problem

652. Benefits and Barriers: Training for Learning Transfer

Goals

- To facilitate learning transfer.

- To identify barriers participants may encounter when they return to work that will keep them from implementing what they have learned.

- To overcome internal barriers and resistance that can block new behaviors.

Group Size

Any.

Time Required

Forty-five minutes.

Materials

- One Benefits and Barriers Planning Work Sheet for each participant.

- A flip chart and markers.

- Masking tape.

Physical Setting

Any.

Process

1. This activity works best near the end of a training session, after participants have been exposed to most of the material. Ideally, the group is feeling positive about the training and is therefore more motivated to integrate the material.

2. Ask the group: "What benefits could you expect if you were able to use the new skills we have learned back at your job?" List as many of the benefits as possible on a flip chart under the heading, "Benefits." Tape all sheets to the wall for easy viewing. For example, some items that might be listed after a session on interpersonal skills include:

   - Improved peer relationships.
   - Greater understanding of others.
   - Less stress.
   - Better morale.
   - Feel more in control.
   - More productive at work.

   (Five minutes.)

3. When the group has exhausted its ideas for benefits, start with a fresh sheet of paper and write the heading, "Barriers." Ask the group, "What are the things in your workplace that may prevent you from using the new skills you have learned?" List all responses and tape the sheets to the wall for easy viewing.

   During this process, people will often list structural or systemic circumstances over which they feel they have little or no control, such as:

   - Boss is unsupportive.
   - Others won't participate.
   - No chance to practice.
   - Office layout not conducive.
   - Work schedules are erratic.
   - Not enough time.
   - Work load too great.

   (Five minutes.)

4. Discuss with the group the issue of external barriers, over which they have no control, and internal barriers, over which they do have control. Label the barriers they have listed as "internal" or "external." Ask again, "What would prevent you from using the skills you have learned here?" The responses will probably emphasize internal barriers, such as:

- I would feel funny.

- I'm not good at it.

- It would make others uncomfortable.

- I'm afraid of looking silly.

- I might do it wrong.

5. Point out that internal barriers usually involve fear: fear of change, fear of the unknown, fear of not looking competent. Facilitate a discussion about fears we have when learning a new skill, using the following points:

- Why do we feel uncomfortable using skills we have just learned?

- What internal barriers do we have that prevent us from practicing new behavior?

- How can we overcome them?

- What types of self-limiting thoughts and feelings do you have on the job?

- What are some ways we can practice new skills in a nonthreatening way?

- What are some ways we can internalize the new skills?

- What would some advantages be? Are the advantages greater than the fears?

(Twenty minutes.)

6. Lead a discussion comparing the value of the benefits to the effort it will take to overcome the barriers by asking such questions as:

- Give some examples of new skills we have just learned that would allow you to work more efficiently or help you better manage your work load or time.

- What will your workplace be like if you do not use these skills?

- How would it be if you did use these skills?

- Are the benefits worth the effort to overcome the barriers?

(Ten minutes.)

7. Help participants understand that we are always reinforcing some pattern of behavior—whether good or bad. If they do not use their new skills, the training will have been a waste of time. To close the exercise, say the following:

> "You are always reinforcing some pattern of behavior. If you don't practice new behaviors, you are practicing old behaviors. Our behaviors are like water that is constantly flowing from the mountains. Each tiny stream flows where there is the least resistance. Over time, the streams turn into rivers and cut deeper and deeper canyons in the patterns of our behavior. To adopt a new set of behaviors takes effort. If we want to change, we must move against the point of resistance until we have cut the canyon in a new, more productive direction. Ask yourself if the benefits you've identified are worth the effort to overcome the barriers. For most people, the answer is a resounding 'yes.' Good luck to you."

8. Hand out the Benefits and Barriers Planning Work Sheet and have participants complete it in pairs. (Fifteen minutes.)

9. Summarize the activity with the following questions:

   ■ What's your greatest barrier to using new methods?

   ■ What ideas do you have to overcome this barrier?

   (Five minutes.)

10. Encourage participants to follow their action plans to practice new behaviors. Suggest that they call one another in a few weeks to reinforce their commitment and offer advice and encouragement. Facilitate an exchange of phone numbers and addresses for this purpose.

Variation

■ The exercise can be used with small groups or self-directed work teams to identify the internal barriers that are obstructing a desired course of action.

Submitted by Steve Sphar.

Steve Sphar, J.D., *is a quality and training consultant for the California State Teachers' Retirement System. He has counseled managers and employees in both the public and private sectors for over fourteen years. He is a published author in national newspapers and professional publications, including the Jossey-Bass/ Pfeiffer 1998* Annual *and the McGraw-Hill 1999* Training and Performance Sourcebook.

BENEFITS AND BARRIERS PLANNING WORK SHEET

What benefits could I expect if I were able to use these new skills back at my job?

What things in my workplace could prevent me from using these new skills?

What are three things I can do to overcome these barriers?

1.

2.

3.

653. Management Wizards: Wrapping Up a Session*

Goals

- To review skills learned in prior management development sessions.

- To apply knowledge gained to typical management dilemmas.

- To wrap up a series of management development sessions in a meaningful, fun, and impactful way.

Group Size

Twelve to twenty-one participants.

Time Required

One and one-half to two hours.

Materials

- A list of key points or action steps from prior management development sessions, either copied or listed on a flip chart.

- Fifteen to twenty 4" x 6" index cards.

- Ten to fifteen index cards on which you have written a variety of difficult management situations, such as:

  - A staff member's personal problems are interfering with job performance.

  - A staff member is very outspoken about his or her negative reaction to upcoming departmental changes.

*The author wishes to recognize Wayne Crimy, director of training at Carroll County Bank, Westminster, MA, who helped develop this activity. The activity itself was inspired by using one of Thiagi's framegames.

- A staff member becomes distraught and emotional when confronted about his or her own poor performance.

- A staff member complains that a co-worker does not complete his or her fair share of the work.

■ Three "Wizard Hats" made from sheets of rolled up heavy paper and decorated with stars or other symbols.

■ Three "Wizard Wands" (optional).

■ Confetti or glitter (optional).

■ A flip chart and felt-tipped markers.

Physical Setting

A room with a "Wizards' Table" at the front with seats for three. Other tables or chairs should be in a U-shaped arrangement, facing the Wizards' Table. There should be enough seats for all participants, including the three Wizards, in the U-shaped arrangement.

Process

1. Explain the goals of the session: To wrap up a management development series. Say that in order to reinforce the skills they have learned, you have prepared a serious activity during which they will have the opportunity to discuss the application of good management skills in real life.

2. Hand out copies of the key points you have prepared or list them on the flip chart. Ask participants to glance through them, refreshing their memories from the sessions in which they were explored. (Five or ten minutes.)

3. Divide participants into three groups of four to seven members each. Give each group five of the blank index cards.

4. Ask groups to look over the list of key actions and, as a group, list five classic management situations that may be challenging for them as they try to achieve these key action steps. They should be very specific, listing situations that are both likely to come up and important for being good supervisors. Tell them to write each of the five situations on a separate card. If needed, provide an example: "Conflict between two staff members who are required to work together."

5. Collect all of the situation index cards and covertly add some of your own. Shuffle the cards well and redistribute them equally among the three groups. (If someone notices that there are more than five cards, confess to adding some situations of your own.)

6. Ask groups to consider their situation cards carefully and to pick three situations that are the most problematic for supervisors. (Five minutes.)

7. Collect the three cards that each group has selected. Reshuffle them, handing three back to each group. Give the groups a few moments to look at the cards they received.

8. Ask each group to decide which person in the group is best at handling the types of difficult situations given on the cards. Designate the people selected as the "Wizards," and invite them, with much fanfare, to sit at the Wizards' Table at the front of the room. Give each of the Wizards a hat and wand and induct them into the "High Wizards Council." (If you are using confetti or glitter, give it to them and explain to the Wizards, privately, that this "Wizard Dust" is for use at the end of the activity.)

9. Explain that the activity will be conducted as a round-robin. Each group will select three situation cards for responses from other groups. The responding group will confer and succinctly explain how the situation on the card should be handled. The High Wizard Council will then confer and award from 1 to 5 points for the answer. They will also provide additional input about how to handle the situation, including anything that may have been left out. This will continue until all groups have used their cards and answered three questions from opposing groups. (Sixty minutes.)

10. Designate the groups as Team 1, 2, or 3, and post the following on a flip chart:

Round 1	Team 1's question	Team 2 answers
Round 2	Team 2's question	Team 3 answers
Round 3	Team 3's question	Team 1 answers
Round 4	Team 1's question	Team 3 answers
Round 5	Team 3's question	Team 2 answers
Round 6	Team 2's question	Team 1 answers
Round 7	Team 2's question	Team 1 answers
Round 8	Team 1's question	Team 3 answers
Round 9	Team 3's question	Team 2 answers

11. Total the teams' points.

12. Conclude the activity with several summarizing questions.

   ■ Were all situations addressed clearly? If not, which ones?

   ■ What can you conclude about management development from this exercise?

   ■ What will you do as a result of what you have learned?

   (Fifteen minutes.)

13. For extra fun, and to end the activity on a high note, ask the High Wizard Council to come up with final words of wisdom (preferably silly and profound) for the participants. Let them sprinkle their "Wizard Dust" on participants.

Variations

■ Using only two situations per group and only six rounds can shorten this activity, or it can be longer if there are a lot of points to be covered.

■ Any other training topic can be used in place of management development.

Submitted by Patti Shank.

Patti Shank, principal, Insight Ed, assesses, designs, facilitates, and develops innovative instructor-led and technology-based educational programs. She is a faculty member at George Washington University and the University of Colorado. Ms. Shank formerly worked as a manager of health education and training for a large health care organization. Her department's creative programming won accolades and awards from accreditation and national training organizations. She is a contributing writer for Lakewood Publishing's Technology for Learning *newsletter and often speaks at training conferences.*

654. COMMUNICATION GAMES: ELIMINATING UNPRODUCTIVE BEHAVIOR DURING PERFORMANCE REVIEWS

Goals

- To help participants understand the types of dysfunctional communication games that are often "played" in performance review discussions.

- To help participants recognize communication games and avoid or stop playing them.

Group Size

Any number of participants.

Time Required

Two hours.

Materials

- One copy of the Communication Games Descriptions for each participant.

- One copy of the Communication Games Work Sheet for each participant.

- One copy of the Communication Games Answer Sheet for the facilitator.

- One copy of the Communication Games Tips for Improving Feedback and Oral Communications for the facilitator.

- One copy of the Communication Games Guidelines for Useful Feedback for each participant.

- A pencil for each participant.

Physical Setting

A room with sufficient space to complete and discuss the work sheet in small groups. Writing surfaces should be provided.

Process

1. Distribute the Communication Games Descriptions to participants, allow them time to read the content, and then discuss each of the various communication games listed on the handout with the group. Solicit real-life examples and comments from participants. (Thirty minutes.)

2. Distribute the Communication Games Work Sheet and pencils and tell participants they will have fifteen minutes to complete it. (Fifteen minutes.)

3. When everyone has completed the work sheet, bring the large group together and ask for volunteers to name the communications game for each statement. Use the Answer Sheet to ensure correct answers are provided. Encourage participants to comment about their results and discuss their answers. (Fifteen minutes.)

4. Use an interactive discussion as you present the Communication Games Tips for Improving Feedback and Communications. (Thirty minutes.)

5. Provide one copy of the Communication Games Guidelines for Useful Feedback to each participant. Have participants pair off and practice giving reassuring and remedial feedback during a performance appraisal. Tell them to "Use a situation in which you have received several complaints from other employees or customers that suggest your employee does not have the necessary skills or knowledge for the job. Tailor it to your job situation." (Fifteen minutes.)

6. Wrap up with a total group discussion of what participants have learned. Use the following questions to focus the discussion:

   - What did you learn from this activity?

   - How will you apply your knowledge to communication on the job?

   - What will you do differently during performance reviews in the future?

   (Fifteen minutes.)

Variation

- Use an observer during the practice session to detect any communication games that are being played.

Reference

Blanchard, K., & Johnson, S. (1981). *The one minute manager.* New York: Berkley Books.

Submitted by Don Morrison.

Don Morrison *is president of Sound Resource Management, a full-service human resource consulting firm. Mr. Morrison is the author of a number of human-resource related publications, including* Employee Performance Planning and Review System *and* Employee Recruitment and Selection in a Post-ADA Environment. *Prior to establishing his consulting firm, he worked as both an HR director and chief executive officer for a number of public corporations.*

Communication Games Descriptions

Unfortunately, feedback sessions, like all forms of human communications, are subject to the games people play, which can interfere with open and honest communication. Everyone plays these games at some time—whether as the giver or the receiver of feedback. Such behavior is particularly harmful to both the employee and the organization when used in a performance review session.

We all need to know the different types of games, how to recognize them, and how to avoid or stop playing them altogether. The communication games played by the sender in the performance feedback situation include:

- *It's My Obligation.* In this game, the sender makes it clear that he or she is giving feedback out of an obligation to the process, with little commitment to sharing observations, solving problems, or using the performance review as a way to improve individual or work unit productivity. The obligatory forms are filled out and used as a shield. The receiver will find the review cold, impersonal, and often negative.

- *Hiding the Real Message.* In this game, the sender avoids direct and clear communication, hiding the real message with verbal qualifiers, reservations, and excess words. By the time the sender gets to the point, the receiver is lost in all the extra verbiage. This game makes it difficult, if not impossible, for the receiver to understand the message.

- *This Isn't Serious.* Sometimes, after giving negative feedback, senders decide they don't want to "hurt" the receivers, so they decide to rescue them. The sender will throw out a comment such as, "Well, don't worry about it; it wasn't important anyway" or "Don't worry; you aren't the first and you won't be the last to make that mistake." The result is that the receiver is led to believe the feedback and the poor performance were unimportant.

- *Leading Questions.* Here, the sender acts like Perry Mason and asks leading and unnerving questions. While this may be all right for Mr. Mason in his efforts to trap a criminal, it is not a good practice in a performance feedback session. The results are mistrust, suspicion, and increased defensiveness on the part of the receiver.

- *Guess What I'm Really Thinking.* In this game, the sender delivers indirect messages and expects the receiver to determine the hidden meaning from nonverbals. This game is commonly played by supervisors, and the employees are expected to divine the true meaning of the message.

These games are all ways for the sender to avoid giving direct and clear feedback. They allow senders to avoid making disclosures and saying what they really mean. The solution is for senders to learn how to say what they mean and mean what they say.

Games can also be played by the receiver. Receiver games are primarily designed to obscure the message, particularly during a performance review session. These games include:

- *Make the Sender Feel Guilty.* During this game, the receiver attempts to make the sender feel guilty by interpreting the feedback to apply to a much broader range of behavior or results than the sender intends. The receiver looks and acts hurt, pouts, and even sulks for days. This type of guilt trip can ruin open, direct communication.

- *Divert Attention.* During this game, the receiver doesn't check for understanding or details, but quickly changes the subject whenever a sensitive issue is broached. The results are that the feedback session goes nowhere because no conclusion is reached and action planning never take place.

- *I'm Not the Only One.* Here, the receiver uses the rule of "safety in numbers." He or she tries to show that the feedback is in error by explaining how many other people are doing the same thing. The result is that the receiver will miss chances for growth and improvement by not "owning" the feedback.

- *Be a Masochist.* In this game, the receiver punishes someone (usually himself or herself) so the sender (usually the supervisor) won't have to. This game is often played by overachievers. It is designed, in part, to force the sender into giving only positive feedback. The result is that the receiver spends so much time in self-talk that the useful feedback may never by heard.

Most of these feedback games are smoke screens to keep the receiver from hearing and acting on feedback. In a performance feedback session, the employee suffers in the long run from these communication games.

COMMUNICATION GAMES WORK SHEET

Directions: Identify each statement below with the letter of the type of communication game being played, as follows:

A = It's My Obligation   D = Leading Questions   G = Divert Attention
B = Hiding the Real Message   E = Guess What I'm Really Thinking   H = I'm Not the Only One
C = This Isn't Serious   F = Make the Sender Feel Guilty   I = Be a Masochist

_____ 1. Joe, why are you always putting me down?

_____ 2. It's company policy to do these performance reviews.

_____ 3. I knew I blew it. Perhaps I should resign.

_____ 4. You're not measuring up, and I think you know why.

_____ 5. Let's not discuss it now. Let's use the time to review the Becker project.

_____ 6. Did you really correct the numbers? Who can confirm that? Do I need to audit your work? Interview staff?

_____ 7. Everybody takes extended breaks.

_____ 8. I think you may tend to get a little too busy and don't always check things out. Not always, but enough to raise questions about your work. The point is, your calculations are often inaccurate.

_____ 9. Don't take this too seriously; it's no big deal.

_____ 10. I work my tail off, and what thanks do I get?

_____ 11. I think everyone in the work group would disagree.

_____ 12. Let's get this over with so we can get back to work.

_____ 13. How many times were you late this month? Do you know everyone's complaining? Can't you get here on time?

_____ 14. Taking that approach can lead to big trouble, if you know what I mean.

_____ 15. Why do you think I gave you this rating on the project?

_____ 16. That's your opinion. Anything else you want to say?

COMMUNICATION GAMES ANSWER SHEET

A = It's My Obligation   2

B = Hiding the Real Message   8

C = This Isn't Serious   9, 12

D = Leading Questions   6, 13

E = Guess What I'm Really Thinking   4, 14, 15

F = Make the Sender Feel Guilty   1, 10

G = Divert Attention   5, 16

H = I'm Not the Only One   7, 11

I = Be a Masochist   3

Communication Games Tips for Improving Feedback and Oral Communications

Feedback is an intense form of communication for both the supervisor and the employee. The supervisor needs to communicate conclusions about performance to employees. On the other hand, employees want to know where they stand, but may find some or all of the feedback hard to take. Feedback must be specific and clear enough that the employee can accept it and make a commitment to an appropriate course of action.

Both the supervisor and the employee must be committed to giving and receiving clear feedback whenever they can. The following five tips, which are expanded below, can help you make the feedback process work:

1. Know what's in it for you;

2. Develop your feedback skills;

3. Don't play communication games;

4. Remember that feedback occurs between human beings;

5. Focus on goals (accomplishments), knowledge, skills, and style.

Know What's in It for You

Feedback is often viewed as either positive or negative, but another way to see performance management is as supportive of employees. Even when feedback is positive, it can produce stress and anxiety. Thinking about the long-term payoffs of successful feedback helps put this short-term discomfort into perspective.

Some of the payoffs for giving quality supportive feedback are:

1. The satisfaction of helping another grow and develop.

2. Working with integrity and in a way that shows respect for others in the workplace.

3. Being open and honest with people.

4. Producing the quality and quantity—bottom-line results.

5. Meaningful interpersonal relations based on open, clear, and supportive feedback.

Develop Your Feedback Skills

During feedback sessions, both the supervisor and the employee give and receive feedback. Both, therefore, need to use key feedback skills. Three of these
skills—listening, empathizing, and questioning—are responsive.

To be responsive, a person must be receptive and non-evaluative. The
other two—concluding and describing—are assertive. To use these skills, a
person must be proactive, be willing to take risks, and be able to evaluate what
is heard.

The responsive and assertive skill groups are two different ways of
thinking and acting. Most people think only of the assertive feedback given
by the supervisor in performance management, but responsive skills are also
critical in these situations. Both the supervisor and the employee must use
all five skills from both groups. The ability to "shift gears" from using responsive skills to using assertive skills and back again is the real "art" of effective feedback.

Listening is a vital skill in all areas of human communications; in a
performance management session, it is critical. Both the supervisor and the
employee must listen! They must set aside their personal opinions, feelings,
and biases so they can hear the other person's point of view. They must be
able to paraphrase the other's observations and conclusions.

A point of view is kind of like a belly button—everyone has one! Your
point of view contains all your values, biases, feelings, emotions, and needs
as you view the world around you. In a feedback session, your point of view
must be "defused" or "suspended" for you to understand the other person
and to empathize with him or her. Listening for and acknowledging feelings
can help remove personal blocks or defensiveness that often threaten a feedback session.

Empathizing occurs when either the supervisor or the employee:

- Asks for information about the other's feelings;

- Shares his or her own similar experiences;

- Make statements that show understanding of the feelings and values of
  the other person; and

- Avoids evaluating the other's feelings and values.

Empathizing and empathic listening keep communication from being
a mechanical process.

Both the supervisor and the employee also need questioning skills to gain understanding of one another's points of view. Questioning shows interest in what the other person is saying. This interest should also be supported through nonverbal behavior. The best questioning technique is to ask open-ended questions, such as "Tell me why that happened," "What do you think about that?" or "How did you proceed?"

The major purpose of performance feedback is to make sure that an employee's performance is on target. During the process, both the supervisor and the employee must judge that performance. Supervisors are paid to judge others' performance, but employees must engage in continuous self-evaluation of their own performance. This process involves:

- Judging the quality, quantity, timeliness, and appropriateness of behavior across a variety of situations and against established goals;

- Making judgments about the strengths and weaknesses of accomplishments, knowledge, skills, ability, and style;

- Controlling personal biases; and

- Determining whether success or failure is due to the individual's behavior or to factors beyond the individual's control.

Supervisors first draw conclusions, then decide what feedback to give, how to evaluate the employee's performance, what additional training or development is needed, what additional work assignments to give, and what support is needed to meet or exceed goals.

Simply observing performance and drawing conclusions is not enough. Both the supervisor and the employee must be able to describe the performance in a clear, concise, and concrete way. This involves:

- Describing the observed behavior, actions, and results;

- Being specific about the time, place, behavior, actions, and results observed;

- Describing one's own reactions and personal feelings about the behavior and the results; and

- Tailoring the timing and the amount of feedback.

Don't Play Communication Games

We all need be able to recognize and avoid communication games. Sender games include:

- It's My Obligation
- Hiding the Real Message
- This Isn't Serious
- Leading Questions
- Guess What I'm Really Thinking

   Receiver games include:

- Make the Sender Feel Guilty
- Divert Attention
- I'm Not the Only One
- Be a Masochist

Remember That Feedback Occurs Between Human Beings

Performance feedback occurs between two human beings, so it will always be a somewhat subjective process. It cannot be effectively computerized or otherwise mechanized. It will always involve judgment, questioning, empathy, and personal commitment.

   It is important for both the supervisor and the employee to try to be as objective, detailed, and concrete as possible. Each must try to avoid playing communication games. They both must be willing and able to give and receive feedback. But they are both human, with their own concerns, opinions, and reactions.

Focus on Goals (Accomplishments), Knowledge, Skills, and Style

What individuals do from day-to-day has both short-term and long-term implications. Evaluating and discussing performance is a complex process. All aspects of the employee's performance should be covered—not only the goals themselves, but also how the goals were accomplished and the impact of the employee's performance on others inside and outside of the organization.

This means discussing the knowledge and skills used by the employee or the absence of critical knowledge and skills. It also means discussing the effectiveness of the employee's style.

Both the supervisor and the employee must be willing to discuss all aspects of performance. There will be short-term anxieties, but the long-term payoffs—an open, honest relationship, strengthened communications, and improved performance—more than offset any short-term anxiety.

Types of Feedback

One of the most important tools a supervisor has for maintaining control and developing employees is the proper use of feedback. Feedback can be either verbal or nonverbal. Nonverbal feedback sends a message, although perhaps not what is intended. For purposes of this discussion, we will focus on verbal feedback. Verbal feedback has often been categorized as either positive or negative, but another way of viewing it is as *reassuring* feedback (reinforcing ongoing behavior) or *remedial* feedback (indicating that a change in behavior is needed). In this sense, all feedback can be considered positive, in that it is for the growth and development of the individual.

Reassuring Feedback. One of the most damaging and erroneous assumptions that supervisors make is that good performance and appropriate behavior are to be "expected" from the employee and that the only time feedback is needed is when the employee does something wrong. Supervisors operating under this assumption rarely give supportive feedback, although in reality it is the more important of the two types of feedback. An axiom of effective supervision (Blanchard & Johnson, 1982) it to "catch them doing something right and let them know it." Use reassuring feedback to reinforce behavior that contributes to organizational goals and values.

If you focus on what employees are doing well, then they will come to value excellent work and see their work in terms of performing as well as possible. What is reinforced has a tendency to become stronger. What is not reinforced has a tendency to fade away, so excellence should be actively reinforced and errors simply mentioned so that employees will focus on excellence. The following example of the two types of feedback illustrates the difference.

Focus on Errors: "The last four letters you typed were replete with typos. I cannot have that kind of sloppy work going out of my office."

Focus on Excellence: "The written communications this week have looked good, except for the last four letters, which contained a number of typos. Perhaps your fingers get ahead of themselves. Please take these back and retype them. Thanks."

Fortunately, however, no one has to make a choice between using only reassuring or only remedial feedback. Both are important and useful, and it is important to understand how each works so that the maximum benefit can be obtained.

Remedial Feedback.   Remedial feedback is as essential to the healing and growth process as is reassuring feedback. It should be thought of as a remedy, a prescription for improved health and performance, used to alter behavior that is ineffective.

A remedial feedback session, although not harmful if done correctly, is not always an enjoyable experience for the receiver. Even under the best of circumstances, the subordinate will probably feel a little defensive or embarrassed. There is no need to apologize for giving remedial feedback. Remedial or otherwise, feedback is a contribution; apologies will discount its importance and lessen its impact. Nevertheless, remedial feedback must be given in a way that does not lessen the recipient's dignity and sense of self-worth.

The supervisor should always have an option ready to explore with the employee. Presenting a behavioral option that the employee might never have considered can be effective and powerful in altering and "healing" bad behavior. The option should be presented immediately after the remedial feedback to help the employee move quickly to a more comfortable position. This reinforces the intrinsic worth of the employee and helps him or her focus on the possibilities and prospects for positive growth.

The following example shows how an option could be presented when giving remedial feedback: "When you criticized Bob during the staff meeting, he seemed very intimidated and upset. When you choose to criticize others' input, it's less disconcerting for everyone to discuss it with the person privately after the meeting."

Guidelines for Giving Effective Feedback

The following guidelines are helpful for anyone who is trying to improve feedback skills:

Be Specific.   Being specific is the most important rule in giving any type of feedback. Unless the feedback is specific, very little learning or reinforcement is possible. The following examples show the difference between general and specific feedback:

General: "I'm happy to see that your work is getting better."

Specific: "I'm happy that you turned in every report on schedule this month."

Although a supervisor's approval ("I'm pleased to see. . . .") or disapproval ("I'm upset that. . . .") can give emphasis to feedback, it should be supported by specific evidence in order to effect a change in behavior.

Center on Actions, Not on Attitudes. Although subordinates should always be accountable for their actions, it is much more difficult to hold them accountable for their attitudes or feelings. Of course, attitudes and feelings are important, yet they are difficult to quantify, so discussing them leads to generalities and may lead to defensiveness. Just as feedback must be specific and observable in order to be effective, it must be nonthreatening in order to be accepted.

One attitude that managers often try to measure is loyalty. Certain employee actions that seem to indicate loyalty or disloyalty can be observed, but loyalty is a result, not an action. The following highlights the difference between giving feedback on actions and giving feedback on attitudes:

Feedback on attitude: "You have been showing disrespect for Tammy again."

Feedback on actions: "You refused to help Tammy with the month-end report, threw the printout down on her desk, and swore at her."

The more that remedial feedback is molded in terms of attitude, the more it will be perceived as a personal attack and the more difficult it will be to deal with the employee's reactions. The more that remedial feedback is cast in specific, behavioral terms, the more likely that it will be accepted by the receiver. The more that reassuring feedback is given in terms of specific actions, the higher the likelihood that those actions and behaviors will be repeated.

Give Feedback as Close to the Actual Event as Possible. Feedback of either type works best if it is given as soon as possible after the behavior occurs. Waiting decreases the impact that the feedback will have on the behavior. The passage of time may make the behavior seem less important to both parties and may mean that specific details are forgotten.

On the other hand, dwelling on something for a long period can cause it to be blown out of proportion. From the subordinate's point of view, the longer the wait for the feedback, the less important it must be. The following example illustrates this point:

Delayed feedback: "Several times last year you didn't submit your monthly capital improvement progress reports."

Immediate feedback: "It's July 3 and you haven't turned in your capital improvement progress reports for June."

Pick an Appropriate Time.   Enough time should be allotted for the feedback session to deal with the issues completely. A manager can undermine the effectiveness of feedback by watching the clock and hurrying through the session. Picking the right time and place is a matter of mixing a little common sense with an awareness of organizational values and the significance of the message.

Do Not Mix Your Agenda.   Frequently, other issues surface during a feedback session. When reassuring feedback is being given, no topic that does not relate to the specific feedback should be discussed if it would undercut the message. For example, the manager could destroy the good just accomplished by adding, "Oh, before I forget, even though you did a great job on the facility plan, I'd like you to pay closer attention to your monthly progress reports. The last one was pretty sloppy." When the parting comment is negative, it has a lingering effect and can completely overshadow and negate the positive.

When remedial feedback is given, however, the situation is different. The feedback should be absorbed as soon as possible, with the employee's negative feelings lasting no longer than necessary. Any reproving should be accompanied by an immediate show of concern and reassurance. As soon as the feedback has been understood and acknowledged, and a commitment has been secured to improve, the manager may want to solicit the employee's input on something else or make some other reassuring statement that reaffirms the employee's intrinsic worth and value. Obviously, the supervisor should not concoct a situation just to provide this type of feedback.

In certain situations, it is appropriate to give both reassuring and remedial feedback at the same time. This is true for training sessions, performance review meetings, and when experienced employees are being assigned new and challenging tasks.

When the situation is appropriate for giving both types of feedback at the same time, don't use the word "but" to connect the two thoughts. The word will dampen nearly everything that was said before it. If it is fitting to give reassuring and remedial feedback within the same sentence, the clauses should be connected with "and." This allows both parts of the sentence to be heard clearly and sets the stage for a positive suggestion. Here are some examples of these sentence structures:

Connected with but: "Your output the first quarter was high, but your second quarter performance should have met the same high standard."

Connected with and: "Your first report was on time, and your others should have been also."

Connected with but: "You were late this morning, but the chief called to tell you what a great job you did on the budget."

Connected with and: "You were late this morning, and the chief called to tell you what a great job you did on the budget."

Alternate the reassuring and remedial feedback. When considerable feedback is being given at the same time, it is frequently better to mix the reassuring feedback with the remedial feedback than to give all of one type and then all of the other.

Regardless of which category comes first, whatever is said last will be remembered the most clearly. If someone with low self-esteem is first given reassuring feedback and then only remedial, he or she is likely to believe the reassuring feedback was given just to soften the blow. Alternating between the two types will make all the feedback seem more genuine.

When feasible, do use reassuring feedback to soften the remedial feedback. When both types of feedback are appropriate, there is usually no reason to start with reassuring. However, this does not mean that remedial feedback should be quickly sandwiched in between reassuring statements. Use reassuring statements as a good teaching aid for areas that need improvement. This is especially true if the employee has done a good job in the past and then has failed under similar circumstances.

Using Feedback Effectively

When using feedback, "seek first to understand, then seek to be understood." The person giving the feedback is responsible for helping the recipient to understand what is being said. Because we all see the world differently, it is important for the recipient to understand the giver's perspective before responding.

Feedback should always be used to develop the employee and support positive growth, not to destroy the individual. The object of giving feedback is not to critique the other person, but to relate what was seen and heard and what effects that behavior has had. One's personal approval or disapproval, even if important, is secondary.

Remedial feedback should be given directly to the person for whom it is intended. If others are present, they should not become an audience. Good eye contact with the recipient is essential.

Receiving Feedback

Just as giving feedback properly requires skill and understanding, so does receiving it. When receiving feedback, many people tend to argue, become defensive, refuse to believe, or discredit the information. Statements such as, "I didn't say that," "That's not what I meant," and "You don't understand what I was trying to do" are attempts to convince the person giving the feedback that he or she is wrong.

However, the recipient must understand that the observer—whether manager, peer, or subordinate—is simply relating what he or she experienced as a result of the recipient's behavior. Right or wrong, perceptions are important and affect behavior. Of course the giver and receiver have different viewpoints, but the purpose of feedback is to give a new view or to increase awareness.

As a rule of thumb, the appropriate response is to acknowledge and thank the person for the feedback. It is also appropriate, of course, to ask for clarity or more detail on any issue—seeking to understand before seeking to be understood.

Feedback can be thought of as food. It is necessary to grow, develop, and sustain life. When people are hungry, food is what they need; but when they are full, food is the last thing they want or need. The same applies to "swallowing" feedback. When people have had enough, they should stop. Attempting to swallow all the feedback that might be available, or that various people would like to give, is like taking another helping just because someone says, "Have some more."

It is reasonable for the receiver to expect specificity in feedback. No feedback should be given or accepted as legitimate if it cannot be clearly demonstrated by an observable behavior. For example, if someone says, "You're not a team player," an appropriate question would be, "What specifically have I said or done to cause you to think that?"

If that response is countered with "I don't know; I just feel that way," then the accusation should be immediately forgotten.

It is impossible to change to meet everyone else's expectations, and the situation becomes more complicated as more and more people express differing expectations or feedback. A single act can generate disparate feedback from different people who observe it. For example, failure to contribute at a staff meeting could be viewed as uncooperative by one person, shyness by another, or merely uninformed by a third. Each person will see it from his or her unique perspective.

Even though an individual is the best authority on himself or herself, there are still parts of each person's behavior that are more obvious to others. Only the individual can decide whether or not to change the behavior. For feedback to be effective, the receiver must hear what the giver is saying, weigh it, and then determine whether or not the information is relevant.

Although people may be the best judges of their own attitudes and intentions, they are better able to grow and develop if they pay attention to the feedback they receive from others, even if the feedback is uncomfortable to receive.

Effective Strategies for Giving Feedback

The strategies below offer one approach to giving feedback during a performance review. First, decide on the desired future objective, whether in the next ten minutes after the session or three years later. Pay attention to the ultimate outcome. Focus on the desired results, not on following the system. Change your methods or even modify your original strategy if conditions change or unforeseen events occur. After you decide on an approach, keep the following rules in mind:

- Be clear about what you want in terms of specific, identifiable outcomes for yourself, your subordinate, and the organization.

- Outline what you expect to say and how you intend to conduct the meeting.

- Have a strategy in mind as you meet with the individual, but don't have it out in the open.

Giving Reassuring Feedback

The following are some suggested strategies for giving reassuring feedback:
- Acknowledge the specific action and result you are reinforcing. Immediately let your subordinate know that you are pleased about something he or she did. Be specific and describe the event in behavioral terms. ("You finished the project on time!")

- Explain the accomplishment and state your appreciation. The person must be able to see the effects of his or her behavior in specific, observable ways. Your appreciation is important, but as an additional reinforcing element. The main reinforcement is the effect. ("It was a major factor in getting the contract, and I am pleased with your outstanding work.")

- Help the subordinate to take full responsibility for the success. If the employee acknowledges the feedback, this step is accomplished. If the employee seems overly modest, more work is needed. Unless he or she can internalize the success and receive satisfaction from it, very little growth will occur.

  Ask how the success was accomplished or if any problems were encountered and how they were overcome. In talking about what happened, the employee is likely to realize how much he or she was really responsible for. It is important for both of you to hear how success was accomplished.

- Ask if the subordinate wants to talk about anything else. While the employee is feeling positive and knows that you are appreciative and receptive, he or she may be willing to open up about other issues. The positive energy created by this meeting can be directed toward other work-related issues, so take advantage of the opportunity.

- Thank the subordinate for the good performance. This assures that your appreciation will be remembered as he or she returns to the work setting.

Giving Remedial Feedback

The following steps are suggested as a strategy for giving remedial feedback:

- Relate clearly in specific, observable, and behavioral terms the nature of the failure or behavior and the effect of the failure or behavior on the work group or organization. If you can say something appropriate to reduce the employee's anxiety, the employee is more likely to accept the feedback nondefensively.

- Before assuming that the subordinate is at fault, ask what happened. In many instances, the subordinate is not at fault or is only partially responsible.

- Help the employee take full responsibility for his or her actions. The more time spent in finding out what happened, the easier this will be. The employee needs to learn from the experience in order to reduce the probability of a reoccurrence, but unless this step is handled effectively, the employee will feel defensive.

- After the employee has accepted responsibility, the next step is to decide what to do to rectify the situation. Jointly devise a plan that will help eliminate errors.

If you both want the same thing (i.e., better performance), then both of you are obligated to do something about it. This is also an excellent opportunity to build on the employee's strengths. ("I'd like you to develop a purchasing policy with the same quality as the investment policy you wrote.")

- Once the issue is resolved, end the session by stating your confidence in the ability of the employee to handle the situation. The object is to allow the employee to re-enter the work setting feeling as optimistic as the situation permits. The employee must also understand that you will follow up and give additional feedback.

Communication Games Guidelines for Useful Feedback

- Useful feedback is descriptive rather than evaluative. By avoiding evaluative language, it reduces the need for the receiver to respond defensively. The receiver may choose to use or reject the feedback on its own merits.

- Useful feedback is specific rather than general. For example, being told that one is "autocratic" and "domineering" will probably not be as useful as to be told, "Just now when we were discussing the issue, you did not listen to what others said, and I felt forced to accept your arguments or to face attack from you."

- Useful feedback takes into account the needs of both the receiver and the giver. Feedback can be destructive when it serves only the giver's needs.

- Useful feedback is directed toward behavior the receiver can change. Frustration is only increased when a person is reminded of a shortcoming over which he or she has little or no control.

- Useful feedback is solicited rather than imposed. Feedback is most useful when the receiver asks a question that those observing him or her can answer.

- Useful feedback is well-timed. In general, feedback is most useful when given as soon as possible after the observed behavior, depending, of course, on the person's readiness to hear it, on support available from others, etc.

- Useful feedback is checked with the sender. The receiver should rephrase the feedback he or she has received to ensure clear communication.

- Useful feedback is checked with others in the group. In a training group, particularly, both giver and receiver can check their feedback with others for agreement.

655. MILLENNIUM MOBILE: LEARNING FOUR FUNCTIONS OF MANAGEMENT

Goals

- To demonstrate the necessity of effective planning as a function of management.

- To demonstrate and investigate methods of organizing as a function of management.

- To demonstrate and investigate leadership as a function of management.

- To demonstrate and investigate control as a function of management.

Group Size

At least two subgroups of six to eight individuals, with a maximum of five subgroups.

Time Required

One and one-half to two hours.

Materials

- One copy of the Millennium Mobile Lecturette for the facilitator.

- One copy of the Millennium Mobile Group Leader Instruction Sheet for each group leader.

- Assorted construction materials for each group—for example, index cards, cellophane tape, colored markers, paper clips, scissors, rubber bands, pipe cleaners, and other such objects—placed in advance on each table.

- A flip chart and felt-tipped markers for each subgroup.

Physical Setting

A room with enough tables to seat the subgroups comfortably while they construct their "millennium mobiles." Round tables work best.

Process

1. Give a brief lecturette on the four functions of management, using the Millennium Mobile Lecturette provided or your own material. Then lead a brief discussion of the main points and the four functions, posting them on a flip chart. Ask for examples from the participants. (Fifteen minutes.)

2. Divide participants into subgroups of six to eight members each and ask each subgroup to select a leader.

3. Give each leader a copy of the Millennium Mobile Group Leader Instruction Sheet. Give the leaders time to read the instructions and then answer any questions they have concerning expectations in broad, general terms only. Say that they are to make whatever decisions are necessary to meet the objectives, but that they must remember to use the four functions of management—planning, organizing, leading, and controlling.

4. Tell everyone to begin. Play the role of an observer, going from group to group noting the following:

   ■ How each subgroup leader communicates with his or her group. Especially note how the leaders provide information to the groups.

   ■ The methods each group uses for planning, especially whether the leader includes others in the planning phase and how.

   ■ Whether each group makes a contingency plan and whether the overall plan meets the objectives of the project.

   ■ The methods the group uses to organize. Are they by function? Product-related? Process-related?

   ■ Any communication issues that occur.

   ■ Methods the leaders use to motivate and provide leadership to the groups. Determine the kind of leadership that is being used and whether it works and what kind of motivation techniques are used and whether they are effective.

   ■ The types of controls implemented and their effectiveness.

   (Sixty minutes.)

5. After the time is up, have each group, in turn, present its millennium mobile. Encourage applause after each presentation. (Five minutes.)

6. Ask each leader to explain the steps and process taken to complete the projects. Seek comments from group members.

7. Share your observations of each group's process with the total group. (Five minutes.)

8. Lead a concluding discussion based on the following questions:

   ■ How effective was your leader in using the four functions of management described earlier?

   ■ What was the most effective planning process used for making the Millennium Mobile? What made it so effective?

   ■ What impact did the way your team was organized have on the completion of the project?

   ■ How appropriate was the leadership style used by your group leader? Why do you think that?

   ■ What kind of power did your group leader exhibit? How effective was it?

   ■ How were you, as a worker, motivated to complete the task? What would have been more motivating for you?

   ■ How were performance standards established and measured in your group? What other ways could have been used?

   ■ Was your "organization" functional? Why or why not?

   (Twenty to thirty minutes.)

Submitted by Erica Nagel Allgood and Terry Carlyle.

Erica Nagel Allgood, principal, Enhanced Training & Development, specializes in communication and management training. She is the lead faculty in the Communication Arts Department at Regis University, Colorado Springs, Colorado. She served as the 1999 president of the Pikes Peak Chapter of the American Society for Training and Development (ASTD). In 1996, Ms. Allgood co-authored The Team Trainer: Winning Tools and Tactics for Successful Workouts, *published by ASTD and Irwin Professional Publishing. She received her master of arts in organizational communication from Kent State University.*

Terry Carlyle, principal, Enhanced Training & Development, has extensive experience in performance management and management/supervisory training. He currently serves as faculty curriculum coordinator for the University of Phoenix and as adjunct faculty at Regis University, Colorado Springs, Colorado. Mr. Carlyle served as the 1999 vice president for membership for the Pikes Peak Chapter of ASTD. His education includes a master's of science in human resource management and development from Chapman College.

MILLENNIUM MOBILE LECTURETTE

Four Basic Functions of Management

Organizational success can be attributed directly to the ability of supervisors and managers to perform the following four functions of management: *planning, organizing, leading,* and *controlling.*

The first function, planning, includes the setting of goals and objectives, which gives organizations a "road map." The planning process must also include a contingency plan to address potential opportunities and threats that may arise. Many organizations create three- to five-year strategic plans. Additionally, they often create short-term operational plans to implement and support their strategic plans.

The second function of management, organizing, puts the right methods, tools, resources, and materials in place to accomplish the objectives identified in the strategic and operational plans. Determining how many employees are needed and the skills these employees must possess is one of the most critical aspects of the organizing function.

Leading, the third function of management, provides the vital direction and motivation of employees to meet established goals. Having the ability to communicate effectively with employees is crucial for this function. Creating an environment that inspires workers to produce, often under difficult situations, separates great leaders from mere managers.

The controlling function of management is used to measure results and create feedback mechanisms. By comparing progress at every point with established standards, managers can determine whether the organization's goals will be achieved. Feedback allows corrective action to be taken. If an established plan is no longer viable, it can be altered or adapted.

If the organization is not performing as expected, the manager must use his or her organizing ability to reexamine the situation. Perhaps workers were put in positions that did not take advantage of their strong skills. Perhaps the organization should increase the emphasis on quality and reduce the emphasis on quantity. If workers are not producing in accordance with expectations and needs, different leadership techniques and motivational tools may be called for. Only by using all available leadership skills can a company be assured of meeting its established goals.

MILLENNIUM MOBILE GROUP LEADER INSTRUCTION SHEET

Instructions: As the leader within your group, your task is to help your group to build a car, the Millennium Mobile, with the supplies provided. The car you build should meet the needs of the average family in the next millennium. All groups are in competition to build the best car. If you win, your group will be awarded a very lucrative contract, and you as leader will receive a large bonus.

You will have one hour to write your group's plan for creating a car for the millennium; organize your "employees"; and provide appropriate leadership and controls as they build their car. At the end of the hour, a judging committee made up of your peers will select the best car.

Things to consider:

- Efficient use of time.

- Economical use of materials.

- Fair and equitable job standards.

- Efficient use of human resources.

- Space for construction.

- Experience of your workers.

- Motivation of your workers.

656. Leadership Style: Learning to Take Risks*

*This activity was adapted from *50 Activities for Developing Leaders* by Lois B. Hart, HRD Press, 1994. Copyright © Lois B. Hart.

Goals

- To identify one's risk-taking style.
- To learn how to recognize the level of risk inherent in a situation.
- To learn how to weigh the pros and cons of taking risks.
- To identify reasons why willingness to take risks is essential for leaders.

Group Size

Twenty-four participants in subgroups of four to six.

Time Required

Eighty to one hundred minutes.

Materials

- One copy of the Leadership Style Risks Work Sheet for each participant.
- One copy of the Leadership Style Planning Sheet for each participant.
- A flip chart and felt-tipped markers.

Physical Setting

Enough open space that subgroups can sit in circles of four to six chairs each.

Process

1. Introduce the topic:

> "The focus of this activity is to look at how each of you looks at taking risks so that you can apply the awareness you gain to your leadership style. Each of you takes risks every day, although you may not think about it at the time. For instance, you may:

> - Drive to work or a meeting location.
> - Eat food in a restaurant.
> - Decide what to wear without knowing whether the weather will change.
> - Give negative feedback to one of your staff members.
> - Deal with a conflict between two employees.

> Leadership requires taking many risks and modeling the confidence to do so to one's followers. Effective leaders must learn to evaluate their preferred style of taking risks, analyze whether the risks they have taken in the past have been appropriate, and be willing to take risks in the future after preparing themselves properly."

(One minute.)

2. Introduce the goals of the activity.

> "The goals for this session are to identify your individual styles for taking risks, learn a way to recognize the level of each impending risk, learn how to weigh the pros and cons of each risk you face, and learn why risk taking is essential for you as a leader."

3. Have participants form small groups of four to six people and arrange each group's chairs in a circle as far from other groups as possible.

4. Give the following directions:

> "I will give you a series of topics to discuss as a group. There is no need to designate a leader for the discussions. The group will have two minutes to discuss each topic in any way you want."

5. Introduce each of the following topics one at a time, listing them on the flip chart. Keep track of the two-minute time limit. Interrupt the discussion, even if all group members have not finished talking, to introduce the next topic:

- Share something personal with others in the group.

- Share with your group something pleasant that happened to you recently.

- Locate something in your wallet or purse you are willing to talk about.

- Tell others about a time you were embarrassed.

- Discuss a time when you were very angry at work.

- Tell about a time when you were very frightened.

- Say something positive about another person in your group.

- Say something positive about yourself (while standing up).

- Ask someone else how much money he or she earned last year.

- Tell everyone about a sexual fantasy you had.

(Twenty minutes.)

6. As you present each topic, observe the participants' reactions so you can give them feedback later. The topics are listed in an escalating order of risk, with the first items generally perceived as low-level risks and the later items perceived as high-level risks.

7. Poll how many people found the last two topics difficult to discuss compared with the earlier ones. Explain that perceived risk usually falls on a continuum from low, through moderate, to high and that the perception of the level of risk is determined by each individual. Describe what you observed as the groups worked.

8. Give everyone a copy of the Leadership Style Risks Work Sheet. Ask participants to read the directions and complete the work sheet individually. (Fifteen minutes.)

9. Have participates form small groups of four to six to discuss what they wrote, taking turns sharing their answers to the questions at the end of the work sheet. (Twenty minutes.)

10. Bring the total group together and have people share some of their responses and what they have learned about themselves or others.

11. Discuss the following points about taking risks and list them on the flip chart:

- Risks are a part of our everyday experience, although we hesitate to take risks we perceive as high-level.

- We can learn from the risks we have taken in the past.

- Before taking a risk, it is helpful to list the pros and cons.

- The environment in which the risk will be taken must be evaluated.

- Sufficient information must be gathered before deciding whether to take a risk.

- Leaders must be confident in taking risks and model their behavior for followers.

(Fifteen minutes.)

12. Distribute copies of the Leadership Style Planning Sheet and review it with everyone. Ask participants to develop individual plans for taking some risks they may face in the future. (Ten minutes.)

13. After participants have completed their planning sheets, have them discuss their plans with either a partner or in small groups. (Five to ten minutes.)

14. Wrap up and summarize what has been learned with questions such as:

- What did you experience with this activity?

- Do you feel differently about taking risks now?

- What will you do differently as a result of this activity?

(Ten minutes.)

Submitted by Lois B. Hart.

Lois B. Hart, Ed.D., is president of Leadership Dynamics in Lafayette, Colorado. She has more than twenty-seven years' experience as a trainer, facilitator, and consultant, presenting programs on leadership, teams, conflict, and facilitation. Dr. Hart earned her doctorate in leadership development and organizational behavior from the University of Massachusetts. She has authored twenty books, including 50 Activities for Developing Leaders, Learning from Conflict, Training Methods That Work, *and* Faultless Facilitation: A Resource Guide for Team and Group Leaders.

LEADERSHIP STYLE RISKS WORK SHEET

Directions: Recall three risks you have taken at work and three you have taken in your personal life, one under each of the three levels of risk: low, moderate, and high. Write them below under the appropriate category. Next, answer the questions about each of the risks you took.

	How did you feel?	What options did you consider?
Work Risk High		
Moderate		
Low		

	How did you feel?	What options did you consider?
Personal Risk High		
Moderate		
Low		

Now answer the following questions as honestly as you can.

How frequently do you take risks at each level?

In what way is the risk different at each level?

What makes something seem high risk for you?

How do you feel before taking a high risk? While you are taking the risk? Afterward?

How many options do you generally consider before taking any risk?

Is there a difference according to level of risk?

LEADERSHIP STYLE PLANNING SHEET

Directions: List three risks that you either are currently facing or anticipate facing in the near future:

1.

2.

3.

Select one of the risks you listed above and answer the following questions about it:

- Is the risk personal or professional?

- What level is the risk?

- What results would you like?

- What are your concerns about taking this risk?

- What do you stand to gain or lose if you take this risk?

- How could you minimize any losses that might occur?

- What options do you have about whether to take this risk?

- How can you lower the level of risk from high to moderate?

Write a short plan of action for how you will face this particular risk when it comes up.

Keep this form and use it to evaluate and make plans to face other risks, whether on the job or in your personal life.

Introduction

to the Inventories, Questionnaires, and Surveys Section

Inventories, questionnaires, and surveys are valuable tools for the HRD professional. These feedback tools help respondents take an objective look at themselves and their organizations. They also help to explain how a particular theory applies to them or to their situations.

Inventories, questionnaires, and surveys are useful in a number of training and consulting situations: privately for self-diagnosis; one-on-one to plan individual development; in a small group to open discussion; in a work team to help the team to focus on its highest priorities; or in an organization to gather data to achieve progress.

You will find that the use of inventories, questionnaires, and surveys enriches, personalizes, and deepens training, development, and intervention designs. Many can be combined with other experiential learning activities or articles in this or other *Annuals* to design an exciting, involving, practical, and well-rounded intervention.

Each instrument includes the background necessary for understanding, presenting, and using it. Interpretive information, scales, and scoring sheets are also provided. In addition, we include the reliability and validity data contributed by the authors. If you wish additional information on any of these instruments, contact the authors directly. You will find their addresses and telephone numbers in the "Contributors" listing near the end of this volume.

Other assessment tools that address a wider variety of topics can be found in our comprehensive *Reference Guide to Handbooks and Annuals*. This guide indexes all the instruments that we have published to date in the *Annuals*. You will find this complete, up-to-date, and easy-to-use resource valuable for locating other instruments, as well as for locating experiential learning activities and articles.

The 2000 Annual: Volume 1, Training includes four assessment tools in the following categories:

Individual Development

The Sexual Harassment Survey: Exploring Gender Differences
by John E. Oliver, Sarah Bartholomew Ellerbee,
and S. Andrew Ostapski

Manager or Scientist: An Attribute Inventory
by Elizabeth N. Treher and Augustus Walker

Consulting and Facilitating

Transfer Climate Assessment by Paul L. Garavaglia

Leadership

Aptitude for Becoming a Mentor Survey by H.B. Karp

THE SEXUAL HARASSMENT SURVEY: EXPLORING GENDER DIFFERENCES

John E. Oliver, Sarah Bartholomew Ellerbee, and S. Andrew Ostapski

Abstract: Much confusion exists in organizations about what constitutes sexual harassment. The legal definition evolves with every case that is decided by the U.S. Supreme Court. Many organizations either overreact or underreact to reports of sexual harassment. Individuals wonder whether they are behaving properly. Recent research indicates that males and females view sexual harassment in very different ways. The Sexual Harassment Survey (SHS) explores the different perceptions of men and women in order to educate both about their differences and their responsibilities under the law. The SHS is designed to be administered in group learning situations. After completing the survey, individuals score their results, and group participants discuss their feelings, strengthen their knowledge of the law, and learn appropriate behaviors. Some research findings and case law developments are offered so that participants can compare their perceptions to other groups and to the latest legal interpretations.

INTRODUCTION

Men and women perceive sexual harassment in very different ways. Both male and female managers in organizations may be confused about what constitutes sexual harassment and how they should handle complaints. Many organizations have developed policy statements concerning sexual harassment and some have detailed procedures for handling complaints, but individuals and organizations still tend to overreact or underreact to complaints. Individuals who have complained of harassment or been accused of harassment are unsure of the proper way to respond. Training programs have helped to develop policies, procedures, and understanding, but some attempts have caused more fear than positive change.

One reason individuals and organizations are confused about sexual harassment is that the legal definition is still being refined. The initial definition provided by the EEOC (Equal Employment Opportunity Commission) guidelines in 1985 left much room for interpretation, and the courts wrestle in applying the law with each new case. The U.S. Supreme Court has dealt with sexual harassment relatively few times since 1986. Lower courts, however, are flooded with sexual harassment cases. The sometimes-conflicting decisions of these courts have led to confusion for individuals, management, and organizations.

One starting point for clarifying the issues surrounding sexual harassment is to have men and women explore their own perceptions and the perceptions of others, discuss the differences in those perceptions, receive new information about sexual harassment law, and learn how to respond to specific circumstances. Individuals can then return to the workplace armed with the tools to change policies, procedures, behaviors, and decisions.

DESCRIPTION OF THE INSTRUMENT

The Sexual Harassment Survey (SHS) consists of twenty statements of behaviors that may be perceived as sexual harassment. Respondents are asked to read each statement and mark the extent to which they agree that the incident describes sexual harassment using a five-point Likert scale from "strongly disagree" (1) to "strongly agree" (5). Then, respondents are asked to describe the action or punishment that they would recommend, using the following codes:

0 = no action	2 = counseling	4 = suspension
1 = education	3 = reprimand	5 = termination

Subjects then respond to Item 21, which states, "There is no such thing as sexual harassment" by using the five-point Likert scale. They respond yes or no to several questions about whether they feel they have been sexually harassed, whether they reported it, and whether they would report it if it happened today. Respondents are also asked the harasser's relationship to them.

A Scoring Sheet is provided so that survey responses of a group can be tabulated, analyzed, and returned to the group. The Scoring Sheet asks subjects to identify their gender so that you can tabulate group totals according to gender, which, in the authors' experience, has an impact on responses. The Scoring Sheet is unnecessary if you choose not to tabulate the data. In that case, the instrument and the Interpretation Sheet may be sufficient for group discussion, or use the Discussion Sheet to focus further on sexual harassment policies, procedures, and actions.

ADMINISTRATION OF THE INSTRUMENT

Participants should be informed that all responses to the survey will be confidential. Respondents will keep their completed surveys in their possession at all times. If data is to be gathered for analysis and feedback to the group, anonymous Scoring Sheets should be provided after the surveys are completed. Any scores revealed to the group will represent group averages only. Be prepared to allow approximately ten minutes for completion of the survey. No further instructions are necessary.

HELPING PARTICIPANTS INTERPRET THEIR SCORES

The Sexual Harassment Survey Interpretation Sheet is provided to help participants understand the meaning of their scores. The Interpretation Sheet contains the generalized results of several studies done by scholars from across the United States using various approaches. Individuals can compare their scores to the generalized results. In addition, the results of a sample of 179 undergraduate university students from all majors can be used as a comparison. Finally, you may want to analyze and report the scores of the participant group if statistical analysis tools and time are available.

DISCUSSING SURVEY RESULTS

After participants have completed their surveys, a brief discussion of sexual harassment is helpful before scoring and interpreting the instruments. The Interpretation Sheet contains a definition of sexual harassment that can be read to participants. Stress the word "unwelcome" when reading the definition. The first two of the three numbered specifications in the definition are known as "quid pro quo" types of harassment. The third kind is known as "hostile environment" harassment.

After discussing the definition with participants, read the next two paragraphs of the Interpretation Sheet regarding the uniqueness and variations of individual responses and the generalization that women and men tend to rate specific behaviors differently. (You do not need to read the mean scores that are presented between these paragraphs.)

If Scoring Sheets are to be used to analyze participant data, they should be handed out at this point, completed, and collected.

Interpretation Sheets should now be distributed. Individuals should be allowed to study their Interpretation Sheets and surveys for about five minutes. Then break the participants into small, mixed-gender groups of four to six members, hand out the Discussion Sheet and allow twenty to thirty minutes for the groups to discuss the questions. (Analyze group data at this point, if desired, or lead a total-group discussion based on the questions.) A Lecturette is also provided for use at any point, but especially suitable for a wrap-up.

VALIDITY AND RELIABILITY OF THE INSTRUMENT

The validity of the Sexual Harassment Survey instrument is best demonstrated by the correlation of the results with the results of other measures of sexual harassment. As discussed in the interpretation section, the results provided by the instrument coincide with the results from several other studies using different measurement methods. Thus, the content, construct, and criteria related validities are established.

The internal consistency reliability (coefficient alpha) of scores on the survey are .85 for the "a" scale and .83 for the "b" scale. However, for a training aid of this type, neither internal consistency nor test-retest reliability are relevant. The instrument is merely a vehicle to guide discussion and learning. Variations among items are expected, and variations between administrations are indicative of learning due to the intervening experiences, that is, discussions and training.

John E. Oliver received his Ph.D. degree from Georgia State University. He is a professor and head of the Department of Management and Information Systems at Valdosta State University. He has published several instruments and experiential learning exercises in the Annuals, *as well as made over eighty other contributions in journals, books, and magazines. His research and consulting interests are in the areas of human resource development, organizational development, and team development. He serves on the editorial review boards of several journals.*

Sarah Bartholomew Ellerbee is an assistant professor of political science in the College of Arts and Sciences at Valdosta State University. She is the legal advisor for the Legal Assistant Services degree program. She earned her doctor of juris prudence degree in 1989 at Mercer University and her LL.M. degree in 1994 at the University of Georgia. Her research and teaching interests include paralegal education and the legal environment of human resource management.

S. Andrew Ostapski, J.D. (Capital University) and LL.M. (University of Miami), is associate professor, Department of Management and Information Systems, at Valdosta State University. He has written numerous articles in research areas of business law and business ethics. As a former attorney for the U.S. Customs Service, he handled labor and personnel law issues, including sexual harassment.

Sexual Harassment Survey

John E. Oliver, Sarah Bartholomew Ellerbee, and S. Andrew Ostapski

Directions: (a) Read each incident below and mark the extent to which you agree that the incident describes sexual harassment, using the following scale:

1 = Strongly Disagree   2 = Disagree   3 = Neutral   4 = Agree   5 = Strongly Agree

(b) Then describe what action or punishment you would recommend for the action if it took place, using the following scale:

0 = no action   1 = education   2 = counseling   3 = reprimand   4 = suspension   5 = termination

1. Sexually oriented kidding, or teasing.

    _____ a. This describes sexual harassment

    _____ b. Appropriate action

2. Telling sexually oriented jokes.

    _____ a. This describes sexual harassment

    _____ b. Appropriate action

3. Flirting.

    _____ a. This describes sexual harassment

    _____ b. Appropriate action

4. Asking a member of the opposite gender for a date.

    _____ a. This describes sexual harassment

    _____ b. Appropriate action

5. "Elevator eyes" (looking down a person's body and back up again).

    _____ a. This describes sexual harassment

    _____ b. Appropriate action

6. Graphic comment about an individual's body.

    _____ a. This describes sexual harassment

    _____ b. Appropriate action

7. Derogatory comment about women or men in general.

———— a. This describes sexual harassment

———— b. Appropriate action

8. Staring at another individual's body.

———— a. This describes sexual harassment

———— b. Appropriate action

9. "Wolf whistle."

———— a. This describes sexual harassment

———— b. Appropriate action

10. Intentionally touching or brushing another's body.

———— a. This describes sexual harassment

———— b. Appropriate action

11. Crude language.

———— a. This describes sexual harassment

———— b. Appropriate action

12. Displaying objects or pictures that are sexual in nature.

———— a. This describes sexual harassment

———— b. Appropriate action

13. Suggesting sexual activities in which you might engage.

———— a. This describes sexual harassment

———— b. Appropriate action

14. Offering to trade sexual favors for something.

———— a. This describes sexual harassment

———— b. Appropriate action

15. Suggesting that sexual favors would be accepted in return for something else.

_____ a. This describes sexual harassment

_____ b. Appropriate action

16. Fraudulently accusing another of sexual harassment.

_____ a. This describes sexual harassment

_____ b. Appropriate action

17. Continuing to pursue another after a relationship ends.

_____ a. This describes sexual harassment

_____ b. Appropriate action

18. One male pursuing another sexually.

_____ a. This describes sexual harassment

_____ b. Appropriate action

19. One female pursuing another sexually.

_____ a. This describes sexual harassment

_____ b. Appropriate action

20. Repeating any of these after being told to stop.

_____ a. This describes sexual harassment

_____ b. Appropriate action

21. There is no such thing as sexual harassment. (Circle one of the following.)

1 = Strongly Disagree   2 = Disagree   3 = Neutral   4 = Agree   5 = Strongly Agree

22. Do you feel you have ever been sexually harassed?   Yes   No

23. If yes, harasser's relationship to you:

co-worker   client   supervisor   subordinate   other _____

24. Did you report the incident formally?   Yes   No

25. If not, would you report it if it happened today?   Yes   No

SEXUAL HARASSMENT SURVEY SCORING SHEET

Information about your gender is requested solely for the purpose of tabulating results by gender; this information will not be used to identify you.

Gender: Male   Female

Directions: Transfer your answers from your survey to this sheet.

	Item a	Item b		Item a	Item b
1.	_____	_____	11.	_____	_____
2.	_____	_____	12.	_____	_____
3.	_____	_____	13.	_____	_____
4.	_____	_____	14.	_____	_____
5.	_____	_____	15.	_____	_____
6.	_____	_____	16.	_____	_____
7.	_____	_____	17.	_____	_____
8.	_____	_____	18.	_____	_____
9.	_____	_____	19.	_____	_____
10.	_____	_____	20.	_____	_____

21. _____

Directions: For the following items, circle your response.

22.   yes   no

23.   co-worker   client   supervisor   subordinate   other _____

24.   yes   no

25.   yes   no

Sexual Harassment Survey Interpretation Sheet

Any of the behaviors described in Items 1 to 20 of the Sexual Harassment Survey may be considered sexual harassment if the behavior is unwelcome, and especially if the behavior is repeated after it has been identified as unwelcome by the recipient. EEOC guidelines define sexual harassment as "unwelcome" sexual advances, requests for sexual favors, and other verbal or physical conduct of a sexual nature that takes place under any of the following conditions:

1. Submission to such conduct is made either explicitly or implicitly a term or condition of an individual's employment.

2. Submission to or rejection of such conduct by an individual is used as the basis for employment decisions affecting the individual.

3. Such conduct has the purpose or effect of unreasonably interfering with an individual's work performance or creating an intimidating, hostile, or offensive work environment.

Individual scores on the survey will be unique. However, you may compare yours to results from other surveys, including a sample of 179 undergraduate university students presented below. In the student sample, ages ranged from eighteen to sixty-eight with a mean of twenty. Seventy-eight percent of the sample was white, 16 percent was African American, and the remaining 6 percent came from other cultures. There were ninety-nine females and eighty males in the sample. Eighty-six percent identified themselves as Christians of several denominations, with the remainder identified as other than Christian. Scores vary by age, race, gender, and religion.

Men's Means

1	a. 2.8	b. 1.1	8	a. 2.9	b. 1.2	15	a. 4.4	b. 3.9
2	a. 2.5	b. .9	9	a. 3.1	b. 1.5	16	a. 3.4	b. 3.4
3	a. 2.1	b. .6	10	a. 4.1	b. 3.0	17	a. 3.3	b. 2.3
4	a. 1.4	b. .3	11	a. 2.9	b. 1.6	18	a. 4.0	b. 3.1
5	a. 2.6	b. .9	12	a. 3.6	b. 2.4	19	a. 3.7	b. 2.5
6	a. 3.7	b. 2.0	13	a. 4.0	b. 2.9	20	a. 4.5	b. 4.0
7	a. 2.9	b. 1.2	14	a. 4.4	b. 3.8			

Women's Means

1	a. 3.3	b. 1.2	8	a. 3.3	b. 1.4	15	a. 4.7	b. 3.8
2	a. 2.6	b. .6	9	a. 3.2	b. 1.1	16	a. 3.2	b. 2.7
3	a. 2.5	b. .6	10	a. 4.1	b. 2.8	17	a. 3.5	b. 2.1
4	a. 1.8	b. .1	11	a. 3.0	b. 1.5	18	a. 3.4	b. 1.7
5	a. 3.1	b. 1.0	12	a. 3.7	b. 2.0	19	a. 3.4	b. 1.7
6	a. 4.5	b. 2.2	13	a. 4.2	b. 2.8	20	a. 4.7	b. 3.9
7	a. 3.1	b. 1.1	14	a. 4.7	b. 4.2			

In general, research has shown that women tend to rate many of the incidents in Items 1a to 20a more severely than men rate them. Men, on the other hand, typically recommend more severe punishments for behaviors they identify as sexual harassment.

On your survey, circle the "a" items you rated 4 or 5. Ratings above 3 indicate that you believe the behavior to be sexual harassment. In the student sample, men (as a group) did not rate Items 1, 5, 8, and 11 as harassment. Women (as a group) did. The highest rated "a" item for both genders was Item 15, which is quid pro quo sexual harassment. Women rated Items 6 and 14 as extremely severe harassment. Women were more tolerant than men on Items 18 and 19, same-sex harassment. In fact, men found Item 18 to be extreme harassment, while women did not. Neither males nor females rated Item 4 as harassment, assuming it was welcome.

Actions or punishments recommended by men and women in the student sample differ significantly. Overall, men (as a group) recommended more severe punishments. Men were particularly severe in their recommendations on Items 10 and 16. The latter may indicate men's fear of being falsely accused of harassment and automatically being presumed guilty. Men recommended more severe punishments (reprimand and suspensions) on Items 18 and 19, while women tended to recommend education and counseling. Both men and women recommended suspension on Item 20. Women (as a group) more often recommended suspension and termination for Item 14, but their responses varied more on that item than for any other for either men or women.

Together both men and women found Items 6, 10, 13, 14, 15, and 20 to be the most serious forms of harassment. Both women and men recommended the most severe punishments for Items 10, 14, 15, 16, and 20.

Sexual harassment appears to exist at all organizational levels and in all job categories. In the student sample, 6.1 percent were supervisors, 11.7

percent held clerical positions, 3.4 percent were production workers, 14 percent classified their positions as professional or technical, 61.5 percent listed themselves as students, and 3.4 percent did not report their positions.

Between 35 and 65 percent of women report that they have been sexually harassed. Approximately 10 percent of men report harassment. Almost 80 percent of women who report being harassed also say they did not formally report it. Over 80 percent of those say they would if they could make the decision again. In the student sample, 42.4 percent of females reported that they had been harassed, while 11.2 percent of the men reported being harassed; 78.5 percent of those who reported being harassed said they did not formally report it. Fifty percent of those who did not report it said they would if it happened today.

In other studies, women who did not report the sexual harassment gave several reasons:

1. Concern for retaliation or increased hostility;

2. Concern about career damage;

3. Personal stress;

4. Concern with ostracism;

5. Concern about being the first woman to complain;

6. Seeing others who complained suffer personally or professionally;

7. Lack of confidence that the harasser would be punished;

8. Concern that the complaint would not be taken seriously;

9. Concern about fairness of the investigation;

10. Absence of policy or complaint mechanisms; and

11. Uncertainty about what constitutes sexual harassment.

Many times, these beliefs existed in spite of sexual harassment policies, complaint mechanisms, fair and speedy investigations, and knowledge of what constitutes sexual harassment.

The women surveyed indicated certain policies that might encourage their reporting incidents:

1. The demonstrated support of top management for enforcing all sexual harassment policies.

2. The guarantee of no retaliation against women who file complaints.

3. The provision that the victim's permission is required for access to the harassment complaint records.

4. The provision that harassment complaint records be kept separate from personnel files.

5. The availability of an external counselor, perhaps by using an 800 number, who would advise them on how to file a complaint with complete anonymity.

6. The use of an intermediary skilled in resolving sexual harassment to investigate all complaints.

7. The availability of a counselor who would advise them on how to file complaints.

8. The victim's right to choose an investigator from a panel of diverse people within the organization.

9. The absence of a provision that the victim of harassment must tell the harasser that his or her behavior is unwelcome before a complaint may be filed.

Unfortunately, to date, there is little research available about how men perceive harassment. Anecdotal evidence suggests that men fail to report harassment for many of the same reasons women fail to report it. However, many men do not even believe it is possible for a man to be sexually harassed! That attitude may be why the responses to Item 21 of the Sexual Harassment Survey were significantly different for males and females. Both genders disagreed that there was no such thing as sexual harassment, but males did not disagree as strongly as females and the difference was statistically significant ($p < .05$).

Sexual harassment is perpetrated by co-workers, supervisors, clients, subordinates, suppliers, and complete strangers. In the student sample, of those who reported being harassed, 37 percent were harassed by co-workers, 35 percent by supervisors, 4 percent by clients, 4 percent by subordinates, and 20 percent by miscellaneous others.

Having been harassed may affect one's attitudes toward harassment. The students who reported having been harassed scored higher on both the severity of the incidents on the survey and the punishments recommended.

Sexual Harassment Survey Discussion Sheet

Directions: The questions below are intended to facilitate discussion and to encourage your focus on important points. Discuss each one in your group, jotting down pertinent points for later discussion in the large group.

1. Which items did you identify as definitely sexual harassment, that is, give a rating of 4 or 5? Compare male responses with female responses. What differences do you see? Why do you think that the differences exist?

2. Which items did you identify as not being sexual harassment, that is, give a rating of 1, 2, or 3? What differences do you see between men's and women's responses?

3. Items 14 and 15 represent quid pro quo harassment. How did the respondents rate them?

4. Did men and women view Items 18 and 19 similarly? Men tend to have stronger feelings about Item 18 than women do about either Items 18 or 19. What could be an explanation for this difference?

5. How did males and females rate Item 4 (asking for a date)? Typically, neither men nor women object if a request is welcome or not repeated after being told it is unwelcome. However, men have learned that they sometimes must persist to get what they want. Participants may want to discuss this attitudinal difference.

6. Turn now to recommended actions or punishments, the "b" answers. Typically, as a group, men recommend more severe punishments than women. For which items did participants recommend suspension and/ or termination (ratings of 4 or 5)?

7. Men tend to recommend suspension or termination for Item 16 (fraudulent accusations). Why might this be? Discuss this implication. This result may indicate men's fear of being falsely accused of harassment and being unfairly presumed guilty.

8. For which items did men recommend no action, education, or counseling? Did women make the same recommendations on those items? In general, both men and women find items 6, 10, 13, 14, 15, and 20 to be the most serious forms of harassment and recommend the most severe punishments for behaviors 10, 14, 15, 16, and 20.

SEXUAL HARASSMENT SURVEY LECTURETTE

Directions: After participants have finished their small-group discussion of the survey, use the following text in conjunction with the Interpretation Sheet to lead a full-group discussion about sexual harassment, the law, and how individuals and organizations respond to sexual harassment claims.

The Law

The definition of sexual harassment given in the Interpretation Sheet provides two basic circumstances in which sexual harassment can occur. The first setting, in which rejection of a supervisor's advances adversely affects the employee's tangible benefits such as promotion or pay, is known as quid pro quo. The second type of claim has come to be known as hostile environment. This situation is arguably more difficult to define and may include all behaviors listed on the survey as well as other behaviors of a sexual nature resulting in adverse effects on the employee's emotional state or job performance. Hostile environment sexual harassment may be perpetrated by supervisors, co-workers, customers, suppliers, or others.

In 1986, the U.S. Supreme Court handed down an important hostile environment sexual harassment decision in Meritor Savings Bank, FSB vs. Vinson. The court ruled, in a five to four decision, that a hostile environment, even without economic hardship and with voluntary participation, is sufficient to constitute harassment if the employer is aware of the conduct.

The Civil Rights Act of 1991 added teeth to the guidelines by permitting victims of intentional discrimination, including sexual harassment, to have jury trials and to collect compensatory damages for pain and suffering and punitive damages in cases in which the employer acted with "malice or reckless indifference" to the individual's rights.

The statute establishes the following liability by size:*

Number of Employees	Maximum Limit of Liability
15–100	$50,000
101–200	$100,000
201–500	$200,000
more than 501	$300,000

---

*Source: Civil Rights Act of 1991, 42 U.S.C. 2000e-5(b)(3).

In 1993, the Supreme Court held in Harris vs. Forklift Systems Inc. that an individual alleging sexual harassment in a hostile work environment need not show psychological injury due to the defendant's conduct. The conduct does not have to cause psychological injury if a "reasonable person" would perceive the conduct to be hostile or abusive and if the individual perceives the conduct as hostile or abusive. Courts will review all of the circumstances surrounding a harassment charge in order to determine whether the conduct is hostile or abusive. The frequency of occurrence, the severity of the conduct, the presence of threat or humiliation, and the extent to which the conduct interferes with the employee's work performance are examples of the kinds of circumstances that might be considered.

In 1998, the Supreme Court ruled in two hostile environment cases that extended important points from the Harris decision. In both Faragher vs. City of Boca Raton and Burlington Industries, Inc., vs. Ellerth, the court held that a hostile environment, even in the absence of tangible job consequences, was sufficient to establish harassment, even when the employer did not know about the conduct. "Both the reasonableness of the employer's conduct in seeking to prevent and correct harassment and the reasonableness of the employee's conduct in seeking to avoid harm" were relevant considerations. The employer must have established policies and procedures that were properly followed. The employee, in turn, must comply with the required action as provided by the employer's policies and procedures.

Recently, two additional issues have arisen in sexual harassment cases: same-sex harassment and fraudulent accusations. In early 1998, the Supreme Court ruled in Oncale vs. Sundowner Offshore Services, Inc., that same-sex harassment was also included in the EEOC definition. In late 1998, a California judge awarded the University of California-Irvine more that $1.1 million in legal fees when he ruled that a sexual harassment lawsuit was baseless.

Organizations are advised to take same-sex sexual harassment complaints as seriously as opposite-sex harassment complaints. Fraudulent accusations are sometimes complicated by the tendency to presume that the accused harassers are guilty. This tendency can be avoided in several ways. First, require accusers to sign written complaints. Make it known in policy statements and other communications that false accusations are themselves harassment and will be handled accordingly. Ensure that objectivity, confidentiality, and due process are followed in investigations. Finally, any actions taken against accused parties should be reasonable. While the guidelines and court cases call for "immediate and appropriate corrective action," the action must be balanced with concern for the rights of the accused. Organizations must ensure due process for both the accuser and the accused. An employer may become liable for actions taken against alleged harassers if the actions include defamation, intentional infliction of emotional distress, wrongful discharge, and breach of contract. To avoid defamation and infliction of emotional distress, confidentiality must be kept during and after the investigation. Actions should be taken only after the harasser's guilt has been established and the disciplinary action should not be "outrageous," but should appropriately match the offense. The establishment of unquestionable guilt of an extremely abhorrent harassment must precede extreme measures, such as termination or referral to law enforcement authorities.

Those individuals falsely accused of sexual harassment might consider giving a sworn statement of the facts when interviewed. It might be advantageous to have an attorney or other advocate or representative present during such sessions. Providing the names of witnesses who can corroborate one's statement of innocence may help investigators get to the truth. Telling the entire truth is in one's best interest, in order to establish innocence.

What Organizations Can Do

Based on the EEOC guidelines and court decisions, the following advice can be given to organizations and individuals:

1. Take all complaints about harassment seriously. Immediately stop the offensive conduct when it is observed in the workplace.

2. Publish a strong policy condemning harassment. The policy statement should include definitions and examples of sexual harassment, spell out possible actions against those who harass, and make it clear that retaliatory action against an employee who presents charges will not be tolerated.

3. Inform all employees of their rights and responsibilities under the policy. Provide several means for filing a complaint.

4. Develop a proactive complaint procedure.

5. Immediately respond to any complaint and investigate with objectivity, confidentiality, and due process.

6. Frequently hold training sessions to educate supervisors, managers, and workers as to the issues and their responsibilities.

7. Discipline managers and employees involved in sexual harassment. Disciplinary actions must be reasonable, that is, the punishment should fit the crime.

8. Keep thorough records of complaints, investigations, and actions taken.

9. Conduct exit interviews to uncover any evidence that harassment might exist.

10. Republish the sexual harassment policy periodically.

11. Keep management informed with upward communication through periodic attitude surveys and other means of feedback to reveal the existence of potential sexual harassment.

What Training Programs Should Include

The following topics might be included in a sexual harassment training program:

1. Definitions of sexual harassment.

2. Examples of all kinds of sexual harassment.

3. The organization's policy statement.

4. Actions to take if harassed.

5. Complaint procedure.

6. Handling a complaint.

7. Methods to provide supportive behavior if a co-worker confides that he or she is being harassed.

8. The importance of due process and confidentiality.

9. The unacceptability of retaliation.

10. The investigation procedure.

11. Possible disciplinary actions.

12. Encouragement of upward communication.

13. The proper response to wrongful allegations.

MANAGER OR SCIENTIST: AN ATTRIBUTE INVENTORY

Elizabeth N. Treher and Augustus Walker

Abstract: In most technical organizations there are clear and important differences between the activity patterns, working styles, motivations, and work values of those who do scientific and technical work and those who manage them and their resources. Years of experience and hundreds of studies point to the problems often encountered when technical specialists and scientists cross the dividing line and become managers. The technical skills that served them well previously are often insufficient for managerial success and, in fact, can create significant roadblocks on the path to effective leadership and management.

The Manager or Scientist Attribute Inventory is based on twenty years of direct observation of the behavior, likes, and dislikes of successful practicing scientists and their managers. It was developed for use in supervisory and management skills workshops held for research and development groups. The inventory leads to valuable discussion and insights into managerial readiness and interests for those considering a managerial path.

INTRODUCTION

Although there is general agreement on the skills necessary for a successful manager of technical groups and specialists, tools to help individuals assess their own readiness are not readily available. We developed and have used this questionnaire in our consulting and training work in order to assist scientists and technical specialists to make the right choice and to become better managers if they move to that level. It is an empirical assessment to help technical professionals address a number of important managerial attributes, compare themselves with other technical managers, and recognize areas that may bring them potential tension and stress.

DESCRIPTION OF THE INVENTORY

The Manager or Scientist Attribute Inventory contains thirty paired items addressing the behaviors, attributes, motivations, and values of scientists (and other technical specialists) and managers. Participants circle items using a six-point scale and self-score their results.

ADMINISTRATION

This inventory can be sent to participants to complete individually before a training program or can be administered in a group setting at the time of training. Be sure to let participants know that their responses are confidential and that they will be the only ones using the data. Emphasize that there are no right or wrong answers and that no results preclude high performance as either a scientist or manager. Explain that the instrument will be helpful to the extent that their answers are as honest as possible.

THEORY BEHIND THE INVENTORY

Extensive research (Badawy, 1982, 1983a, 1983b; Bailey & Jensen, 1965; Boyton & Chapman, 1972; Lea & Brostrom, 1988) into differences between managers and scientists or technical workers has yielded consistent, distinct behavior patterns and preferences for these two groups. Data from the literature (Badawy, 1982, 1983a, 1983b; Boyton & Chapman, 1972) and from the authors' experience in managing technical managers and groups was distilled to produce this self-report inventory, which highlights individual preferences toward managing others and doing technical work.

You, the facilitator, must have a good grounding and understanding of the research and be able to describe the typical differences in characteristics, motivations, and behaviors of technical managers versus technical professionals. For further reading, see the list of references before the survey.

SCORING AND INTERPRETATION

To obtain a score, respondents transfer their responses to the Answer Sheet, and their numeric value is totaled by column. The following calculations are then done:

$$2M_1 + 1.5M_2 + M_3 = \text{Total Value for Managerial Attributes}$$

$$2S_1 + 1.5S_2 + S_3 = \text{Total Value for Scientist Attributes}$$

The smaller of M or S is then subtracted from the larger. The difference represents the respondent's preference for being either a manager or a scientist.

It is important to note that a strong profile for either dimension does not preclude success in the other. It does, however, indicate that there may be difficult transition issues.

FACILITATING DISCUSSION OF THE INVENTORY

It is useful to present the data on which the inventory is based after respondents fill out the inventory, but before they score it. After the discussion have the respondents predict their S and M scores relative to one another: S > M, S < M, or S = M.

Lead a discussion to review the observed and published characteristics and differences between scientists and managers. As part of that discussion, it is helpful to divide the participants into two or more small groups, each with a discussion assignment, such as listing motivators for scientists or managers, describing attributes of scientists or managers, or listing work values of scientists or managers. After these discussions, have each subgroup present its views to the total group. Such presentations are generally very consistent with published research on the topic.

Another approach is to divide the participants into four subgroups according to their scores and then assign each group the discussion questions below. Those whose scores do not place them into any of these categories can rotate and sit in on different discussions.

Group 1: Those Who Score High S and Are S.   Do these results fit you? What issues might you face if you become a manager? What are likely to be your biggest challenges on becoming a manager? Do you really want to become a manager?

Group 2: Those Who Score High M and Are M.   Do these results fit you? What has helped you develop management skills? Where might your views differ from those of your staff? How can you help others to develop the attributes of a good manager?

Group 3: Those Who Score High S and Are M.   Do these results fit you? What are some of your frustrations in managing technical work? What gives you the greatest satisfaction at work? How could you develop your management skills and interests further? How could you gather feedback on how you are doing as a manager?

Group 4: Those Who Score High M and Are S.   Do these results fit you? What gives you the greatest satisfaction at work? How could you develop your management skills? How could you demonstrate your interest in management? Who could help you to develop into a manager? How can you combine your technical responsibilities with your management interests? What are the roadblocks, if any, to your becoming a manager.

OTHER SUGGESTED USES

This inventory has been used primarily for management and supervisory skills training. It can also be used in one-on-one coaching and in career counseling settings. It is not intended to limit or discourage individuals from becoming technical managers, but to help them better understand and prepare for potential roadblocks and sources of frustration on the road to management excellence. The inventory is also useful in helping to target areas for personal development.

RELIABILITY AND VALIDITY

The Manager or Scientist Attribute Inventory is intended for use as an analytical tool, not a psychometric or rigorous data-gathering instrument. The inventory has shown a high level of face validity with the hundreds of technical specialists and managers who have used it.

References

Badawy, M.K. (1982). *Developing managerial skills in engineers and scientists.* New York: Van Nostrand Reinhold.

Badawy, M.K. (1983a). Managing career transitions. In *The first-level manager: Selected papers from research management.* Washington DC: Industrial Research Institute.

Badawy, M.K. (1983b). Why managers fail. In *The first-level manager: Selected papers from research management.* Washington DC: Industrial Research Institute.

Bailey, R.E., & Jensen, B.T. (1965, September/October). The troublesome transition from scientist to manager. *Personnel,* pp. 49–55.

Boyton, J.A., & Chapman, R.L. (1972). *Transformation of scientists and engineers into managers.* (NASA SP-291.) Washington DC: NASA National Academy of Science Administration.

Boyton, J.A., & Chapman, R.L. (1985). Making managers of scientists and engineers. In *The first-level manager: Selected papers from research management.* Washington DC: Industrial Research Institute.

Lea, D., & Brostrom, R. (1988, June). Managing the high-tech professional. *Personnel,* pp. 12–22.

Manners, G.E., & Steger, J.A. (1979). Implications of research on R&D manager's role to selection and training of scientists and engineers for management. *R&D Management, 9*(2), 85–91.

McBean, E.A. (1991, May/June). Analysis of teaching and course questionnaires: A case study. *Engineering Education,* pp. 431–441.

Medcof, J.W. (1985). Training technologists to become managers. *Research Management,* pp. 41–44.

Oppenheim, A.N. (1966). *Questionnaire design and attitude measurement.* New York: Basic Books.

Overton, L.M., Jr. (1969). R&D management: Turning scientists into managers. *Personnel, 46*(3), 56–63.

Pearson, A.W. (1993, January/February). Management development for scientists and engineers. *Research Technology Management,* pp. 45–48.

Walker, A.C. (1990). *Effective technical management.* Washington DC: American Chemical Society.

Elizabeth N. Treher, Ph.D., *is co-founder of The Learning Key, a training and consulting firm working with technology-based organizations. She has held research and management positions in industry and academia and has more than sixty publications and patents. She has designed several innovative training games to teach about business (The PHARM Game® and Big Buck$$™), team-development consulting, and executive coaching.*

Augustus Walker *is a long-time associate of The Learning Key and president of Effective Research. He has provided specialized training and consulting services to technical organizations for more than thirty years. Mr. Walker is known for his work in group and individual problem solving and technical management consulting. He is author of many publications and patents, including the book* Effective Technical Management *published by the American Chemical Society.*

Manager or Scientist Attribute Inventory

Elizabeth N. Treher and Augustus Walker

Directions: Read each of the pairs of statements that follow. If you strongly agree with the statement on the left, circle 1. If you strongly favor the statement on the right, circle 6. If you do not strongly agree with either statement, circle the number that best represents your feelings about the two statements in general. There are no right or wrong answers. Use your own views, not those you think others might have or prefer that you have.

1. In solving nonroutine problems, the leader should provide support.

In solving nonroutine problems, the leader should give directions and ideas.

| 1 | 2 | 3 | 4 | 5 | 6 |

2. I prefer to have all the facts before making a decision.

I am comfortable making decisions based on partial information.

| 1 | 2 | 3 | 4 | 5 | 6 |

3. The organization I work for is my primary source of satisfaction and professional recognition.

I obtain satisfaction and recognition from outside professional contacts and associations.

| 1 | 2 | 3 | 4 | 5 | 6 |

4. I prefer to do many varied things and not go into any one activity too deeply.

I prefer to focus my attention on one important thing and get to the bottom of it.

| 1 | 2 | 3 | 4 | 5 | 6 |

5. I prefer to work in my own area of expertise and not become involved in projects crossing several technical disciplines.

I enjoy working as a generalist or on interdisciplinary problems.

| 1 | 2 | 3 | 4 | 5 | 6 |

6. I like to generate new information and results on problems.

I like to see that available information is found and used effectively.

| 1 | 2 | 3 | 4 | 5 | 6 |

7. Decisions should be made analytically on the basis of the facts.

Political and human considerations should influence all decisions.

| 1 | 2 | 3 | 4 | 5 | 6 |

8. I like to run things and be highly visible.

I prefer to influence decisions quietly through my own expertise and reputation.

| 1 | 2 | 3 | 4 | 5 | 6 |

9. I prefer to consider my ideas carefully and put them in writing.

I prefer discussing my ideas with others and giving presentations.

| 1 | 2 | 3 | 4 | 5 | 6 |

10. When something goes wrong, the individual responsible should take the blame.

When something goes wrong, the manager should take the blame.

| 1 | 2 | 3 | 4 | 5 | 6 |

11. I enjoy working with people from other departments and functions.

I prefer working with people with similar backgrounds and interests.

| 1 | 2 | 3 | 4 | 5 | 6 |

12. It is usually better to figure out what the real problem is rather than to take quick action.

I have a strong sense of urgency and like to react quickly when something goes wrong.

| 1 | 2 | 3 | 4 | 5 | 6 |

13. When my colleagues have arguments, I like to help resolve them.

When my colleagues have arguments, I prefer not to become involved.

| 1 | 2 | 3 | 4 | 5 | 6 |

14. People and decisions interest me more than things and ideas.

| 1 | 2 | 3 | 4 | 5 | 6 |

Things and ideas interest me more than people and decisions.

15. The most important thing is to understand and solve the problem.

| 1 | 2 | 3 | 4 | 5 | 6 |

The most important thing is to meet goals and objectives.

16. I work well under stress and with urgent schedules. Things can drift without deadlines.

| 1 | 2 | 3 | 4 | 5 | 6 |

I work best when the pressure comes from my own interests and when schedules are realistic.

17. I enjoy interpreting the business goals of the organization and deciding how technology can help achieve them.

| 1 | 2 | 3 | 4 | 5 | 6 |

I enjoy theoretical and experimental work. In the long run it is the principal basis for growth and profit.

18. I like to identify a problem and solve it myself.

| 1 | 2 | 3 | 4 | 5 | 6 |

I like to see that problems are identified and solved as efficiently as possible.

19. I like to get to work early and leave late. A sense of urgency is important to the organization.

| 1 | 2 | 3 | 4 | 5 | 6 |

I like flexibility to come and go as my work demands. Creative insights cannot always be produced by schedules and pressure.

20. Generally, I study something only long enough to satisfy an immediate need.

| 1 | 2 | 3 | 4 | 5 | 6 |

Generally, I study something thoroughly so that I can understand and use it well.

21. I prefer shared accountability and interdependence.

| 1 | 2 | 3 | 4 | 5 | 6 |

I prefer individual accountability and independent work.

22. I believe that independent groups of specialists pursuing their own projects accomplish the most.

| 1 | 2 | 3 |

I believe that integrating technical groups is essential to accomplishing the most.

| 4 | 5 | 6 |

23. Organizational politics play a necessary role in setting goals and doing the work.

| 1 | 2 | 3 |

Organizational politics waste time and energy and get in the way of quality, creative work.

| 4 | 5 | 6 |

24. I sometimes ignore others' views in defending my position when I believe I am right.

| 1 | 2 | 3 |

I am flexible and willing to compromise my ideas for the organization's good.

| 4 | 5 | 6 |

25. A technical manager is a manager of people with technical training.

| 1 | 2 | 3 |

A technical manager is a technically trained person with additional management responsibilities.

| 4 | 5 | 6 |

26. I like to solve problems in clever and unusual ways.

| 1 | 2 | 3 |

I like to solve problems in familiar and established ways.

| 4 | 5 | 6 |

27. Understanding how things work is a major source of stimulation for me.

| 1 | 2 | 3 |

Getting things done and seeing practical results is what motivates me.

| 4 | 5 | 6 |

28. I enjoy helping others find their own answers and solve their own problems.

| 1 | 2 | 3 |

I prefer to answer questions and solve problems on my own.

| 4 | 5 | 6 |

29. To be respected, a technical manager should always know more than his or her subordinates.

    To be respected, a technical manager must be able to recognize, use, and acknowledge subordinate strengths.

1   2   3   4   5   6

30. I like to speculate and approach problems from a theoretical and abstract point of view.

    I like to identify the goal and work toward it in a practical and realistic way.

1   2   3   4   5   6

MANAGER OR SCIENTIST ATTRIBUTE INVENTORY SCORING KEY

Directions: To score the inventory, first circle the number corresponding to your answer on each question on the scoring key below. Next, add the numbers you circled in each column and enter each of the totals at the bottom of the six columns.

Use these formulas to calculate your final score:

$$M = 2M_1 + 1.5M_2 + M_3$$
$$S = 2S_1 + 1.5S_2 + S_3$$

Example: Add the numbers in each column on the manager side of the scoring sheet. Say your totals are $M_1 = 19$, $M_2 = 29$ and $M_3 = 7$. Your calculation would look like this: $M = [2(19) + 1.5(29) + 7] = 89$. Now add the numbers in each column on the scientist side of the scoring sheet. Say you have $S_1 = 6$, $S_2 = 18$, and $S_3 = 24$. Then your S calculation would look like this: $S = [2(6) + 1.5(18) + 24] = 63$.

Now subtract the smaller of M or S from the larger. The difference represents your level of preference for either the manager or the scientist attributes.

For example, if your scores had been $M = 70$ and $S = 90$, you would find an excess S of 20. See the interpretation below.

Number	Manager's Profile			Scientist's Profile		
1.	1	2	3	4	5	6
2.	6	5	4	3	2	1
3.	1	2	3	4	5	6
4.	1	2	3	4	5	6
5.	6	5	4	3	2	1
6.	6	5	4	3	2	1
7.	6	5	4	3	2	1
8.	1	2	3	4	5	6
9.	6	5	4	3	2	1
10.	6	5	4	3	2	1
11.	1	2	3	4	5	6

Number	Manager's Profile			Scientist's Profile		
12.	6	5	4	3	2	1
13.	1	2	3	4	5	6
14.	1	2	3	4	5	6
15.	6	5	4	3	2	1
16.	1	2	3	4	5	6
17.	1	2	3	4	5	6
18.	6	5	4	3	2	1
19.	1	2	3	4	5	6
20.	1	2	3	4	5	6
21.	1	2	3	4	5	6
22.	6	5	4	3	2	1
23.	1	2	3	4	5	6
24.	6	5	4	3	2	1
25.	1	2	3	4	5	6
26.	6	5	4	3	2	1
27.	6	5	4	3	2	1
28.	1	2	3	4	5	6
29.	6	5	4	3	2	1
30.	6	5	4	3	2	1

Add and enter the total for each column.

$M_1 =$	$M_2 =$	$M_3 =$	$S_3 =$	$S_2 =$	$S_1 =$
_____	_____	_____	_____	_____	_____

$$\underline{} + \underline{} + \underline{} = \underline{}$$

$2M_1 \qquad 1.5M_2 \qquad M_3 \qquad M$

$$\underline{} + \underline{} + \underline{} = \underline{}$$

$2S_1 \qquad 1.5S_2 \qquad S_3 \qquad S$

Interpretation

If you have a total score of M – S equal to or greater than 25, it suggests you are somewhat more comfortable with the activities and work patterns of a manager than with those of a scientist. If your S – M number is equal to or greater than 25, the reverse is true. The greater the difference, the greater the discomfort level is likely to be for someone attempting to work in the other domain. Differences of 25 or less cannot be interpreted.

Please note that even a large difference between your scores does not necessarily mean that you cannot perform well in the other domain. It does suggest that you may find it uncomfortable to do so. As a first-line technical supervisor, your work would probably continue to be highly "hands on." However, as a technical expert advances to higher levels of management, the differences become more important and apparent between those with greater technical attributes versus those with greater managerial attributes. The pressure may be very difficult for those with large differences between their S scores and their M scores.

TRANSFER CLIMATE ASSESSMENT

Paul L. Garavaglia

Abstract: For over thirty-five years the issue of transfer of training has been studied. Although opinions
on what works and what does not work vary, the fact
remains that little of what is taught in training is applied on the job. This instrument assesses factors in
the back-home environment shown to be relevant
to retention of newly acquired skills. The learner's
motivation, the organization itself, the work environment, and teamwork issues all affect transfer. By
using this assessment, the trainer can predict potential failure and take corrective action.

INTRODUCTION

Sending employees to training and experiencing improvements in performance do not necessarily go hand-in-hand. It is easy to register employees for training; the hard part begins when employees return to the job. For the knowledge and skills gained in training to be applied on the job, a transfer climate must be established. If trainees fail to apply skills gained in training to the job, it reflects badly on training departments.

How much transfer of training can we realistically expect? According to Baldwin and Ford (1988) there are basically five potential outcomes for training: (1) Trainees transfer skills initially but then taper off, slowly moving toward the pre-training level; (2) Trainees fail to transfer skills at all, and the post-training level of knowledge drops immediately after returning to the work site; (3) Trainees attempt to use the new skill(s) on the job, but after a period of time there is a sharp decline in the use of the skill(s), which then quickly approach the pre-training level; (4) Trainees' learning and retention are minimal, with little chance for transfer; and (5) Trainees' skill levels increase over time after they return to the job.

Factors that influence outcomes vary.

- Systemic and instructional design factors of the training program itself can determine whether skills are learned and retained (number 4 above).

- Maintenance system factors back on the job (see 1, 2, 3, and 5 above) can affect how skills are used or whether they are used on the job.

Richey (1992) suggests that 20 to 45 percent of the variance in post-training behavior is because of design (systemic and instructional) factors. We can conclude from this that 55 percent to 80 percent is because of maintenance system factors in the organization itself. If indeed up to 80 percent of transfer failures (many would say more) are due to the organization's maintenance system, it makes sense for an organization to establish a climate for returning trainees that facilitates the use of new skills and knowledge on the job.

Maintaining the status quo and explaining away performance problems is a lot easier for many companies than innovatively solving the problem, according to Garavaglia (1997). This attitude on the part of organizations is a major reason transfer fails. The Transfer Climate Assessment provides a tool for assessing an organization's transfer climate. An organization can then take the necessary steps to change the environment and increase the likelihood that knowledge and skills will be transferred, rather than lost.

DESCRIPTION OF THE ASSESSMENT

The Transfer Climate Assessment addresses the following four problem areas:

- Learner Motivation
- The Organization Itself
- The Work Environment
- Teamwork Issues

Each problem area is addressed by different questions on the assessment, as follows: Learner motivation (1 through 4); the organization itself (5 through 9); the work environment (10 through 12); and teamwork issues (13 and 14).

The respondent rates each component of the transfer climate in terms of the degree to which it is true in his or her work group on a continuum from "rarely" to "consistently." The five-point scale allows users to score findings quickly and summarize results easily. After the assessment has been scored, results should be compared to the norms, which are provided for total transfer climate scores, as well as for each of the fourteen components.

ADMINISTRATION

This assessment is not intended for individual use, but as an organizational information-gathering tool. Typically, the information is obtained from trainees, that is, anyone who is sent to training or who is affected by the problem of transfer failure. Supervisors and managers who want to use the assessment are advised to consult first with an HRD professional. Following are some general guidelines for using the assessment:

1. Give the assessment to individuals, work groups, or meeting participants. Administer it company-wide or in segments to represent each department or work group.

2. The assessment is simple, easy-to-complete, yet profoundly powerful, so use it to sample as many trainees as possible.

3. Provide a brief explanation of the purpose of the assessment. Build commitment by explaining the benefits, such as to identify and remove obstacles to transfer and to increase organizational performance.

4. Provide an explanation for the rating scale. Inform respondents that they will be asked to circle the answer that best describes their organization on each item.

5. The assessment takes five to fifteen minutes to complete. After everyone has finished, close with appropriate remarks.

Alternatively, the results of the assessment can be used to decide the support that supervisors and managers need, as they ultimately have responsibility for establishing a transfer climate. For this purpose, identify problem areas and recommend solutions. Recommendations can be made regarding different types of training or coaching for managers, and other organizations can serve as models of good transfer climates.

PRESENTATION OF THEORY

The best way to present the theory behind the Transfer Climate Assessment is to review the results that can be normally expected from training. Show, using a flip chart that looks like the chart below, the five outcomes:

(1) Trainees transfer skills initially but then taper off, slowly moving toward the pre-training level;

(2) Trainees fail to transfer skills at all and the post-training level of knowledge drops immediately after returning to the work site;

(3) Trainees attempt to use the new skill(s) on the job, but after a period of time there is a sharp decline in the use of the skill(s), which then quickly approach the pre-training level;

(4) Trainees' learning and retention are minimal, with little chance for transfer; and

(5) Trainees' skill levels increase over time after they return to the job.

Explain that both systemic and instructional-design factors can determine whether skills are learned and used back on the job (see 4 above) and that factors in the workplace (see 1, 2, 3, and 5 above) can affect how skills are used or not used on the job. As you review the outcomes of the assessment, place a check mark in the category that each outcome represents. For example, the first item is related to the organization's maintenance system; therefore a check mark should be placed in that category. When all five possible outcomes have been reviewed, summarize by saying that 20 percent of the possible outcomes are due to instructional-design factors and 80 percent due to maintenance-system factors.

Beginning Chart		Completed Chart	
Design Factors	Maintenance System Factors	Design Factors	Maintenance System Factors
		✔	✔ ✔ ✔ ✔
		1 out of 5 = 20 percent	4 out of 5 = 80 percent

SCORING

Respondents give all items on the assessment a rating between 1 and 5 on a continuum from "rarely" to "consistently." In each case, the respondent should circle the answer that best represents his or her own work group. When respondents are finished, ask them to add the numbers they have circled to obtain one number that represents their assessment of the transfer climate at the organization.

INTERPRETATION

The highest possible score is 70. Give respondents copies of the Interpretation Sheet, which is also shown below, to help them interpret their scores.

Score	Description
0–14	Climate needs much improvement.
15–28	Climate needs improvement.
29–42	Climate has potential.
43–56	With a little more effort, a transfer climate will exist.
57–70	Transfer climate exists. Keep up the good work.

Next, ask respondents to compare their scores with the norms established for this assessment:

High Score = 68
Average Score = 38
Low Score = 23

In addition, ask participants to calculate their percentage scores by dividing their own scores for the assessment by the total possible of 70. For example, a score of 38 would yield a percentage score of 54 (38/70 = 54). Next ask respondents to compare their percentage scores with the chart and the norms associated with the cumulative transfer climate scores shown below. Post them on a flip chart for ease of discussion.

Grading Scale	Cumulative Transfer Climate Scores
A = 90 – 100	1 percent
B = 80 – 89	0 percent
C = 70 – 79	10 percent
D = 60 – 69	20 percent
E = 50 – 59	26 percent
F = 0 – 49	43 percent

Now have respondents look at each of the fourteen items individually and total the scores they gave the organization for each. Tell them to use the same method as before to determine the percentage of the possible total score that they gave the organization. Tell them to use the grading scale from their Interpretation Sheets to give the appropriate grade for each component. The chart below provides the normative data for each individual transfer climate component.

Broader Context	Transfer Climate Component	Percent of Possible Score Obtained	Grade
Motivation	Rewards and incentives	65 percent	D
	Positive reinforcement	64 percent	D
	Feedback on performance (prior to training)	45 percent	F
	Feedback on performance (after training)	47 percent	F
Organization	Removal of obstacles	41 percent	F
	Changes in the system	44 percent	F
	Well-defined work process (structures roles and responsibilities)	67 percent	D
	Well-defined work process (empowers employees)	61 percent	D
	Well-defined work process (aligns work processes with organizational values and culture)	65 percent	D
Work Environment	Equipment, tools, and materials	69 percent	D
	Ergonomics	66 percent	D
	Job/performance aids	68 percent	D
Teamwork	Booster session	34 percent	F
	Buddy system	41 percent	F

POSTING

Ask participants to share their scores. Then post the cumulative transfer climate scores, as well as cumulative scores obtained for each of the transfer climate components, on a flip chart. If data was obtained from different work groups, cumulative group scores should be compared to the organization's totals, as well as to the normative data. Ask respondents to break into subgroups and then develop some action plans for raising any low transfer climate component scores. In order to increase the likelihood of success, ask group members to hold one another accountable for taking action to make necessary changes. Have them commit in writing what they will do and by when and share their plans with the group.

RELIABILITY AND VALIDITY

This assessment tool provided very interesting results regarding reliability. Over 150 assessments were completed, which provided the normative data above. Interestingly, the only normative data that changed after the first ten assessments were administered was the cumulative transfer climate score, which moved from 37 to 38. To devise the transfer climate components that make up the assessment, over one hundred possible transfer references were reviewed, which provide face validity.

References

Baldwin, T.T., & Ford, K.J. (1988). Transfer of training: A review and directions for future research. *Personnel Psychology, 41*(1), 63–105.

Garavaglia, P.L. (1997). Lack of application means elimination. *The Transfer Agent, 3*(2), 1–5.

Richey, R.C. (1992). *Designing instruction for the adult learner.* London: Kogan Page.

Paul L. Garavaglia is a principal consultant for The ADDIE Group, Inc. He is the author of the book Transfer of Training: Making Training Stick. *He is also a two-time winner of the American Society for Training and Development's Instructional Technology Blue Ribbon Award, once for the job aid Making the Transfer Process Work and again for the handbook Managers as Transfer Agents. Mr. Garavaglia has published transfer-related articles in Corporate University Review, Educational Technology, Performance Improvement, and Training & Development.*

TRANSFER CLIMATE ASSESSMENT

Paul L. Garavaglia

Organization: _____

Directions: Circle the number that best represents how the following are practiced in your organization after a training session, with 1 representing "rarely" and 5 representing "consistently":

	Rarely				Consistently
1. Trainees who perform new skills are rewarded more than those who do not perform the new skills.	1	2	3	4	5
2. Trainees are encouraged in their efforts to use new skills on the job.	1	2	3	4	5
3. Trainees discuss anticipated objectives with their managers prior to attending training.	1	2	3	4	5
4. Trainees discuss progress toward achieving objectives with their managers after training.	1	2	3	4	5
5. Obstacles to transfer of the skills and knowledge learned in training are identified and removed.	1	2	3	4	5
6. Changes in the system are made in order to facilitate the transfer of learning from training.	1	2	3	4	5
7. Trainees work within a work process that defines and structures roles and responsibilities.	1	2	3	4	5
8. Trainees work within a work process that empowers employees.	1	2	3	4	5
9. Trainees work within a work process that is aligned with organizational values and culture.	1	2	3	4	5

	Rarely		Consistently		
10. Trainees have the necessary equipment, tools, and materials to perform their work.	1	2	3	4	5
11. Trainees work in an ergonomically correct environment.	1	2	3	4	5
12. If necessary, job/performance aids are provided.	1	2	3	4	5
13. Trainees meet with trainers to discuss post-training performance.	1	2	3	4	5
14. Trainees are paired together to reinforce post-training performance.	1	2	3	4	5

Total of Numbers Circled _____

TRANSFER CLIMATE ASSESSMENT INTERPRETATION SHEET

Interpretation Scale

Score	Description
14	Climate needs much improvement.
15–28	Climate needs improvement.
29–42	Climate has potential.
43–56	With a little more effort, a transfer climate will exist.
57–70	Transfer climate exists. Keep up the good work.

Calculation of Percentages

Grading Scale	Cumulative Transfer Climate Scores
A = 90 – 100	1 percent
B = 80 – 89	0 percent
C = 70 – 79	10 percent
D = 60 – 69	20 percent
E = 50 – 59	26 percent
F = 0 – 49	43 percent

Normative Data

Broader Context	Transfer Climate Component	Percent of Possible Score Obtained	Grade
Motivation	Rewards and incentives	65 percent	D
	Positive reinforcement	64 percent	D
	Feedback on performance (prior to training)	45 percent	F
	Feedback on performance (after training)	47 percent	F
Organization	Removal of obstacles	41 percent	F
	Changes in the system	44 percent	F
	Well-defined work process (structures roles and responsibilities)	67 percent	D
	Well-defined work process (empowers employees)	61 percent	D
	Well-defined work process (aligns work processes with organizational values and culture)	65 percent	D
Work Environment	Equipment, tools, and materials	69 percent	D
	Ergonomics	66 percent	D
	Job/performance aids	68 percent	D
Teamwork	Booster session	34 percent	F
	Buddy system	41 percent	F

The 2000 Annual: Volume 1, Training/© 2000 Jossey-Bass/Pfeiffer

APTITUDE FOR BECOMING A MENTOR SURVEY

H. B. Karp

Abstract: Mentoring is quickly becoming a major force for developing people within organizations. Opinions vary, however, as to what role mentoring should play, the areas it should cover, and the skills necessary to become an effective mentor. The Aptitude for Becoming a Mentor Survey (ABMS) is a twenty-item instrument that asks the respondent to assess his or her disposition toward becoming a mentor for less experienced employees of the organization. The underlying assumption of this survey is that effective mentoring, at a minimum, requires that the mentor be good at both coaching and counseling, be interpersonally competent, and possess a keen political sense.

The ABMS can be used as a diagnostic tool to allow people to gain a sense of their own proclivities toward mentoring or as part of a formal mentor training program. The author also makes the point that the desire to be a mentor is a necessary, but not the only, condition for becoming one.

INTRODUCTION

As organizations become more complex and start to use new technology, mentoring is becoming an important means of developing professional and managerial talent. Training continues to be as important to personal and professional development as it has ever been; however, in today's more complicated work environment, training alone is rarely enough. Training can be used to provide a set of skills—technical, professional, or interpersonal—for a large group of people at the same time in a consistent manner. Training is usually conducted by using a fairly uniform format with emphasis on acquiring a skill, rather than using the skill.

Because most skills are retained and/or practiced *uniquely,* a second step—development—is necessary to maximize the training, and this is where mentoring comes in. A mentor is someone with skills, experience, and perspective who has reasonable organizational influence and is willing to develop a personal working relationship with someone of lesser status in order to help that person become more effective.

Mentoring has been a recognized form of personal development for thousands of years. It was first depicted by Homer, who described Odysseus entrusting the education of his son, Telemachus, to Mentor, his chief retainer, before departing for the Trojan Wars. From that day to this, the role of the experienced guide has been revered as a means of developing the newer members of the organization.

Mentoring today takes on many aspects. It can be a single supportive encounter; an informal supportive relationship between an older, more experienced organizational member and a younger one; or a formal program sponsored and supported by an organization.

There is also a wide range of opinion regarding what types of activities comprise mentoring. Some possible activities include: training, role modeling, sponsoring, advising, coaching, counseling, guiding through organizational politics, and providing social and emotional support. The Aptitude for Becoming a Mentor Survey focuses on the last four functions: coaching, counseling, political guidance, and providing social and emotional support.

Coaching. A coach is someone with experience in a specific area of competence whose task is to help someone else correct performance problems or find new ways to use existing skills more creatively. The main focus of coaching is task-centered, and the coach concentrates more on the protégé's cognitive abilities.

Counseling. A counselor is typically someone with excellent interpersonal skills who assists another person in coping with personal problems and/or inappropriate behavior on the job. Counseling is people-centered, and the counselor deals with issues that are usually more emotive in nature than cognitive. Effective counselors must be able to establish empathy with the protégé, without allowing themselves to have feelings of sympathy.

Providing Political Guidance. A political guide is an experienced and savvy organizational member who understands the system's norms and values; knows where the spheres of influence are and has access to them; and is willing to share this information with those less experienced. This is probably the most unique and helpful of all the mentoring functions. There are no training programs in "How to Be an Influential Member of the System." This can only be learned from someone who already understands the process and is willing to pass on that knowledge.

Providing Social and Emotional Support. Mentoring calls for more than just cognitive abilities and good intentions. An effective mentor provides a place for the protégé to air partially thought-through ideas and vent feelings of anger or indecision safely. The effective mentor also provides continual encouragement as the protégé takes on new and more difficult challenges.

DESCRIPTION OF THE SURVEY

The Aptitude for Becoming a Mentor Survey is comprised of twenty items that measure the respondent's suitability for becoming a mentor. Each of the items deals with a skill or characteristic that is essential for effective mentoring, based on one or more of the categories described above.

Respondents rate themselves on each question using a five-point scale, then self-score the surveys to obtain a single score indicating their aptitude for becoming organizational mentors. A Rationale Sheet is provided for the facilitator to share with the respondents. The rationale for each preferred response is provided. An Interpretation Sheet is also provided that allows respondents to assess their current readiness to be a mentor by reading the implications of their particular range of scores.

There are no reliability or validity data available, as the survey is purely descriptive, rather than predictive, in nature. The survey, however, does have very high face validity in that the intention of each statement is quite clear. For that reason it is important that the facilitator state at the beginning that there are no right or wrong answers.

ADMINISTERING AND SCORING THE SURVEY

The respondents answer each item by indicating their reactions to it on a five-point scale. The survey is self-scoring. Respondents simply add the numeric values of their answers together.

On all items except numbers 4, 6, 15, and 18, the items are scored from 1 through 5, from "Strongly Disagree" through "Strongly Agree." The scale is reversed on items 4, 6, 15, and 18.

Once the participants have scored their surveys, the facilitator can go over the rationale for each item by referring to the Rationale Sheet or can distribute it for later reference. The underlying assumption of the survey is that the higher one scores, the higher the probability that one has the necessary skills and outlook to become an effective mentor.

The facilitator then distributes the Interpretation Sheet and leads a discussion on the implications that can be drawn from each of the categories. This can lead to a deeper discussion of what it takes to be an effective mentor and the fact that *wanting* to be one is a necessary, but not a sufficient condition for being an effective mentor.

H.B. Karp, Ph.D., is presently on the faculty of management of Christopher Newport University in Newport News, Virginia. He also is the owner of Personal Growth Systems, a management-consulting firm in Chesapeake, Virginia. He consults with a variety of Fortune 500 and governmental organizations in the areas of leadership development, team building, conflict management, and executive coaching. He specializes in applying Gestalt theory to issues of individual growth and organizational effectiveness. He is the author of many articles, including Personal Power: An Unorthodox Guide to Success and The Change Leader: Using a Gestalt Approach with Work Groups.

APTITUDE FOR BECOMING A MENTOR SURVEY

H.B. Karp

Instructions: Twenty statements are listed below that pertain to effective mentoring. Please read each item carefully and circle the number on the scale that corresponds with how much you agree with the statement. Respond to each item as honestly as you can, keeping in mind that there are no right or wrong answers. When you have completed the survey, add up the numeric value of your responses and place the sum in the designated place at the end of the survey.

Please note the following scale designations:

SD = Strongly Disagree   D = Disagree   N = Neutral   A = Agree   SA = Strongly Agree

1. I am at least as people-oriented as I am task-oriented.	1 SD	2 D	3 N	4 A	5 SA
2. I see part of my job as contributing to the professional development of others.	1 SD	2 D	3 N	4 A	5 SA
3. Ordinarily, I am a good listener.	1 SD	2 D	3 N	4 A	5 SA
4. I am quick to sympathize with others' problems.	1 SA	2 A	3 N	4 D	5 SD
5. I am good at showing others better ways of doing things.	1 SD	2 D	3 N	4 A	5 SA
6. I think that political savvy is a poor substitute for professional competence.	1 SA	2 A	3 N	4 D	5 SD
7. I am good at helping other people make decisions.	1 SD	2 D	3 N	4 A	5 SA
8. I am aware of my own strengths and potential areas for growth.	1 SD	2 D	3 N	4 A	5 SA

9. I am recognized as a competent professional.	1 SD	2 D	3 N	4 A	5 SA
10. I understand how the political structure of my organization works.	1 SD	2 D	3 N	4 A	5 SA
11. I am comfortable networking with peers and those above me in the organization.	1 SD	2 D	3 N	4 A	5 SA
12. I am good at generating alternatives.	1 SD	2 D	3 N	4 A	5 SA
13. I am patient when working with the problems and concerns of others.	1 SD	2 D	3 N	4 A	5 SA
14. One of my strengths is defining problems clearly.	1 SD	2 D	3 N	4 A	5 SA
15. I have difficulty operating on the "feeling" level with other people.	1 SA	2 A	3 N	4 D	5 SD
16. I find assisting others to be personally satisfying.	1 SD	2 D	3 N	4 A	5 SA
17. I am held in high regard by those with whom I work and to whom I report.	1 SD	2 D	3 N	4 A	5 SA
18. I like making decisions for other people.	1 SA	2 A	3 N	4 D	5 SD
19. I can recognize when people need guidance or nurturing and when they need to be independent.	1 SD	2 D	3 N	4 A	5 SA
20. I have actively sought mentors myself.	1 SD	2 D	3 N	4 A	5 SA

Total Score: _____

APTITUDE FOR BECOMING A MENTOR INTERPRETATION SHEET

There is no predetermined preferred score for this survey; however, you can get a feel for how ready you are to be mentor by reading the following interpretations of the various ranges of scores on the survey.

If You Scored Between 100 and 85

You clearly have the awareness and the confidence to be an effective mentor. You understand what it takes to support the growth of others and have a willingness to put in the necessary time and effort to do this well. You also understand and are comfortable with the role of a mentor as a political guide in the organizational "jungle."

If You Scored Between 84 and 70

You have the necessary skills and perspective to provide support for someone with less experience. You also require some growth and/or more confidence in certain areas yourself. Take the time to become clear about what it is you want to do and where your present strengths lie.

If You Scored Between 69 and 50

You have the ambition and talent to be an effective mentor in certain specific areas. It is important that you be very clear about where your talents lie and where you require some growth as well. Negotiate carefully with your protégé to decide on realistic positive outcomes from the mentoring process. When you feel less than confident or somewhat confused about what do next, discuss this with *your own mentor.*

If You Scored Between 49 and 0

Your ambition to be a mentor is exemplary and should not be ignored. To assure that the process goes well for both you and your protégé, you would do well to do some pre-work before taking on the role and responsibilities of being a mentor. If you do not have a mentor yourself, actively seek one out who can show you the ropes of mentoring. This will not only provide you with the guidance you need, but will help you to appreciate the mentoring role from the protégé's perspective. In addition, look for an opportunity to go through some formalized training to learn more about the mentoring process.

Aptitude for Becoming a Mentor Rationale Sheet

The rationale for each of the twenty items that make up the Aptitude for Becoming a Mentor Survey are given below. Although there are no right or wrong answers to the survey, some responses may indicate that one may be more or less suited for the role of a mentor. The preferred response is indicated after each item.

1. I am at least as people-oriented as I am task-oriented.   **SA**

   Effective mentors do put a high value on the protégé's task performance. However, it is essential that the mentor be at least as interested in the personal development of the protégé as he or she is in the protégé's successful completion of a task.

2. I see part of my job as contributing to the professional development of others.   **SA**

   This perspective is important for both the mentor and the organization. If the mentor sees mentoring as simply an add-on or additional burden, there is less chance of commitment. If helping to develop others is viewed as part of the job, commitment is deeper.

3. Ordinarily, I am a good listener.   **SA**

   The ability to listen well is the mentor's most important skill. To be able to hear and understand the protégé's concerns and problems from the protégé's perspective is the essential first step in providing any support needed.

4. I am quick to sympathize with others' problems.   **SD**

   On the surface, being sympathetic to a protégé's problems might seem like a positive attribute; in reality, sympathy tends to encourage protégés to take on a "victim" or "martyr" role. Empathy, on the other hand, is essential for the mentor to stay in good contact with a protégé.

5. I am good at showing others better ways of doing things.   **SA**

   The ability to show others better ways of doing things is comprised of two parts: (1) the capacity to see a better way of doing something and (2) the ability to explain this option clearly, concisely, and in a nonpatronizing way. Effective mentoring requires not only the ability to create better solutions, but also the ability to present new options in ways that do not injure the protégé's self-esteem.

6. I think that political savvy is a poor substitute for professional competence.   **SD**

   Understanding and knowing how to work effectively within the political structure of the organization is one of the most important skills a mentor can pass on.

Thinking that political astuteness and professional competence can be separated displays a naiveté that would be destructive to most mentoring efforts.

7. I am good at helping other people make decisions.   SA

Being able to assist others in making personal and professional decisions that affect their lives is an essential mentoring skill. This is quite different from actually making decisions for other people or assuming that you know what is best for them. The mentor shares his or her perspective and the protégé makes the decision.

8. I am aware of my own strengths and potential areas for growth.   SA

Effective mentors "buy what they sell." Unless the mentor is concerned about his or her own growth and development, he or she will not be effective with the protégé.

9. I am recognized as a competent professional.   SA

Acknowledging that one is a competent professional is important. Being either incompetent or falsely humble about one's accomplishments is a poor attribute for an effective mentor.

10. I understand how the political structure of my organization works.   SA

Recognizing the importance of being politically astute is the first step; understanding how the system works is the second. New protégés probably need more guidance in this area than in any other.

11. I am comfortable networking with peers and those above me in the organization.   SA

Being comfortable with those on an equal or higher level is one mark of an effective mentor. If the protégé must rely on the mentor's guidance in learning how to work comfortably within the system, the mentor must first be able to display that ability.

12. I am good at generating alternatives.   SA

Whether the mentor is engaged in coaching or counseling, the key is to assist the protégé in solving problems. Generating alternatives prior to choosing a solution is a critical problem-solving skill.

13. I am patient when working with the problems and concerns of others. ·   SA

The key to effective problem solving is having the patience to stay with the process, rather then going for the quick or easy solution. Being patient when helping a protégé with a problem not only results in a better outcome, it provides a model for the protégé to follow in the future.

14. One of my strengths is defining problems clearly.   SA

Whether the problem is personal or professional, a good mentor must stifle the impulse to go for a solution immediately. Experienced mentors understand that the more time spent analyzing the cause and nature of the problem, the easier it will be to arrive at a permanent solution.

15. I have difficulty operating on the "feeling" level with other people. SD

    Comfort with the feeling level is necessary for mentors, both in terms of providing a support base for the protégé and in acting as a counselor for specific problems.

16. I find assisting others to be personally satisfying. SA

    If the mentor-protégé relationship is to last over the long term, it must be a source of personal satisfaction for the mentor. If helping is not satisfying to the mentor, it's probably best for him or her to be available for short-term consulting, but make no attempt to establish an enduring relationship.

17. I am held in high regard by those with whom I work and to whom I report. SA

    The more prestige the mentor has in the organization, the higher the probability that some of it will be reflected onto the protégé. Although this is not the ultimate purpose of mentoring, it does not hurt the protégé to be seen as someone who is being guided by a person of substance.

18. I like making decisions for other people. SD

    Mentors who make decisions for their protégés or who encourage protégés to follow their advice are creating an unhealthy state of dependency. Liking to make decisions for others is a control issue and hardly supports the growth of the protégé. There is nothing wrong with the mentor occasionally offering advice, so long as the protégé is encouraged to make up his or her own mind.

19. I can recognize when people need guidance or nurturing and when they need to be independent. SA

    The long-term objective of mentoring is to help the protégé become self-supporting and independent. This is a weaning process that can happen slowly over time. It is essential for the mentor to recognize when the protégé needs the support of others and when he or she is capable of standing alone. Incidentally, the move toward protégé self-support and the eventual ending of the relationship is something that the mentor usually will be aware of long before the protégé is.

20. I have actively sought mentors myself. SA

    This is a straightforward question. Does the mentor buy what he or she sells? A low score on this question does not preclude anyone from being an effective mentor, and it still demands an answer to the question, "If not, why not?"

Introduction
to the Presentation and Discussion Resources Section

The Presentation and Discussion Resources Section is a collection of articles of use to every facilitator. The theories, background information, models, and methods will challenge facilitators' thinking, enrich their professional development, and assist their internal and external clients with productive change. These articles may be used as a basis for lecturettes, as handouts in training sessions, or as background reading material.

This section will provide you with a variety of useful ideas, theoretical opinions, teachable models, practical strategies, and proven intervention methods. The articles will add richness and depth to your training and consulting knowledge and skills. They will challenge you to think differently, explore new concepts, and experiment with new interventions. The articles will continue to add a fresh perspective to your work.

The 2000 Annual: Volume 1, Training includes ten articles, in the following categories:

Communication: Clarity and Precision in Communication

The Influence Continuum by Marlene Caroselli

Communication: Coaching and Encouraging

A Pragmatic Primer for Mentoring by H.B. Karp

Communication: Technology

An Overview of Web-Based Training by Brandon Hall

Problem Solving: Models, Methods, and Techniques

Is This a Good Decision? A Manager's Checklist
by Janet Winchester-Silbaugh

Facilitation Skills for ETD by Simon Priest and Michael A. Gass

Ground Rules for Training by Brian Gordon

Consulting: Organizations: Their Characteristics and How They Function

How Training Departments Can Add Value
by Rita S. Mehegan and Robert C. Preziosi

Facilitating: Theories and Models of Facilitating

Facilitating Effective Debriefings by Joe Willmore

Facilitating: Techniques and Strategies

Improvisational Theater Games: A New Twist for Training
by Cher Holton

Obtaining Results from Technical Training by Brooke Broadbent

As with previous *Annuals,* this volume covers a wide variety of topics. The range of articles presented encourages thought-provoking discussion about the present and future of HRD. Other articles on specific subjects can be located by using our comprehensive *Reference Guide to Handbooks and Annuals.* The guide is updated regularly and indexes the contents of all the *Annuals* and the *Handbooks of Structured Experiences.* With each revision, the *Reference Guide* becomes a complete, up-to-date, and easy-to-use resource for selecting appropriate materials from the *Annuals* and *Handbooks.*

Here and in the *Reference Guide,* we have done our best to categorize the articles for easy reference; however, many of the articles encompass a range of topics, disciplines, and applications. If you do not find what you are looking for under one category, check a related category. In some cases we may place an article in the "Training" *Annual* that also has implications for "Consulting," and vice versa. As the field of HRD continues to grow and develop there is more and more crossover between training and consulting. Explore all the contents of both volumes of the *Annual* in order to realize the full potential for learning and development that each offers.

The Influence Continuum

Marlene Caroselli

Abstract: To work is to sell, regardless of whether you are "in sales" and whether you hold a position of authority over others. When you interact with people, generally you are either presenting an idea or listening to the ideas of others—either selling or being sold on something. To sell successfully, you must convince others that it is worth their time to listen to a proposal and to take action in accordance with it. This article offers a process for influencing others, consisting of five stages: balk, talk, caulk, walk, and stalk. Recommendations are given for each stage: for influencing others, for overcoming negative reactions and obstacles that may be encountered, and for fostering successful implementation of the idea being sold.

THE INFLUENCE CONTINUUM

Often when you want people to comply with your wishes, you will either not have or not want to use position power to accomplish your goal; instead, you will want to influence them. This article offers an approach to influencing that can be used by anyone in an organizational or team setting. With some adaptation, the approach can also be used in one-on-one situations. The process of influencing is separated into five stages, each named for the characteristic action of that stage (on the part of the audience, the influencer, or both): Balk, Talk, Caulk, Walk, and Stalk. Figures 1 and 2 illustrate the five stages. Figure 1 presents them as a continuum. Figure 2 shows that, during the process of influencing, investment in terms of time and effort is greatest at the beginning and gradually decreases, as those influenced become increasingly committed.

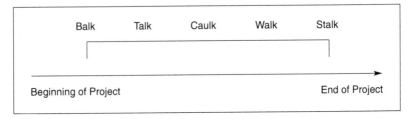

Figure 1.   The Five-Stage Influence Continuum

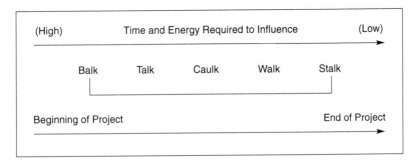

Figure 2.   Time and Energy Required to Influence During the Five Stages

Stage 1: Balk

When you want to influence others to listen to an idea and to take action that is different from their accustomed behavior, you must anticipate resistance. During the first stage, called "balk" because of this characteristic audience reaction, prepare to present your idea in ways that lower resistance.

Most people do not feel a need to give up a current practice and adopt another unless they believe that the new practice will be significantly better in some way. Reactions may range from hesitation or agreement on a surface level only ("It sounds okay, but let me think it over") to questions about potential benefits ("What's in it for me?") or direct challenges ("The way I'm doing things now works just fine; I don't need to change"). Influencing others successfully during the "balk" stage, when people know little or nothing about your proposal and probably do not care to know more, calls for preparing an introduction to your idea that will create interest.

Lay the Groundwork.   Before you unveil your proposal, set a tone of anticipation. Let people know that they can look forward to the change as a positive experience.

Prepare for Resistance.   Develop strategies for handling resistance to the change. Anticipate people's questions and qualms; devise appropriate responses and rehearse them before you meet with people to present the change.

Gather Precedents to Cite.   Collect facts, figures, and benchmarking data from comparable situations to include in your initial presentation of the idea. These precedents will go a long way toward persuading others of the validity of your idea.

Plan a Powerful Presentation.   Work on making your presentation powerful or dramatic. You might try an experiential approach. Let's say you previously trained three colleagues from another department in a new problem-solving technique that you now want your team to adopt. You could invite these colleagues to a team meeting, explaining to them in advance that you want them to use the technique for solving a particular problem. At the meeting you would ask the team members to suggest a real workplace problem that needs to be solved. You would form three subgroups, each to be led by one of the colleagues. Then you would give each colleague a specific amount of time to come up with a solution and walk through it with the subgroup members. After the subgroups finished the task, you would reassemble the entire group to review the new technique, discuss ways in which it may be superior to techniques currently being used, and answer any questions. Also, you would encourage your three colleagues to share their experiences with the technique, its benefits, any difficulties they encountered, how they overcame those difficulties, and their personal reactions to the technique.

STAGE 2: TALK

The "talk" stage refers to the actual presentation of your idea, during which you not only explain it but also engage your audience in a discussion of it. To make your presentation as effective as possible, consider the following questions and incorporate resulting insights:

- What draws my attention?

- What factors are compelling enough for me to try something despite my belief that I don't need it?

- What persuades me? How am I persuaded?

Seasoned influencers often begin their presentations by acknowledging the negative emotions that people experience when confronted with change. One approach to exploring these emotions involves offering some simple snacks that most people in your audience are not likely to have tried. Examples of foods that are largely unfamiliar to an American audience, for example, are plantain chips and sesame tahini spread. Minutes before you start your presentation, place the food items along with any necessary serving utensils, napkins, and so forth on a table. Tell people to help themselves; then deliberately occupy yourself with paperwork or some other unrelated activity. Meanwhile, have an observer make notes about who tries the food, who avoids it, and what comments people make. After everyone has had a chance to sample or refuse the food, ask the observer to share his or her notes. Then start a discussion by stating that you fully understand people's preference for what is familiar over what is unfamiliar, in eating as well as other activities. Lead people to the realization that trying something new can yield gains, regardless of whether those gains are apparent at the outset. Following are recommendations of ways to influence successfully during the "talk" stage, when you are ready to present your idea to people who are willing to listen to it and discuss it.

Use Visual Aids. Use visual aids to supplement your message, but make sure that they do not constitute more than half of your presentation. Visual aids can be highly effective, but they cannot replace a passionate proposal and an effective rationale for implementing that proposal. Remember that visual aids are only one of the three essential "V's" of an influential presentation: voice, verbiage, and visuals.

Paint a Vivid Picture. Use metaphors and vivid verbal pictures to engage the members of your audience and to help them envision your idea. When your purpose is to inspire and motivate rather than simply to edify, you need to appeal not only to people's minds but also to their emotions and imaginations.

Acknowledge Disadvantages and Risks. Present and explain any potential disadvantages and risks associated with your idea. People know that every new venture has a "downside." By readily acknowledging the particulars of that downside, you will be seen as honest, and you will probably preclude some audience attacks on your idea. Discussing disadvantages and risks also allows you to appeal to the courage and adventurous spirit of others in trying your idea.

Encourage Discussion. Make sure that you establish a dialogue with your audience. By inviting and welcoming feedback, you will arouse people's interest and enhance the likelihood of buy-in.

Ensure Viability and Value. First ensure that the idea you are proposing is both doable and worth doing. Then assure your audience that it is viable and beneficial. Don't worry about aiming slightly higher than existing comfort levels; that is the basis of continual improvement.

STAGE 3: CAULK

The third stage, "caulk," extends throughout the process of implementing your idea. At the beginning of implementation you scrutinize your idea, looking for and "caulking" or repairing cracks or weak spots that might jeopardize the outcome. For example, if you find that you lack essential organizational support, you can cultivate a relationship with a top manager who is willing and able to champion your idea. Then, once implementation has begun, you and others involved in the process continue to assess progress. The "caulking" responsibilities that must be fulfilled consist of solving any problems that arise, obtaining any additional resources that are needed, and strengthening commitment when it begins to wane. Recommendations for successfully influencing others during the "caulk" stage, when you and they are working to reinforce implementation, are as follows:

Agree on Measurements of Success.   Because we human beings have such a capacity for misunderstanding one another, it's important that you establish clear and measurable gauges of success. Quantitative measures, although they need not be used exclusively, will tell you when and where caulking is needed.

Focus on Accomplishments.   When setbacks occur, remind people of their accomplishments to date. Sometimes during implementation the future seems too far away, the goal less distinct than it once was, the need for your idea less pressing. If you are to be effective as an influencer, expect such developments and be prepared to caulk any fissures by restoring people's flagging spirits. For example, Jack Kahn, CEO of Manco Inc., a manufacturer of duct tape, spurs his sales staff to ever-greater achievement by making "fun" promises (*Incentive*, 1997). In one case he promised that if sales quotas were met, he would let his staff shave his head. Altered pictures of the executive, with hair deleted, were posted throughout the workplace. A new record was set in sales and, as promised, the staff shaved the head of their chief executive.

Avoid Defensiveness.   Don't let defensiveness impair your ability to identify and solve problems. You won't be able to caulk if you don't know where the leaks are, and you won't know where the leaks are if you refuse to listen to feedback. If you doubt the importance of paying attention to feedback, consider the following news story: As reported in *USA Today*, "If repairs had been made when leaks in the city's infrastructure were first noted, the cost would have been about $10,000. However, the problems were not addressed; caulking was not done. Consequently, 250 million gallons of water from the Chicago River spilled into faulty underground pipes and then into the city, causing a loss of $1.5 billion attributable to repairs, lost revenue, and property damage."

Identify the Real Causes of Problems.   Use what is called the "five-why technique" to determine causes. This method consists of asking why a problem exists and continuing to ask why as each answer is received until you are certain that you have uncovered the real causes, rather than superficial reasons. You scrape through the various layers on the surface until you can clearly identify the cracks; then you can caulk appropriately.

Stage 4: Walk

Eventually you will cease to be the impetus behind your idea; after implementation the idea continues on the strength of its own momentum. By the time you reach this fourth stage, known as "walk," you have conceived the idea, nurtured it through a period of gestation, helped to give it birth, facilitated its continued growth, and seen it reach maturity. Your idea has become standard operating procedure; now you can walk away and turn your attention to another project. Recommendations for influencing others during the "walk" stage, the process of releasing yourself from the day-to-day execution of your idea, are as follows:

Recognize People's Efforts.   Think of appropriate ways to recognize those who helped you to implement your idea. For example, you might write a formal letter of commendation to everyone who participated in the process and then send a copy to each person's supervisor.

Celebrate Successful Implementation.   It is important to hold some kind of celebration or ceremony to signify the end of the project. Not only does the hard work of those involved deserve public and lavish praise, but such a ritual also helps the participants to achieve closure and move on. People often remember the closing celebrations or ceremonies with as much intensity as they remember the many months preceding the project's conclusion.

Encourage Networking.   Encourage networking among those who have been part of the project. Frequently, all people need is a nudge in the right direction. Keep in touch with them, and ensure that they keep in touch with one another. Some teams find the initial success so heady an experience that they decide to undertake a second project. Other teams disband after the initial success, but their members network to keep alive their memories of the past, to learn about opportunities for other projects, and to encourage their hopes for the future.

Connect Implementers with Influencers.   Make plans to inform your implementers when new opportunities arise, in connection with either your own new projects or the developing projects of others. Such referrals are appreciated by those being referred, as well as by those who need implementers.

STAGE 5: STALK

Despite the usual negative connotation of the word "stalk," it is used here in a positive sense to designate the fifth and final stage of influencing. It consists of dropping in on those who have implemented your idea and who continue to support it and maintain the implementation.

Recommendations for influencing others during the "stalk" stage, during which you strive to catch others in the act of doing the right things in the right way, are as follows:

Seek Periodic Progress Reports.   Even though you are no longer associated with the day-to-day operation of your project, you will want to keep apprised of progress. Periodically seeking progress reports will assure you that the plan is being executed as you envisioned and that those responsible are able to function without your intervention. Your "stalking" efforts need not consume much of anyone's time or effort. You may make phone calls, visit people's offices, or hold "reunion" social gatherings; or you may choose to receive occasional memos. Keeping yourself updated in this way allows you to monitor progress and to continue to show your interest in the project.

Publish What Has Been Learned.   After you have witnessed that the right things are being done in the right way, spread the word about what has been learned. For example, you might oversee the publishing and disseminating of special reports or articles in the organization's newsletter. Another idea is to set up a system whereby other employees who are interested in influencing can meet with and receive advice from those who served on the implementation team. In this way you can help to spread the knowledge gained from implementation.

Encourage Continual Improvement.   Meet with your implementers to discuss ways of continually improving on the progress that's been made. You might create and maintain a record of the team members' suggestions during implementation or a log of lessons learned and insights gained; then make that record or log available to all of your implementers as well as others in the organization who are interested in similar pursuits.

Conclusion

It's long been observed that if you fail to plan, you can plan to fail. This adage serves as the philosophy behind the five-stage model presented in this article. Whether you use this model in influencing others or in teaching others to influence, your emphasis at each stage needs to be on careful planning to accomplish a goal.

References

A hairy challenge. (1997, December). *Incentive,* p. 12.

The Chicago flood. (1992, April 21). *USA Today,* p. 10A.

Lewin, K. (1982). Group decision and social change. In G.E. Swanson, T.M. Newcomb, & E.L. Hartley (Eds.), *Readings in social psychology.* New York: John Wiley.

Marlene Caroselli, Ph.D., has authored thirty-five books. She also writes for the National Business Employment Weekly, *the* ICSA Journal, *and Stephen Covey's publications. A popular trainer and keynote speaker, she travels extensively and writes intensively. Her expertise lies in the areas of communication, creativity, and management.* Principled Persuasion: Influencing with Integrity, Selling with Standards *is her most recent book.*

A PRAGMATIC PRIMER FOR MENTORING

H.B. Karp

Abstract: As organizations become more complex and individualized, mentoring is becoming increasingly important for developing less experienced, high potential organization members. There are many views, some contradictory, as to what constitutes mentoring, who should do it, and what are the appropriate values and roles that define the effective mentor.

This article offers a pragmatic, rather than an idealistic, view of the mentoring process. It contains key definitions, descriptions of the roles that the mentor can take on, benefits and pitfalls for both the mentor and the protégé, and some of the conditions necessary for success.

Introduction

Today's organizations are becoming more value-driven, technology is becoming more complicated, organizational structures are becoming more complex, and the rate of change is increasing. Because new people in an organization have to reach their highest levels of contribution as quickly as possible, the traditional ways of training and orienting them are no longer as effective as they once were. Although formal training, which is designed to provide the greatest number of people with the same information, is still appropriate for some purposes, the demand has increased to find ways to personalize employee development. Because mentoring is one of the best ways to do this, it has been adopted by many organizations in the past several years.

There are many different opinions regarding what mentoring is, who should conduct it, and what its values and functions are. This primer provides a pragmatic view of the mentoring process.

What Is Mentoring?

Almost any act of support from a person with more experience to one with less experience could be categorized as mentoring. However, mentoring is much more than that. To begin with we need to define some terms. The two key roles in the relationship are "mentor" and "protégé."

A *mentor* is someone with the skills, experience, and perspectives that are needed by the organization; who has a reasonable amount of organizational influence; and who is willing to develop a personal working relationship with someone of less experience and status in order help that person to become more effective.

The *protégé* is the person who is being helped.

The mentoring role can include any number of functions that are designed to assist the protégé. A few of the more common mentoring functions include:

- *Sponsor:* A person with some status who serves as an advocate for the advancement of the protégé.

- *Role Model:* An experienced person whose actions and/or values are held in such high regard that others are encouraged to emulate him or her.

- *Trainer:* A highly competent professional whose task is to impart specific skills to the protégé.

- *Coach:* A person with experience in a specific area of competence who helps others to correct performance problems or find ways to use their existing skills more creatively.

- *Counselor:* Someone with excellent interpersonal skills who assists others in coping with personal problems and/or inappropriate behavior on the job.

- *Political Advisor:* A person who understands the norms and values of the organizational system, knows where the spheres of influence are, has access to them, and is willing to act as a guide to someone else.

THE MENTOR'S ROLE

A good mentor is able to perform any one of many supportive roles. The major mentoring functions are: trainer, sounding board, coach, counselor, and political advisor.

Trainer

Going back to our definitions, a trainer is a "highly competent professional whose task is to impart specific skills to the protégé." Although this is not included in many definitions of mentoring, there are times when a protégé needs special instruction that is more appropriate coming from a mentor than from a boss or an HR professional. There are several aspects of the mentoring role that facilitate training in a unique way.

1. The mentor is more likely aware of rapid changes in the organization's industry or service.

2. The mentor can offer experienced-based shortcuts.

3. The mentor can provide a context to support the learning from his or her background.

4. The protégé may have an opportunity to observe the mentor on the job, performing the function skillfully.

In providing training, the Socratic approach is best. Rather than providing the protégé with the right answers, it is better to respond to the protégé's questions with, "First, tell me what you would do, and then I'll fill in the blank spaces."

Sounding Board

One very valuable function that a mentor can provide is listening while the protégé expresses frustrations and ideas. Frequently, people do not know what they really think about something until they hear themselves say it out loud. No matter how safe the organizational environment is purported to be, there are always some things that are too risky to voice openly. Because the function of the mentor is to provide support, the protégé should be able to speak openly, or even impulsively, to the mentor, with no risk. Not only does this provide an opportunity for catharsis, it also allows the protégé to receive feedback and perceptions about the sensitive or unclear issue from the mentor.

Coach

Coaching is similar to training, but differs in one major way. Training is teaching something new to the protégé, whereas coaching is helping the protégé to use existing skills more effectively. Coaching generally comes into play when the protégé is having some kind of performance problem and/or needs to increase the quality of his or her output.

The mentor needs to have coaching skills and experience and know how the protégé's work fits into the organization's "big picture." Coaching frequently entails showing the protégé shortcuts to better performance; explaining how the protégé's work interfaces with that of others in the system; helping the protege to develop alternatives to what is currently being done; and helping the protégé to improve existing skills (e.g., how to make better presentations).

Counselor

A counselor is someone with excellent interpersonal skills who assists others in coping with personal problems and/or inappropriate behavior on the job. Whereas coaching generally applies to issues concerning job performance, counseling deals with situations that can affect the job indirectly. A protégé will usually go to his or her mentor when confused, concerned, or in trouble. Counseling can address stressful issues that arise at home and are negatively affecting the protégé's job performance. Examples of these are the illness of a family member, financial worries, and problems with substance abuse. Counseling is also useful in addressing on-the-job behaviors that are negatively affecting the protégé's performance, such as chronic lateness, poor interpersonal skills, or behaviors that others find disruptive or annoying.

Political Advisor

Every organization has its own norms and values, its own way of doing things, and its own political structure. The most important duty of the political advisor is to help the protégé to see that politics are neither good nor bad, but simply the way that power is distributed in the particular organization. Explaining how the system works, providing the protégé with some of the do's and don'ts, and seeing that the protégé is introduced to the appropriate people are important roles of the mentor.

BENEFITS AND POTENTIAL PROBLEMS

The most common view of mentoring is that both the mentor and the protégé profit from the relationship. However, experience suggests otherwise. Altruism is a driving force in many mentoring relationships, but it is by no means the only one. As with any relationship, problems and failures can occur. Some of the benefits and potential problems are listed below:

Benefits for the Mentor

- *Enhanced Self-Esteem.* It is flattering to be asked to serve as a mentor, and mentors are respected in most organizations.

- *A New Perspective on the Work.* Bringing a protégé in to work on something that the mentor is well-known for brings a fresh view to the process and new life and interest to the working environment.

- *Leaving a Mark.* The mentor leaves his or her mark on the organization. Probably the biggest benefit of being a mentor is that it is a key to organizational immortality. The mentor has often spent years developing his or her own processes and unique ways of accomplishing things. Passing them along to a protégé keeps them, and the mentor, alive in the organization.

- *An Ear in Other Parts of the System.* Unless the protégé is a direct report, he or she is working in other parts of the organization. This presents the mentor with a valuable source of information about what is happening in those areas.

- *Being a Mentor Looks Great on One's Performance Appraisal.* Being a mentor, while not formally recompensed, helps one to be perceived as someone who is influential, is willing to go the extra mile for the organization, and genuinely cares about the development of people.

Potential Problems for the Mentor

- *Time Taken from Other Things.* Being a mentor takes a lot of time if it is done right. The time spent with a protégé is time that is not available to pursue personal objectives.

- *Possessiveness.* The mentor can so strongly identify with the protégé that he or she views the protégé's other supportive relationships with jealousy.

- *A Protégé's Failure Lies at the Mentor's Doorstep.* Even though the protégé is completely responsible for his or her decisions and actions, the mentor often is held accountable (unfairly) for the protégé's failures. It's not right, but it comes with the territory.

There also are pros and cons to being a protege. Going in with one's eyes open is the best way to maximize the opportunity.

Benefits for the Protégé

- *Targeted Developmental Activities.* The protégé's professional development can be planned with the mentor, rather than dealt with on a haphazard basis.

- *Increased Likelihood of Success.* Having a more experienced professional on hand for personal guidance gives a protégé a distinct edge over those who are not being mentored.

- *Less Time Spent in the Wrong Position.* A mentor who knows the organization can help the protégé to match his or her individual needs to those of the organization. Although this could certainly apply to promotions, it more often than not refers to wrong choices that have little to do with politics.

- *The Pygmalion Effect.* The mentor usually has positive expectations of and for the protégés. This can be a strong reinforcement for the protégé.

- *Increased Awareness of the Organization.* The mentor can share his or her more experienced view of the organization's systems, processes, and people with the protégé, pointing out the opportunities and pitfalls.

- *Having a Friend in High Places.* The mentor may be able to serve as a champion within the organization for the protégé.

Possible Problems for the Protégé

- *Being the Object of Gossip or Jealousy.* There always is a cost to being in a favored position. If the protégé's peers have not been selected for mentoring, they may not be supportive of the protégé, whom they regard as being in a preferred situation.

- *Having a Mentor Who Does Not Keep Commitments.* Even with the best of intentions or the most enthusiastic of beginnings, some mentors are more committed to the mentoring process than others. New priorities for the mentor may get in the way. The protégé must take responsibility for getting his or her needs met or take the initiative in finding another mentor.

- *Having Unreal Expectations for Promotion.* Although being mentored often indicates that a protégé is on the fast track, it rarely implies that the protégé is on the "inside" track. The protégé should not assume that a promotion is automatically the next step. Being clear about the difference between being sponsored and being mentored is critical in establishing a long-term, mutually supportive relationship.

- *Hitching One's Wagon to a Boulder.* Sometimes a mentor will run afoul of the organization's political system. This can happen in any one of several ways: A mentor can make a mistake that causes the boss or the organization embarrassment; a new CEO can bring in his or her personal favorites; or the in-group can suddenly become the out-group. Regardless of the cause, if the mentor falls into disfavor, it is likely that the protégé will also lose favor by association with the mentor.

CONDITIONS FOR SUCCESS

Mentoring is more a position of influence than it is a specific function. Although there are no hard and fast rules for effective mentoring, there are several conditions that increase the probability that it will go well.

1. *A mentor should not be an immediate supervisor of or in a direct reporting line with the protégé.* Because the supervisor is responsible for the subordinate's performance appraisal and is accountable for the subordinate's performance, there is something to lose. This does not make for an effective mentoring relationship. By the same token, if the supervisor's boss is the mentor, the supervisor is effectively cut out of the chain of command.

The rule of thumb is that the mentor should be at least two steps up and one over from the protégé. A father isn't a good mentor; an uncle is.

2. *Mentoring must be purely voluntary.* Regardless of how people "should" feel, you cannot force one person to care about another. Mentoring takes a lot of time, effort, and involvement. If the mentor does not really care about how the protégé does, his or her advice can be haphazard and potentially dangerous, particularly if the protégé trusts the mentor.

3. *Being a protégé must be purely voluntary.* There are times when a younger employee or manager could benefit from the sage advice of an older member of the organization and just doesn't realize it. It is certainly appropriate for a supervisor to point this out and to volunteer to help the junior member find a mentor. It is never appropriate to insist that the individual be mentored. Regardless of how accurate the observation is, a person who is forced into a mentoring relationship will not value the experience and, at worst, will actively resent it.

4. *The mentor can be no more committed to the protégé's success than the protégé is.* The possibility always exists that the mentor can become more involved in the mentoring process than the protégé. When this happens, the mentor begins to lose effectiveness and could even begin to resent the protégé for being unappreciative of the mentor's time and efforts. If the mentor begins to sense a lessening of interest on the protégé's part, he or she should discuss this with the protégé. If the protégé's interest has waned, the mentor needs to cut back by a like amount.

5. *The protégé sets the pace.* It is important to establish who is responsible for what. While it certainly may be appropriate for the mentor to suggest a course of action, it is the protégé who must see the need and state what is wanted as much as possible.

6. *The mentor needs to become obsolete as soon as feasible.* Some mentors stay in position for years, while others do it only for a specific or brief period of time. Although there is no right or wrong approach to this, there is a potential pitfall. In some circumstances, the longer the relationship lasts, the more ego-massaging it is for the mentor, and the more safe and dependent the protégé becomes. Periodically, the mentor and the protégé need to re-evaluate the relationship and make a conscious choice to continue it or plan to end it.

7. *The mentor is a source of encouragement.* Regardless of the function that the mentor is engaged in with the protégé, the mentor needs to be a continual source of encouragement. Most mentors can empathize with their pro-

tégés because they have experienced the frustrations and challenges at the front end of any career. Pointing this out and providing sincere reassurance can go a long way toward helping the protégé to overcome what appears to be a never-ending uphill climb.

Summary

Mentoring is a time-honored way of passing on effective processes and procedures and is a prime source of individual development. Mentoring is really an art form, with each mentor passing on his or her insights and skills in a way that is unique to that mentor. The more that trainers of mentors can assist them in focusing on their uniqueness, the higher the probability that these mentors, in turn, will do the same with their protégés.

Resources

Bell, C.R. (1996). *Managers as mentors.* San Francisco, CA: Berrett-Koehler.

Carew, J. (1998). *The mentor Donald I.* New York: Fine Books.

Clutterbuck, D., & Megginson, D. (1995). *Mentoring in action.* London, U.K.: Nichols.

Ferguson, T.W. (1997). Who's mentoring whom? *Forbes, 159*(10), 252–253.

Hay, J. (1995). *Transformational mentoring.* New York: McGraw-Hill.

Hegger, H. (1993). *The mentor handbook.* London, U.K.: Nichols.

Karp, H.B. (1995). *Personal power: An unorthodox guide to success.* Lake Worth, FL: Gardner Press.

Lawson, K. (1996). *Improving workplace performance through coaching.* West Des Moines, IA: American Media.

Phillips-Jones, L. (1997). *The new mentors and proteges.* Grass Valley, CA: Coalition of Counseling Centers.

MacLennan, N. (1995). *Coaching and mentoring.* Amherst, MA: HRD Press.

Murray, M. (1991). *Beyond the myths and magic of mentoring.* San Francisco, CA: Jossey-Bass.

Shea, G.F. (1994). *Mentoring: Helping employees reach their full potential.* New York: AMA Management Briefing.

Shea, G.F. (1997). *Mentoring: A practical guide.* Menlo Park, CA: Crisp Publications.

Stevens, P. (1995). *How to network and select a mentor.* San Jose, CA: Resource Publications, Inc.

Stursberg, P. (1994). *Your dream mentor.* Salt Lake City, UT: Northwest Publishing.

Zey, M. (1993). *The mentor connection: Strategic alliances in corporate life.* New Brunswick, NJ: Transaction Publications.

H.B. Karp, Ph.D., *is presently on the faculty of management of Christopher Newport University in Newport News, Virginia. He also is the owner of Personal Growth Systems, a management-consulting firm in Chesapeake, Virginia. He consults with a variety of Fortune 500 and governmental organizations in the areas of leadership development, team building, conflict management, and executive coaching. He specializes in applying Gestalt theory to issues of individual growth and organizational effectiveness. He is the author of many articles,* Personal Power: An Unorthodox Guide to Success, *and* The Change Leader: Using a Gestalt Approach with Work Groups, *and is a co-author of* X Marks the Spot: Building Teams for the 21st Century.

AN OVERVIEW OF WEB-BASED TRAINING*

Brandon Hall

Abstract: Web-based training (WBT) is instruction delivered by means of a Web browser, through the Internet or through an organization's intranet. This article explains the terms, concepts, and technologies of Web-based training. It compares the following types of Web-based training programs: text and graphics, interactive, and interactive multimedia. It describes the advantages and disadvantages of Web-based training and provides considerations for determining whether to use it. It tells where Web-based training can best be delivered and lists the criteria used to evaluate it. The article also explores the costs and issues related to investing in Web-based training, including selling it to decision makers and motivating employees to use it. Finally, it describes the processes of designing and presenting such training.

*Adapted with permission from the *Web-Based Training Cookbook* by Brandon Hall. Published by John Wiley & Sons. Copyright © 1997 by Brandon Hall.

Introduction and Definitions

Web-based training (WBT) is instruction that is delivered by means of a Web browser, such as Netscape Navigator®, through the Internet or an organization's intranet. The Internet includes all electronic transmissions, including e-mail, file transfers, and the World Wide Web. The Web is just one part of the Internet, but it is the fastest growing, most promising part, especially in relation to training.

Other terms are often used for delivering training over a network (remote access training), including Internet-based training, intranet-based training, online training, and net-based training. They are defined below.

- Internet-based training is any training that can be accessed over the Internet. Usually this is done with the World Wide Web, but e-mail correspondence courses and file transfers also fall into this category.

- Intranet-based training is based on an organization's internal computer network. Web browsers are used to access company pages, but they are only accessible within the organization.

- Online training refers to any training done with a computer over a network, including an organization's intranet or local area network and the Internet. This is also called net-based training.

Web-based training and Internet-based training are the two most widely used terms for this type of training. There is no clear first choice, and both terms are likely to remain popular. As technology evolves, so does terminology.

Multimedia Training

Multimedia training is a type of computer-based training (CBT) that uses two or more media, including text, graphics, animation, audio (sound/music), and video. In practice, multimedia uses as many of these media as is practical to produce a colorful, engaging program delivered via the computer. A typical program allows users to control their progress and pace through the course so that everyone can learn at his or her own speed. A phrase that reflects this impact is, "With CBT, we capture their heads; with multimedia, we capture their hearts."

Other Technologies

Computer-based training is an all-encompassing term used to describe any computer-delivered training, including CD-ROM and the World Wide Web. However, some people use the term CBT to refer only to old-fashioned, text-only training.

- Distance learning historically refers to a broadcast of a lecture to distant locations, usually through video presentations.

- Desktop training is any training delivered by computer at the learner's desk.

- Desktop videoconferencing means a real-time conference using live pictures between two or more people on a network who communicate via computer.

- Interactive training is an umbrella term that includes both computer-based and multimedia training.

- Computer-assisted instruction is a term commonly used in the field of education for any instruction for which a computer is used as a learning tool.

- Self-paced training is training that is taken at a time and a pace determined by the user. Historically used for text or audio/video self-study courses, the term is now used by some organizations to include computer-based, Web-based, and multimedia training.

User Hardware and Software

The basic hardware required for a user to take a Web-based training course is:

- A computer fast enough to handle the training program. For computers that use Windows® programs, a 486 processor may work, but a Pentium® or better is preferred.

- A sound card that is capable of playing back any audio files the training program uses.

- A network connection, whether it is a digital line connected directly to the organization's server or a modem that can dial in to the Internet.

If the training is delivered via the organization's local area network (LAN) or intranet, for example, the users do not need a separate Internet connection. The same technology used for the Internet exists on many organizations' intranets. Although the Internet is getting all the publicity, the fastest growing segment of the market for Web browsers and servers is organizational intranets.

The basic software that the end user must have includes:

- A Web browser.

- Any specialized browser plug-ins or controls that are required by the particular training program, such as those needed to play audio or video files.

The user does not need the same computer system as the developer. One of the major advantages of Web-based training over other types of computer-based training is cross-platform compatibility. Web browsers can access Web-based training using a language that is platform-independent.

EXAMPLES OF WEB-BASED TRAINING

Web-based training is often less expensive and more convenient than other ways of delivering training. There now are effective programs on the World Wide Web in each of the three main categories of training: computer training, technical training, and soft-skills training. The technology for delivery over the Internet or an intranet is improving rapidly and, in a year or so, the state of the art for multimedia Web-based training will be at the level of state-of-the-art multimedia CD-ROM-delivered training.

Because this is such a new medium, distinctions among the various types of Web-based training are still being made. The main distinctions are the levels of interactivity and the amounts and types of media. Because training programs are developed to meet specific training needs, training programs that do not include the latest Web-based multimedia technologies may be highly appropriate for specific situations. There can be too many bells and whistles. However, there is rarely too much interactivity. Holding the attention of the student and engaging his or her mind is necessary for learning to occur. Interactivity makes the difference between a program that simply presents information and one that trains. As a general rule, training programs should emphasize interactivity.

Text and Graphics Web-Based Training Programs

Text and graphics programs may simply be paper-based course materials placed on the Web so that students can access them in an electronic format. The worst of these programs are called "page turners." Although that is a positive comment for a book, it is a negative one for computer-delivered training, as no one wants to use a program that mainly involves reading off a computer screen. On the other hand, text and graphics programs designed from the ground up for Web delivery can be appropriate for a given training need. Many contain hyperlinks to other materials or to charts and graphs that further illustrate the desired learnings. These usually provide a low level of interactivity, although not necessarily a low level of information.

The majority of sites that utilize the text and graphics approach utilize no authoring tools other than what is necessary to create hypertext markup language (HTML) coded text. One example of a text and graphics model is the Cyber Travel Specialist from New Media Strategies, Inc. This training program is designed to teach travel agents all over the country how the Internet will be useful to them as a business tool. The curriculum is a combination of a Web-based training module, a hands-on workshop, and a lecture. The program is designed for an audience that may not yet be comfortable with a training course delivered completely over the Web; it helps to ease the participants into the new technology.

The text and graphics model is the place many people start in the development of Web-based training, because it is the easiest to create and is accessible to the most people. However, in many cases it can only minimally be considered training. To gain greater effectiveness from this medium, one needs to move to the next level and add more interactivity.

Interactive Web-Based Training Programs

Engaging the learner with stimulating interactivity is the promise and the future of computer-delivered instruction, whether delivered on CD-ROM or the Web. What a good story line is to a movie, what game play is to a computer game, so interactivity and instructional design are to Web-based training. Interactivity at its best is a simulation of the work situation. At a minimum, it can include application exercises, drag-and-drop, column matching, testing, text entry, and even programming code entry. These go beyond the simple presentation of text and graphics; they bring the learner into the program to engage with the content and practice the skills.

A terrific example of interactive WBT courseware is that developed by Randy Hootman of Randysoft (*www.randysoft.com*). He has designed a series of tutorials that teach programming languages, including HTML, Perl, and others. The unique aspect of these courses is that they provide a simulated programming environment that allows students to actually enter code into an open text area, submit the code, and immediately see the results of their new programming skills. Assessment is done in real time, so the user receives immediate feedback on what he or she did.

Interactive Multimedia Web-Based Training Programs

Most Web-based training programs are truly interactive; they allow the user to manipulate graphic objects in real time, sometimes taking on the quality of a game-playing exercise. The simulations are realistic, and the situations are often difficult. Appropriate use of audio and/or video helps from an instructional point of view and from the human side as well.

The promise of interactive multimedia training was realized with CD-ROM technology. It allowed large audio and video files to be stored on a portable disk and presented nicely on the computer screen, without the wait times of the Internet. The Web provides improved transfer speeds and is an improvement on the CD-ROM in terms of storage space and ease of update. Data on a CD-ROM is there forever. Information on a Web site can be easily updated as often as necessary.

An interactive multimedia course allows the student to enter into a world that attempts to mimic a part of real life, providing immediate, real-life responses to user input. If something goes wrong, such as the student taking the wrong action in response to a hazardous situation, the program lets him or her know by simulating a meltdown.

An excellent example of interactive multimedia WBT is the Web Interactive Training Program at NASA's Kennedy Space Center. The program makes use of simulations, video, online testing, and plenty of graphics. Two courses include the Nondestructive Evaluation Overview and an Introduction to Statistical Processes. The first teaches users how to test the material integrity of a part, component, or system without damaging it; the second presents a method to monitor processes and to determine whether adjustments are needed.

The Eddy Current Simulation of NASA's NDE Overview is an example of courses designed to train NASA managers who work on quality control, safety, and reliability efforts. NASA is reportedly pleased with these products and is saving money on first-time development costs, in-class instructor costs, and travel costs with the implementation of Web-based training.

Another example of an interactive multimedia WBT course is Oracle Simulator, developed by Empower for database administrators. The program emulates real-life backup and recovery situations for server manager software, from the ringing telephone with a distraught user's call to implementing the software solution. The simulation takes place in the hot-line office of a fictitious company called DBA. The user acts as the hot-line contact. Customers call to report database administration problems. The screen shows a typical office, including a file drawer that contains information on hot-line customers' companies and their database problems. The user clicks on a file folder tab to choose a customer.

In the program, a customer calls, outlines the basic database problem, then sends an e-mail message detailing the problem. The user can click on the telephone at any time to listen to the customer's message again. The computer in the simulation is used for videoconferences with an on-call expert, for interactions with the customer via e-mail and videoconference, and for viewing a log of the information received from the expert and the customer.

As the user solves the database problem using the server manager, the on-call expert (mentor) guides the user through various choices, using a desktop videoconference-window metaphor. A progress-log screen records all interactions with the customer and the expert.

The software simulation includes a series of screens from the actual software program. Certain screens ask the user to select commands and show the results of those commands with instructional feedback. As the user progresses through different pathways of the simulation, the system keeps track of the steps the user has taken to solve the problem.

Web-based interactive multimedia is an effective way to provide training in a risk-free environment. Users can see the results of their actions immediately. The inclusion of graphics, audio, and video provides the multimedia advantage of making the environment more realistic and the training more effective and enjoyable.

DECIDING WHETHER TO USE WEB-BASED TRAINING

Is Web-Based Training Right for Your Organization?

The following are considerations in determining whether Web-based training is appropriate for your organization.

1. Do you have management support?
2. Do you have enough potential users to justify the cost of purchase or development?
3. Are your potential users computer-literate?
4. Will they accept a Web-based program?

5. Will they learn from this particular program?

6. Will the program provide a method of instruction that is easier, faster, less expensive, safer, or more engaging than the alternative?

Advantages of Web-Based Training

Some advantages of Web-based training are flexibility, accessibility, and convenience. Users can proceed through a training program "at their own pace and at their own place." They can access the training at any time and only as much as they need. This is known as "just in time and just enough."

Worldwide distribution is inexpensive, as Web-based training can be delivered to any computer that can access the Internet or an intranet, anywhere in the world. No separate distribution system is needed, which keeps delivery costs low. Web-browser software and Internet connections are widely available. Most computer users have access to a browser, are connected to the organization's intranet, and/or have access to the Internet. Cross-platform Web-based training can be accessed by Web-browsing software on any platform: Windows, Mac, UNIX, OS/2, Amiga, and so on. You can deliver the training program to any personal computer over the Internet or the organization's intranet without having to author a program for each platform.

The centralized nature of a Web-based training program means that it can be disseminated in a standardized, easily updated version to multiple users. If changes need to be made in the program after the original implementation, they can be made on the server that stores the program, so users worldwide can instantly access the update. Courses can be designed to access designated current information, such as the latest new-product specifications, from any other server worldwide, permitting instant updating whenever and wherever the program is run.

There are no travel costs for bringing remote employees to a centralized workshop because the Web is available from the desktop. According to the report "Return on Investment and Multimedia Training," the actual time required for training by computer averages about 50 percent that of instructor-led training. Web-based training is often less expensive and more convenient than the alternatives.

More and more information services and programs within organizations are moving to the World Wide Web. Web-based training is a fascinating new field, which will likely have a vast impact on all professionals. With careful attention to instructional design during the development phase, Web-based training can be a valuable addition to an organization's training and performance-support offerings. The future of the Web and Web technologies is long-term and will have a big impact, according to all estimates.

Disadvantages of Web-Based Training

Limited bandwidth (the actual speed available at the time of the transmission) results in slower performance for sound, video, and intensive graphics, causing long waiting periods during downloading, and this can affect the ease of the learning process. The more users there are on a network, the less bandwidth is available for transmission. The problem is greater over the public Internet, where more traffic jams occur, and tends to be less on organizational intranets, which usually have greater bandwidth. Future technologies will no doubt help to solve this problem.

There's a general concern that as we move toward more computer usage, computers are replacing human contact to a dysfunctional degree. Decreasing instructor-led training makes some trainees uneasy. If this is a concern, consider a gradual introduction of WBT technology.

As with any emerging technology, the level of interactivity in Web-based training is often limited. This is gradually improving; as it does, the impact of Web-based training on performance also improves.

Like any first-time challenge, learning about and implementing new technology can require more resources than may be expected. Make it easier by starting with a simple program and building on success. Remember that the greater portion of costs associated with Web-based training are start-up costs. Programs can be delivered and reused with fewer costs than with traditional methods.

Some training topics require a more personal touch and are not best served by computer-based training. Team-building activities and dealing with emotional issues such as downsizing are examples. Web-based training and other technologies for training are mainly for assisting the learning process and are not intended to replace methods that already work well.

Criteria to Use in Evaluating Web-Based Training

The following are ten criteria used in the judging of the annual Multimedia and Internet Training Awards sponsored by the *Multimedia and Internet Training Newsletter:*

1. *Content:* Does the program include the right amount and quality of information?

2. *Instructional Design:* Is the course designed in such a way that users will actually learn?

3. *Interactivity:* Is the user engaged through the opportunity for input?

4. *Navigation:* Can users determine their own ways through the program? Is an exit option available? Is a course map accessible? Are the meanings of icons and labels clear, so that users don't have to read excessive documentation to determine program options?

5. *Motivational Components:* Does the program engage the user through novelty, humor, game elements, testing, adventure, unique content, surprise elements, and so forth?

6. *Use of Media:* Does the program appropriately and effectively employ graphics, animation, music, sound, video, etc.? Is the gratuitous use of these media avoided? Is the soundtrack pleasant, not annoying?

7. *Evaluation:* Is there some type of evaluation, such as:

   ■ Completion of a simulation?

   ■ Mastery of each section's content before proceeding to the next section?

   ■ Section quizzes?

   ■ A final exam?

8. *Aesthetics:* Is the program attractive and appealing to the eye and ear? Does the structure of the screen add to the program?

9. *Record Keeping:* Are student performance data, such as time to complete the program, question analyses, and final scores, recorded? Is the data forwarded to the course manager automatically?

10. *Tone:* Is the program designed for the audience? Does it avoid being condescending, trite, pedantic?

INFLUENCING DECISION MAKERS TO USE WEB-BASED TRAINING

The costs for a Web-based training program are often lower than those associated with instructor-led training. The biggest stumbling blocks often are the start-up costs for investment in the technology and the development time. But the costs associated with delivery are much lower than for traditional methods.

Investing in Web-based training can be justified, based on the following:

- Significant cost savings have a way of catching management's attention. Lower training costs result from the reduction in time and resources for delivery, including eliminating the costs of traveling to learning centers.

- Because Web-based training programs are designed to be completed at the user's own pace, many programs have administrative features that keep track of where students are in the course and how well they are doing.

- Any motivational strategies used for other training can be applied to Web-based training. By using a computer, some reward structures can be automated. In addition, the tracking and reporting available with Web-based training allow the organization to structure rewards and requirements for completion and mastery.

Making the Transition to Web-Based Training

To make the transition easier for trainers as well as students, some organizations combine elements of Web-based training and instructor-led training (ILT) in some early programs. There are a variety of new roles and career opportunities for those who are willing to adapt to the new technologies.

DEVELOPING WEB-BASED TRAINING PROGRAMS

Web-based training development teams range from just one, very dedicated, person who does it all to project teams of over forty professionals. In general, at a minimum, you will need:

- A project manager capable of dealing with diverse work styles and personalities.

- An instructional designer familiar with computer-delivered instruction.

- A programmer or author to use the authoring tool.

- A graphic artist.

- A subject-matter expert.

- A Webmaster for maintaining the program on the server.

- Someone who can obtain funding for Web-based training from management.

The Use of Multimedia and Other Issues

With languages like Java® and plug-ins for authoring tools like Shockwave® and Neuron® making it possible, multimedia on the Web is growing in popularity. Bandwidth is the major limitation, and right now the vision and the potential are greater than the reality. Emerging technologies will provide greater bandwidth and greater compression for delivering audio and video. It is only a matter of time before multimedia over an organization's intranet and the Internet is commonplace. In the meantime, hybrid CDs, also known as Internet CDs, are an alternative. In these, the program with audio and video are delivered on a CD-ROM, with updates and tracking handled automatically over the Web.

The type and amount of interactivity and the media required vary with the instructional objectives of each program. It is generally not possible for a program to be too interactive. However, it is possible for a program to suffer from too many media, which are gratuitous when they don't contribute to meeting the instructional objectives.

From an instructional-design perspective, Internet-based training differs from multimedia training. Designing for the Internet presents a special problem. Connection speeds can be slow and downloads can be long due to factors over which trainers have no control. Until bandwidth improves, it is a good idea to eliminate the "fat media" in a program, especially video, and to design in interactivity, discussion, and access to other resources that are part of the benefits of training online. Web-based training is different from CD-ROM-based training in the following ways:

- CD-ROM-based training programs usually have their own unique interface.

- Web-based training requires a Web browser, so the basic navigation scheme is usually familiar to the student.

Students who will be receiving Web-based training should know how to use a browser. In general, the student should see little difference in the actual training once it has been accessed. If the training is over an intranet, the difference is not very noticeable, but over the Internet, the connection speeds and download times are often much slower than with CD-ROMs.

More and more, CD-ROM and the Web are being seen not as two different methods, but as two parts of the same method: content delivery. CD-ROM is useful for intensive media, and the Web is useful for information distribution. Combine the two and you have a real solution.

Online Learning Assistants and Facilitators

A learning assistant or facilitator available online can be helpful to the users, although successful training programs can be designed without these. A learning assistant online can help the user to handle customer-service issues and technical problems. A facilitator can help with content issues and can guide discussions. Web-based training—especially within an organization—is usually designed to be a stand-alone process to be taken at any time of the day or night. Even in the latter case, having e-mail access to a Webmaster, course manager, or content expert can be helpful.

Creating Programs

The major authoring tools allow you to create both a stand-alone version of a program and a Web version of the program. Depending on which authoring tool you use to create a pre-existing CBT program, you may be able to convert most of it for delivery over the Web. You do not need to learn complicated programming languages in order to create Web-based programs. In general, you should be familiar with HTML, although this is not required if you are using one of the high-level HTML editors, such as Microsoft's FrontPage®, which allows you to create Web pages without knowing HTML. The major authoring programs are nearly the same whether you are developing for CD-ROM or the Web. There are also "object oriented" visual tools for programming with Java, such as Aimtech's Jamba® and Symantec's Visual Cafe®.

Authoring programs, such as Authorware®, ToolBook II®, IconAuthor®, Quest®, IBTAuthor®, and many others are currently available, with training components built in. If you want to start with a simple program, an HTML editor or Web page layout program such as Netscape Navigator Gold®, Microsoft FrontPage, Claris Home Page,® or Asymetrix Web Publisher® may be all you need. Java is a programming language that allows the developer to create small applications called applets that control specific aspects of a Web-based training program, such as creating interactive animations. Shockwave is a plug-in for programs developed with Macromedia's Authorware so these programs can be viewed with a Web browser. The Neuron plug-in allows ToolBook II applications to be viewed with a Web browser. Interactive multimedia WBT programs are usually authored with a software tool that allows for the programming necessary to add the multimedia and manage the high levels of interactivity and record keeping. Java applets can be built to manage this, but most authors prefer the traditional full-scale authoring tools, such as Authorware or ToolBook II, which have plug-ins for delivery over the Internet. You should be aware of what Java is capable of, although the specifics of programming a Java applet are not necessary if you use the right authoring tool.

Whether training should be interactive on the Web or downloaded and used offline depends on the type of training and administration desired. Real-time administration, as the user is taking the course, can be achieved while the user is online. Offline programs can be set up to send completion information and test scores at the end of the course, and, if necessary, download another portion of the course. But if a student is taking a course offline, he or she may not be aware of any updates to the program that occur while the course is in progress. If the online course requires a change or update of some part of the data or coding, the student is not disrupted and does not have to initiate another download of the entire course.

The speed of connection needed to access Web-based training effectively depends on the program. If the program will utilize video, animation, and audio, the connection should be as fast as possible. For home office users, this means ISDN or 33.6Kbps and 56Kbps modems. If the training utilizes limited graphics and no audio or video, a minimal connection via a 28.8 modem can be adequate. It is difficult to calculate how fast a program will be delivered over a network because bandwidth varies so. One second, the program might be delivered at 6.5Kbps, the next it may be 1 or 2 Kbps or less. In general, computer files are calculated in bytes (MB, KB), and bandwidth is measured in bits (Mb, Kb). To determine how many bits your program is, multiply the number of bytes by 8. A program that takes up 4 megabytes of space takes up 32 megabits. If your connection speed is 2Mbps (megabits per second), this file would take 16 seconds to download. Alternatively, over an Internet connection of 33.6Kbps (.336 Mbps) a 32-Mb training program would take about 96 seconds to download. All this is assuming ideal conditions but, of course, conditions are always less than ideal.

A Web server is needed to make the training program available to others. The options are a server maintained by the training department or information technology (IT) department or a public Internet service provider (ISP), such as America Online, Compuserve, AT&T, and others.

Once the program is developed, you will need to place the program and its accompanying files on your server, then test to ensure it works properly. Ask your network administrator, Webmaster, or ISP provider how to upload the files to the Web site. After that it is a matter of marketing.

The most utilized method of charging for a WBT program is to have the users pay in advance by credit card and then give them a password that lets them into the program. Security for taking payment over the Internet is relatively good. For internal programs over an intranet, course registration software can automate chargebacks to the purchasing department.

Security

An organization's intranet should be protected from hacker intrusions by a firewall, a hardware and/or software security measure taken to keep unwanted transmissions or visitors from the Internet from entering the organization's intranet. An effective firewall will keep out hackers, casual users, and accidental queries while allowing access to legitimate users of the company's intranet, even from remote locations. In order to keep out viruses, some firewalls limit the ability of employees within the organization to download files from the Internet. Your IT department or network administrator also can recommend virus protection software, such as Norton's AntiVirus® or McAffee VirusScan®.

Although security problems exist and make big news in the media, the percentage of incidents is quite small and should not deter your work deploying Web-based training. A large part of the future of training will be online. Get started today.

Brandon Hall, Ph.D., *is the editor and publisher of the* Multimedia & Internet Training Newsletter *and author of the* Web-Based Training Cookbook. *He monitors the use of technology in the field of training and shares his observations with colleagues. He has a doctorate in educational psychology and has worked in training with Fortune 500 companies over the last twenty years. He presents regularly at major conferences and has been interviewed by the* New York Times, Fortune, Training, Training & Development, *and other periodicals.*

Is This a Good Decision?
A Manager's Checklist*

Janet Winchester-Silbaugh

Abstract: How can you tell a good decision from a poor one? A good decision (1) supports the organization's strategic plan, (2) fits an environment full of unknowns and conflicting needs, (3) is creative and based on a range of input, and (4) generates support and successful action.

This article contains a checklist that can help you to evaluate any decision in terms of its goals, its underlying assumptions, the information considered, the people involved, the process, the implementation, and other critical factors. It does not, of course, promise that the decision will work out well, but it will tell you whether the decision-making process is sound.

---

*This checklist is based on the ideas of Teresa Amabile on creativity, John Bryson and Peter Schwartz on strategic planning, Harlan Cleveland on ambiguity and paradox, Eliayhu Goldratt on dealing with natural conflicting needs of the system, and Noel Tichy on leadership.

CHARACTERISTICS OF GOOD DECISION MAKING

How often have you been given recommendations that sound good on paper but give you an uncomfortable feeling? This checklist is designed to help you figure out what is wrong with such recommendations. A good decision-making process has certain characteristics:

- It is based on the organization's strategic plan.
- It considers the ever-changing, conflicting needs of the environment, customers, and the organization.
- It is creative and based on a wide range of input from many sources with different points of view.
- It generates enough support and energy to result in useful action.

Good Decisions Support the Organization's Strategic Plan

John Bryson (1995) says that strategic planning encourages organizations to address major organizational issues, respond wisely to internal and external demands, and deal effectively with rapidly changing circumstances. Decisions translate the strategic plan into action. The more decisions that point in the strategic direction, the faster an organization will move.

Many executives and managers give lip service to strategy, but few integrate it into the core of their thinking. It is important to consider how each decision fits into the bigger picture and with other decisions, other time periods, and other departments. A decision should feel like one piece of a larger puzzle, rather than the most important one. A decision should be consistent in both its goals and its method for achieving them. Watch out for the decision that seems to solve all the organization's problems. Such grandiose decisions feel good, but rarely support other decisions.

Good Decisions Take into Account a Complex, Changing Environment

Harlan Cleveland (1989) states that "Executive leadership is above all a taste for paradox, a talent for ambiguity, the capacity to hold contradictory propositions comfortably in a mind that relishes complexity." Many decisions make perfect sense in a perfect environment (customers' needs don't change, raw materials are available, computers work, and key employees don't quit), but environments are not perfect; they contain uncertainty and contradictions. Your most critical assumption may be based on your worst data. Good decisions consider likely, as well as less-likely scenarios. If a decision is based on average revenues or the median customer response, it may fail in other conditions. A good decision will consider the expected environment as well as some very different scenarios (Schwartz, 1991).

Good Decisions Are Creative and Are Based on a Wide Range of Input from Many Sources with Different Points of View

Environments are not as tidy as most of us want them to be. There is not one right answer. What may be the perfect answer from a marketing point of view may be the wrong answer for production. What will help one customer may hurt another. An effective decision-making process will approach a problem from different perspectives (e.g., financial, strategic, operational, and customer needs). Eliayhu Goldratt (1998) uses systematic analysis to identify when a conflict is the result of two legitimate organizational needs. A good decision takes these legitimate but conflicting needs into account.

A good decision also incorporates many different sources of information: some hard data, some soft, some conflicting. Beware the decision based on a single cost-benefit analysis.

Creativity also involves considering different options. Teresa Amabile (1998) states that "Homogeneous teams do little to enhance expertise or creative thinking." It is time to worry if all members of a decision-making group think the decision is obvious and do not see any drawbacks. The group that agrees on everything is probably not exploring all the possibilities. If decision makers are truly exploring possibilities and options, they will disagree about many things—at least initially.

Good Decisions Create Energy in Others and Lead to Successful Action

Decisions you cannot implement are not very useful. Tichy and Cohen (1997) state that "Winning leaders create energy in others." The same can be said for good decisions. People who have to implement a decision should (1) know about it, (2) be excited about it, and (3) know what they need to do to implement it. Before finalizing an action plan, it is a good idea to talk to the people who have to do the work. Many decisions sound good on paper, but just will not fly.

Once a decision has been made, it should be communicated to all those who may be affected by it. It also is important to clarify what specific actions are necessary to implement the decision and by whom. When people are clear about what is expected of them, they generate the energy for action.

You can use the following checklist to evaluate a decision-making process to assess whether it is likely to produce a good decision.

Is This a Good Decision? A Manager's Checklist

Questions to Ask

What to Look for in an Answer

Strategy: Does the decision fit into the strategic plan?

1. If you state both the decision and the strategy in one sentence, do they sound consistent?

2. Will it help your customers?

3. Does it support other strategic decisions you've already made?

4. Does it reflect your organization's values?

5. Does it move the organization closer to what it wants to be?

6. Does it fit your organization's strengths and limits?

Strategy may be either a guiding light or a buzzword. Does this decision put strategy into action or does the decision seem to use strategy to justify what people want to do anyway?

Strategy: What are the fundamental assumptions?

1. Do they support the organization's strategy?

2. Will the outcome of this decision be resilient when the environment changes?

3. Are the goals and the methods consistent?

4. Does it try to do too much ?

Try to figure out what assumptions the decision is based on. Unstated assumptions limit thinking and bias the outcome.

Questions to Ask	What to Look for in an Answer
Strategy: How does this decision help the whole organization?	Good decisions build strength into the organization and, often, into the industry. Risk is involved in many decisions, but unknown risk may do the most damage.

Strategy: How does this decision help the whole organization?

1. Does this decision create synergy with other decisions you've made this year?
2. Does it help customers in the long run?
3. Does it help your industry?
4. Can it generate support?
5. How does it affect other departments?
6. Does it create constructive pressure?
7. Does it make some organizational conflicts worse?
8. What are the possible negative consequences?
9. Does it create movement toward your goals?
10. Is it consistent with other decisions made in the past?

Good decisions build strength into the organization and, often, into the industry. Risk is involved in many decisions, but unknown risk may do the most damage.

Environment: Is the decision resilient under different conditions?

1. Does the decision consider a changing environment?
2. Does it recognize that needs of different customers, departments, and goals may be in conflict?
3. Does it give too much weight to the needs of one area at the expense of another?
4. How does it deal with unknowns? Is it based on the assumption that everything is known?
5. Does it address trade-offs?

Decisions are often made from one point of view, even if based on rational information. A strong decision, however, is based on many different points of view and takes into account changes in the environment, less-than-perfect conditions, and other unknowns.

Questions to Ask	What to Look for in an Answer

Questions to Ask

6. Has the decision-making group thought about the best and worst outcomes?

7. How much risk is involved?

Process: Who is involved in the decision?

1. Are the decision makers from different backgrounds or departments?

2. Do some people have unusual viewpoints?

3. Do the decision makers have different thinking styles?

4. Are some from inside and others from outside the organization?

5. Are they from different levels in the hierarchy?

Process: What types of information are used in making the decision?

1. Is hard data balanced with soft data?

2. Are multiple tools from several disciplines used?

3. Is the discussion dominated by a few people or viewpoints?

4. Were measurements of customer reaction considered?

5. Did analysis include unlikely scenarios as well as likely scenarios?

6. Did information come from several departments?

What to Look for in an Answer

A good decision is based on many different ideas and points of view.

Think of different information as shining light into the same dark room from different windows. The more views the better. Every type of data and analysis tool has a bias. If you rely on little data or only one type (such as financial), you cannot see the full picture. The strategic information is often ignored because it is difficult to quantify.

Questions to Ask

Process: What was it like?

1. Was there open discussion and disagreement?

2. Were multiple viewpoints discussed?

3. Were impractical ideas used to lead to practical solutions?

4. Did the opinions of group members change during the process?

5. Did truly new ideas emerge, based on existing ideas?

6. Was there a sense of excitement and fun?

7. Did the group members talk about risks?

8. Were the trade-offs and the limits of each idea well-thought-out?

9. Did ideas flow into and out of the group, or was it insulated?

Implementation: Can the decision be put into action?

1. Do you understand and support the decision?

2. Will other people understand it, especially at lower levels and different areas of the organization?

3. How do you know the timeline is sensible?

4. Are some departments protecting themselves from responsibility?

5. Does the level of support equal the needed level of action?

6. What are the resource limitations and conflicts?

What to Look for in an Answer

Creativity is like evolution in the sense that you need lots of ideas bumping into one another openly to create new, better, more practical ideas. The process is messy. People disagree. They experiment, play, and argue. They know the downside of their decisions, the risks. Look for movement and change in ideas during the process.

For a good implementation, a decision has to be understandable, generate support, and result in concrete actions. Ask whether this decision will generate the support needed for the desired implementation to happen.

Questions to Ask

7. Are there too many competing projects?

8. Is it obvious what actions are to be taken?

9. Does the action sound as big as the decision?

10. Are there polarized centers of resistance that you should learn from?

References

Amabile, T.M. (1998, September/October). How to kill creativity. *Harvard Business Review,* pp. 76–87.

Bryson, J.M. (1995). *Strategic planning for public and nonprofit organizations.* San Francisco, CA: Jossey-Bass.

Cleveland, H. (1989). *The knowledge executive.* New York: Truman Talley.

Goldratt, A.Y. (1998). *Empowerment.* Avraham Y. Goldratt Institute. *www.goldratt. com/empower.htm.*

Schwartz, P. (1991). *The art of the long view.* New York: Currency Doubleday.

Tichy, N., & Cohen, E. (1997). *Leadership Engine.* New York: HarperCollins.

Janet Winchester-Silbaugh, MBA, CEBS, CCP, is an organization development consultant with Change Resources Management in Albuquerque, New Mexico. She works with organizations to remove the barriers to change by developing strategy, planning action that has leverage, and developing compensation and other human resources systems that support change.

FACILITATION SKILLS FOR ETD

Simon Priest and Michael A. Gass

Abstract: The evolution of experiential training and development (ETD) or "adventure training" facilitation can be traced through six distinct generations. These six generations are summarized in order of occurrence from the 1940s through the 1990s. This article examines each of them in more detail and provides examples of using each with a common group activity called "Spider's Web."

INTRODUCTION

Experiential training and development (ETD), also called adventure training, includes such programs as "ropes" courses, "outdoor adventure" courses, and the like. The facilitation of such programs has evolved in sophistication, complexity, and difficulty over the last six decades. The following listing summarizes the facilitation approaches favored during these decades.

- *1940s:* Letting the experience speak for itself (learning by doing);

- *1950s:* Speaking on behalf of the experience (learning by telling);

- *1960s:* Funneling or debriefing the experience (learning through reflection);

- *1970s:* Front-loading the experience directly (direction with reflection);

- *1980s:* Framing the experience isomorphically (reinforcement in reflection); and

- *1990s:* Front-loading the experience indirectly (redirection before reflection).

This article examines each of these methods in more detail and provides examples of using each with the common group activity called "Spider's Web."

A Spider's Web is approximately a six-foot by six-foot square of elastic mesh, with openings large enough to let a person pass through, strung between two posts to look like a giant web. Group members pass through openings, from one side to the other, without touching the strands. Contact with a strand wakes the spider, which "bites," and the person has to start over. A second contact with the web means that the entire group has to start over.

SIX GENERATIONS OF SKILLS

Letting the Experience Speak for Itself

Letting the experience speak for itself is a facilitation method, used since the 1940s, found in numerous ETD programs. Clients are left to sort out their own personal insights after the experience. When the activities are properly sequenced and well-designed, their inherent qualities often do serve to lead clients to the relevant insights, that is, "learning by doing." This approach works well provided that no prescriptive intrapersonal and interpersonal outcomes are sought. Clients may have a good time and possibly become proficient at new skills, but they are less likely to have learned anything about themselves, how they relate with others, or how to resolve issues in their lives if they have to figure it out for themselves.

In letting the experience speak for itself, the leader would not add any suggestions or insights about the Spider's Web exercise when the experience was completed. If any comments were made, they would pertain to how much fun the experience was and would encourage the group to move on and try the next event (e.g., "That was great, good job! Now let's try something new and different.").

Speaking on Behalf of the Experience

In an effort to enhance client learning, several programs use a second-generation approach, speaking on behalf of the experience, a method popular since the 1950s. Here the leader (often in the role of an expert) interprets the experience for the clients, informing them of what they should have learned and how they can apply their new knowledge in the future. This "learning by telling" approach can be suited for role plays and simulations, in which the results are predictable and reproducible time and time again. However, in the adventure experience, people bring unique individual histories to the way they react under stress. The results from ETD experiences also seem to be less predictable and more unique. Due to this, client learning is generally quite varied and personal. Telling individuals what they are supposed to have learned from an experience can disempower and alienate them and can disconnect the leader from group members, thus restricting their future learning opportunities.

When using this approach, the leader provides the group members with feedback about their general behaviors after the activity is over. The leader might include what was done well, what the group needs to work on, and what was to be learned from the experience (e.g., "I notice that your intergroup communication is poor; everyone is talking and no one seems to be listening. The level of trust seems to be improving, since no one appeared to worry about being picked up by the others. You could have benefitted from having a coordinator for this activity!").

Funneling or Debriefing the Experience

One solution to the problems that come from using learning by telling has been to encourage "learning through reflection," encouraging clients to reflect on what happened during the experience and to discover learnings through group discussion. Clients are more likely to work on issues or on personal commitments to change if they bring them up themselves. This increases their "ownership" of the issues, a 1960s concept. The leader facilitates the debriefing process by asking questions, rather than by telling participants what happened. The group members discuss what took place and why. Obviously, for an experience to have true meaning for clients, they must accept responsibility for how they functioned during the experience. Although numerous methods of debriefing exist, the most common approach in North America is the group discussion.

One example of a successful debriefing approach is "funneling"—sequenced questions that funnel learning from the broad experience to the narrow behavioral change people may wish to make as a result. The leader fosters a group discussion, focusing on the details and an evaluation of the group's behavior during the activity. Sample questions in the funneling style are, in order: "What happened?"; "What was the impact of this?"; "How did that make you feel?"; "What did you learn from this?"; "What aspects of this activity were metaphors for your own life?"; and "What will you do differently next time back on the job?"

Front-Loading the Experience Directly

Leaders typically explain how the activity should work (tasks, rules, and safety concerns) and then debrief afterward by guiding reflective discussions, as described above. However, because most reflection occurs after an experience, benefit may be added by briefing the clients ahead of time so they gain more from the experience. This is known as front-loading, which gained popularity in the 1970s. For this approach, the leader emphasizes several key points during the pre-briefing, such as:

- *Revisit:* What behaviors or performances can be learned from the activity;

- *Objectives:* The aims of the activity and what can be learned or gained from it;

- *Motivation:* Why experiencing the activity might be important and how it relates to real life;

- *Function:* What behaviors will help bring about success and how to optimize these; and

- *Dysfunction:* What behaviors will hinder success and how to overcome them.

In essence, the clients are focused toward certain distinct learning outcomes determined by the leader. When the learning is front-loaded, debriefing is a review of the previous discussion and what has been learned, rather than focused on reactions to the experience itself.

In front-loading the Spider's Web activity, the leader would give the same logistical briefing as usual, asking in addition a series of questions to focus the learning (e.g., "What do you think this exercise might teach you?" "Why is learning this important?" "How might what you learn from this activity help you in the future?"). Because this pre-briefing covers many of the topics usually raised in the debriefing, the concluding discussion can be focused on actual learnings and planned changes.

Framing the Experience Isomorphically

A fifth generation of facilitation, popular since the 1980s, involves isomorphically framing the experience. Isomorphs are hints added to the adventure experience by the leader so that clients are encouraged to make certain metaphoric linkages between the adventure experience and their real lives. For example, a leader may use the word "marriage" to describe paddling a canoe, purposefully creating an isomorph to link the skills of tandem paddling to the skills of living with a partner. When strong linkages are meaningful and relevant, client motivation is increased and transfer of learning is usually enhanced. If the leader can "frame" an activity with several isomorphs that reflect reality for the clients, any behaviors they use during the adventure experience may match those they desire to learn for daily living. When framing is successfully accomplished, transfer is effective, and the dynamics and processes of the two experiences are not so different. Again, only a little debriefing is needed afterward and serves mainly as reinforcement, because the clients discuss the similarities between the adventure experience and "real life" and are able to see the obvious connections.

This is still a relatively uncommon approach in ETD programs, but can be successful. For example, for warehouse workers, the Spider's Web might be described as a distribution network (the web) through which goods and services (team members) are passed from the warehouse (one side) to the customer's many outlets (the other side). Passage takes place along unique routings (openings), and contact with the network (brushing up against a strand) damages the goods and services, which means they need to be returned to the warehouse. A trainer might explain that if damaged goods and services are purposely passed on to the customer, then all shipments will be refused by the customer and returned to the warehouse to be repaired and shipped again. If the framing is done well, the debriefing need only focus on which needs of the group were attained in the activity and which were not achieved due to particular shortcomings.

Front-Loading the Experience Indirectly

Indirectly front-loading the experience is even more rare in facilitating adventure experiences, but has been used during the past decade in standard training as a last resort when all other approaches have failed, only in the clients' best interests, and for the purpose of addressing continuing problems, for example, if the harder a client tries to eliminate an unwanted issue, the more it occurs or if the more a client tries to attain a desired result, the more elusive the result becomes.

Indirect front-loading can take several paradoxical forms, with double binding being the most common. An example of a use of double binding for a problematic group with sexist behaviors using the Spider's Web follows. At the beginning, the group may mill around, with lots of people offering suggestions. After some time, a couple of dominant males tend to start the group off. They may station a few men on the other side of the web and then throw the women through like sacks of potatoes, often with embarrassing remarks about female anatomy disguised as humor. Then the same group of dominant males decides how to do the hardest part of the task, which is getting the last few people through. Afterward, during the discussion of the exercise, everyone agrees that the leadership was more-or-less sexist, and there are various emotional reactions to that. Using the positive double bind, the leader might say, "There are other ways to do the Spider's Web" and then leave it up to the group to decide what they could be.

Stated in this way, the front-loaded double bind is positive, and a "win-win" situation is created. If the group chooses to perform the task in a sexist manner, the members "win" because their behaviors become painfully obvious, and the awareness or denial of the group's sexist behaviors is heightened for the debriefing. If the group chooses to perform in a nonsexist and equitable manner, the members also "win" because they have clearly demonstrated that they can act differently and may continue to do so in the future. One way brings dysfunction to the forefront of discussion, while the other breaks old habits and provides new learning. With this indirect front-loading technique, the leader has positively "bound" this resistant client group to a unique learning opportunity. The approach is one of "redirection before reflection"; the debriefing is simply an opportunity to punctuate key lessons learned before and during the experience.

Other forms of indirect front-loading are symptom prescription, symptom displacement, illusion of alternatives, and proactive reframing. These interventions are primarily used in psychotherapeutic settings.

CONCLUSION

Experiential training and development can be categorized on the basis of whether the primary focus for learning and change emphasizes feelings, thinking, functional behavior, or dysfunctional behavior. Various "generations" of facilitation methods have been popular, beginning in the 1940s and continuing until the present. In recreational ETD programs, where the purpose is to have fun, learn a new skill, and be entertained, the first and second generations (learning by doing and learning by telling) tend to be the most appropriate approaches to facilitation. In educational ETD programs, where the purpose is understanding new concepts, enriching the knowledge of old concepts, and generating an awareness of the need for change, the third generation (learning through reflection) is the most commonly used method of facilitation. In developmental ETD programs, where the purpose is to improve functional behavior and train in new and different behaviors, the third, fourth, and fifth generations (learning through reflection, direction with reflection, and reinforcement in reflection) appear to fit best. In therapeutic ETD programs, where the purpose is reducing dysfunctional behaviors and conditioning less negative behaviors, the fifth and sixth generations (reinforcement in reflection and redirection before reflection) are the most effective techniques.

Adventure program leaders have a responsibility to their ETD programs (which provide a service) and to their clients (who consume that service) to be clear about the level of facilitation they can provide. The reputation and credibility of the profession suffer when a customer requests therapy (with the intent of receiving specific prescriptive behavioral changes), but the program provides education (with a more general focus of learning new ideas), and the leader offers recreation (with little or no facilitation). Those who facilitate ETD programs have the responsibility to consider the types of program they can offer, which type of facilitation is most appropriate to a particular program, and how their choice of approach will impact their clients. Failure to do so can damage the reputation of the entire profession.

Reference

Priest, S., & Gass, M.A. (1997). *Effective leadership in adventure programming*. Champaign, IL: Human Kinetics.

Simon Priest, Ph.D., *is a leading researcher and writer on the topic of corporate experiential training and development. He consults for a handful of progressive corporations interested in staying ahead of their international competition by focusing on the development and maintenance of human resource relationships. His consulting expertise primarily lies in leadership, executive programs, and creating internal corporate universities.*

Michael A. Gass, Ph.D., *is a leading researcher and writer on the topics of facilitation and metaphoric transfer in experiential programming. He consults for leading global organizational learning providers. His consulting expertise primarily lies in facilitator training and isomorphic framing.*

GROUND RULES FOR TRAINING

Brian Gordon

Abstract: Those who facilitate adult learning based on
Knowles' principles of androgyny realize that adults
have control over whether they remain and participate in a training program and that self-motivation
is the best stimulus to learning. Therefore, ground
rules for adult education should encourage the self-
direction of the learners and their responsibility for
availing themselves of the opportunity for learning.
The ground rules first proposed by Schwartz are
based on the work of Argyris and Schon, who believe
that, given valid information and a free and informed choice, people will become internally committed to an action. Such rules, which set high
expectations for both the trainer and the trainees,
help to create an environment of honesty and open-
ness that leads to enhanced learning.

$\mathbf{A}$dult learning theory (Knowles, 1972, 1975, 1990) clearly demonstrates that the "I talk, you listen" method of teaching is not nearly as effective as more interactive methods. Indeed, adults require more experiential involvement in their own learning. With this realization, trainers treat learners (trainees) as equals in the learning process and expect them to question and participate. In order to facilitate learning, some ground rules are needed. These rules highlight the differences between adult learning and childhood learning and form a contract between the trainer and the trainees.

CHANGING TRADITIONS

Unfortunately, much training in organizations today is still done in the old college style, in which a lecturer stands at the front of the class and dispenses wisdom to the trainees. Some trainers have trainees sit in groups around tables instead of in rows, the trainers wander around instead of standing at the front of the room, and questions are permitted. However, the essential method is still lecturing. John Cone, vice president of Dell University states that, "The teaching philosophy of most companies today is similar to that of the schools I went to. Lots of people sitting in a classroom, with an expert up front telling you things" (Dahle, 1998). Dell University is the internal training department for the extremely successful Dell Computer Corporation. Cone's goal is to have 70 percent of training delivered by nontraditional means.

Pedagogical teaching (the way in which knowledge traditionally has been imparted to children) may be attractive to bottom-line, linear thinkers because it offers a high trainee-to-trainer ratio and it is so "neat"—easy to prepare for and control. It may also be attractive to trainees who want to snooze through a class that they are forced to go to! There may be some cases in which the classroom-lecture model is most effective. Most often, however, it is not as effective in helping people to increase their knowledge and skills as more experiential, participative methods. It is now generally recognized that people learn best by "doing" rather than just "hearing." People also learn much better in a supportive environment in which they are treated with respect.

How to Create a Learning Environment

Some organizations require a minimum number of training hours per employee per year. Others make certain courses mandatory. Both will fill training classes with people who are required, but may or may not want, to be there. Neither is likely to produce much of a commitment to learning by the trainees or the trainers.

This situation can be improved by creating a healthy learning environment that stimulates interest and commitment on the part of the trainees. Even people who are only somewhat interested in the topic will stay tuned in if the way the material is presented maintains their interest. A hands-on experience that trainees can relate to their previous knowledge and experiences or to their current jobs or lives will encourage them to participate and take responsibility for their own learning.

First, it is important to encourage participation and interaction. If trainees are chatting among themselves, doodling, or finding reasons to leave the room, they are not engaged in the learning process. "It is very easy to shift the blame or the responsibility to the students for not paying attention or learning what was taught" (Rochelle, 1998). Second, make sure that the only trainees in the room are those who want to be there. This may be difficult to do, especially if the organization mandates the training. Of course, mandated training guarantees minimum enrollments; however, if your objective is to facilitate learning, rather than to fill the room, you will have to change the ground rules.

Ground Rules for Training

Effective ground rules are based on those developed by Roger Schwarz and derived from ground rules and theory first postulated by Chris Argyris and Donald Schon. The theory on which the ground rules are based is that, given valid information and a free and informed choice, people will become internally committed to an action (Argyris, 1982). Argyris and Schon felt that continuous and effective learning would only occur if these three variables existed.

The Importance of Valid Information

Valid information means that potential trainees receive all the information they need to decide whether or not to participate in the class. All the information includes what will be taught, when, how they will use the knowledge, what the delivery method will be (including experiential methods), what the trainer's expectations are, and the expected outcome of the training. Typical course descriptions state the topic of the training, the learning objectives, and the background of the trainer. They usually do not include the class schedule, the delivery methods, or the trainer's expectations. Trainees generally learn these things in the first hour of the class, after it is too late to negotiate attendance. For example, if the training is two days long, and the first afternoon will be devoted to a topic that a trainee already knows, with advance notice, he or she may negotiate to skip that session in order to attend to something else. Stating the delivery methods (e.g., hands-on skill practice, group activities) and the relevance of the training to the trainees' work or personal lives may help to increase their commitment to the training course and to their active participation.

Free and Informed Choice Leads to Internal Commitment

Once a prospective trainee has all the valid information, a free and informed choice can be made. When a trainee makes a conscious, free, and informed choice to participate in your training class, he or she has made an internal commitment to learning the material in the way you have committed to presenting it.

The Rules

Ground rules serve much the same purpose as the initial information about the course: they serve as guidelines for the trainer and the trainees and establish a set of mutual expectations. The following ground rules are adapted from Schwartz (1994):

1. Test assumptions and inferences.

2. Share all relevant information.

3. Focus on interests, not positions.

4. Be specific—use examples.

5. Explain the reasons behind your statements, questions, and actions.

6. Disagree openly with any member of the group.

7. Make statements, then invite questions and comments.

8. Jointly design ways to test disagreements and solutions.

9. Keep the discussion focused.

10. Participate in all phases of the process.

These ground rules are designed to keep trainees committed to being in the learning group. Although all trainees will not necessarily agree with everything you teach or how you teach it (just as you may not agree with everything they do or say) the ground rules help to bring sources of disagreement out in the open and resolve them so that an open learning environment exists. For example, suppose that a trainee, who did not seem very attentive in the first morning of your three-day class, misses the entire afternoon but shows up the second morning. You can assume why he or she did not show up, but the only way you will know is to ask. The trainee may have needed to attend to urgent business or may have already been very familiar with the material you covered in the first afternoon. You will not know unless you ask, and if the trainee's learning is suffering for some reason you could help with, you will want to know.

Note that none of the ground rules says anything about being on time for sessions, coming back in a timely manner from breaks, or not talking out of turn. These are things to be discussed at the start of the training and on an ongoing basis if problems arise. Such things will be less of a problem with trainees who want to be there. Should you perceive that there is a problem, state the problem and put the responsibility for solving it on the trainees. For example, if there are two people who are continually talking to one another while the class is going on, and you suspect this may be distracting to other students, you can say in a nonjudgmental way, "I've noticed John and Jane talking and am concerned that it may be distracting to others. Does anyone find it distracting?" If any of the other trainees speak up, you are then in a position to ask the talkers to stop talking without them being resentful toward you and thus impairing their learning.

The Rules Are for Trainers, Too

For these types of interventions to be effective, you must follow the rules yourself and encourage the trainees to point out things that would help them learn better. Do you tend to talk quickly? Write illegibly? Skim over areas you assume that the trainees know or would not be interested in? Ask trainees to do things without explaining the reasoning behind them? If you are open, people will mention these things to you, so create the kind of environment in which trainees feel comfortable doing so. You can help to get that started by asking some questions, for example, "Before we get into statistics, does everyone understand the reasons for learning statistics?" If trainees see a purpose in learning the material, their interest level will rise.

In many cases more than one ground rule applies. In the example where John and Jane are talking, the trainer used Rule 1 to test an assumption that the talking was distracting. The trainer also was specific (Rule 4), naming the behavior and the people involved, which allows everyone access to the same information. An argument could easily be made that other rules, such as numbers 5 and 10, were also used in the intervention.

It is useful to post the ground rules where all can see them during the training program, so they serve as reminders and so that they can be referred to in case of disputes. Following these ground rules may even help you find areas in which your training style could be made more effective.

CONCLUSION

In addition to making learning more experiential, one way to encourage learner commitment and participation is to establish ground rules for both trainees and trainers that create an open, supportive, responsible learning environment. By being open and honest with trainees and with themselves, and by expecting trainees to share responsibility for learning, trainers can increase the probability of successful training interventions.

References

Argyris, C. (1982). *Reasoning, learning, and action: Individual and organizational.* San Francisco, CA: Jossey-Bass.

Dahle, C. (1998, December). Interview with John Cone. *Fast Company,* 20.

Knowles, M. (1972). *The modern practice of adult education.* Chicago, IL: Association Press/Follett.

Knowles, M. (1975). *Self-directed learning.* Chicago, IL: Association Press/Follett.

Knowles, M. (1990). *The adult learner: A neglected species* (4th ed.) Houston, TX: Gulf.

Rochelle, D. (1998, December). *Suntracks: How to deal with generation X'ers in the classroom.* Tempe, AZ: American Society for Training & Development, Valley of the Sun Chapter.

Schwarz, R. (1994). *The skilled facilitator: Practical wisdom for developing effective groups.* San Francisco, CA: Jossey-Bass.

Brian Gordon *is co-founder of Live to Learn, a consulting firm offering facilitation and training services, among others. He has attended Roger Schwarz' The Skilled Facilitator Intensive Workshop and has a bachelor of science degree in technical management.*

How Training Departments Can Add Value

Rita S. Mehegan and Robert C. Preziosi

Abstract: The impact that a training department has on an organization is determined by how much value it contributes to the organization's value stream. A wide variety of strategies and tools can be used to add value. This "how-to" article identifies and explains how to use some of these strategies and tools. Suggestions also are offered for one-person and small training departments.

Linking Training to the Organization's Needs

Most training departments are in the business of selling knowledge-based intangibles, rather than tangibles. From the viewpoint of "customers" within the organization, results equate to value. So a training department can be viewed as adding value to the organization by linking training initiatives to customer requirements. The question is: What does the organization want the training group to do? Training professionals must involve customers (the organizational stakeholders whom the training serves) in defining their training requirements. This requires formal strategies to access and stay close to the voice of the customer.

Figure 1 lists multiple, concurrent strategies that can be employed by training professionals who are successfully linked to their customers. Each strategy is discussed below, with an emphasis on practical implementation.

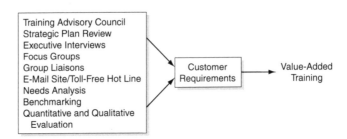

Figure 1. Ways to Link Internal Training to Organizational Needs

Training Advisory Council

An advisory structure, such as a training advisory council, is a partnership between the training department and the customers it serves. A council provides a formal mechanism for identifying and prioritizing training needs, making resource allocation decisions, and evaluating and accounting for results. It also leverages the above-average rapport and relationship-building skills most trainers possess, especially when it comes to selling the value of results.

The composition of the council membership can vary, from a high-level executive committee to mid-level managers. It should, in all cases, be cross-functional, truly representing the breadth of the organization that training serves. The senior training leader should chair council meetings.

For maximum impact, training advisory council members should be nominated by senior management and the council should include two members of senior management. Nominees should have strategic views of their functional areas, good networks into the daily operational issues of their respective areas, and schedules that will realistically allow their participation. Biannual or quarterly meetings are recommended, depending on the culture of the organization and the amount and intensity of training interventions.

Agendas for the council should include specific discussion of user requirements, strategic directions for training, prioritization of training resources, and evaluation of training initiatives in terms of organizational value. In addition to obtaining valuable input from customers, the advisory role of the council typically fosters a sense of ownership for the council members who, in turn, frequently become "ambassadors" articulating training's value. Indeed, they should arm themselves with performance improvement data and promote the perception of training value throughout the organization.

Strategic Plan Review

To continue to seek greater alignment with management, trainers should proactively obtain and review the organization's strategic plan, annual reports, executive presentations, and division business plans. Training professionals should examine their training plan relative to these strategic sources of information about customer requirements. The training business plan should provide the following value-added information:

1. A list of specific challenges facing the organization and the strategies and goals that have been established for dealing with these challenges.

2. The training implications of each challenge, including the training priorities:

   - Who will be affected;

   - The new skills and knowledge those people will need and when they will need them;

   - The cost of providing this training;

   - The cost of not providing this training; and

   - The expected return on the training investment (Svenson & Rinderer, 1992).

Executive Interviews, Focus Groups, and Group Liaisons

In addition to analyzing strategic business documents, the trainer should hold brief meetings with executives and customer groups in order to expand and validate his or her document analysis. Three effective meeting methods are executive interviews, user focus groups, and group liaison programs.

Executive interviews should be brief and focused. A key question to ask is: "Very specifically, how can training create value for the organization?"

Small *focus groups* of mid-level to upper-level managers, containing five or six people each, can be highly effective in discussing and expanding on the information gained from the document analysis.

Group liaisons further link training staff members with functional areas within the organization. A liaison is the primary, visible, and ongoing link between the internal customer and the training department. The person appointed as liaison should attend functional area department meetings and receive all departmental information that is distributed. To realize the full value of a liaison program, the members of the training department should meet at least quarterly to debrief specific customer issues and requirements within their assigned functional areas.

Web/E-Mail Sites and Toll-Free Hot Lines

Two additional sources of information about customer requirements utilize a more real-time, high-technology approach: a training web/e-mail site and a toll-free hot line number. Both provide immediate, user-friendly mechanisms for receiving a broad range of customer input regarding training. In particular, the ease of access allows customers to offer recommendations and/or complaints regarding training quickly. These "golden complaints" offer opportunities for the training department to enhance its perceived value to the organization (Peters & Austin, 1985).

There are two basic approaches to complaints. The first and most typical views the complaint as a disease to be cured, with the memory of the pain rapidly suppressed. The second views the complaint as a golden opportunity (Peters & Austin, 1985).

Needs Analysis

Customer requirements can also be identified by means of a data-based process known as needs analysis. Information about performance and the possible need for training is gathered throughout the organization. An analysis of the data collected is undertaken to identify performance problems that could be solved or improved by training or other interventions. Both training and nontraining interventions are recommended. A training needs analysis is analogous to an architect's blueprint. A thorough analysis provides a clear set of mutual expectations between the training professional and the customer. In addition, the customer is involved in the direction of the training, creating a sense of ownership. Figure 2 is an example of a form that can be used for conducting a performance-based needs analysis.

[Department Name]
Analysis Report

Name of Project:

Author: Date:

Audience	
Project Goals	To
Methodology Used for Needs Analysis	(((
Overall Analysis	
Analysis (What, Why & Recommendations)	1. *(Performance gap)* *(Why/performance conditions)* Recommendations
Savings/Costs	

Analysis completed by (name of developer, title): _____

Signature of Training Manager: _____ Date: _____

Figure 2.   Sample Needs-Analysis Form

Benchmarking

Organizations get in trouble when they assume that performance and other factors that create value for the organization's customer are constant. Value, as perceived by the customer, is subject to continual revision. One strategy to avoid such problems is external benchmarking, collecting information about the best practices of other organizations within the industry or service area. The goal is to discover what practices other high performance and high value training departments offer their internal customers. A comparative gap analysis then is conducted to identify opportunities to increase value-added processes. This strategy is proactive and offers much added value.

Quantitative and Qualitative Evaluation

Listening to what the customer has to say is critical. A well-constructed questionnaire can yield detailed quantitative and qualitative information on customer satisfaction with the training department. Such a questionnaire typically uses a Likert scale to gather quantitative ratings and open-ended questions to gather qualitative information.

To fully leverage the value of this tool, the data is statistically analyzed. Qualitative comments are examined for themes and codified. Finally, a double-loop model of communication is used to coach trainers for continuous improvement and advise the customers of the actions being taken in response to their feedback.

CONDUCTING A STRATEGIC TRAINING AUDIT

Another primary strategy for adding value to the training function is by auditing the measurement systems, processes, and technologies. If more traditional training departments conducted more proactive audits of themselves, they might not be such visible and vulnerable candidates for reengineering (Shandler, 1996). The operative word in this observation is *proactive*. By conducting a strategic training audit and linking benchmarking data with audit results regularly, the training department can examine itself against the characteristics of world-class systems. Because value is driven by perception and subject to change, regular audits and benchmarking comparisons provide the training department with data on which to base continuous improvement.

Figure 3 presents the key components of a strategic training audit. In the figure, "technologies" refers to training methodologies, as well as to tech-

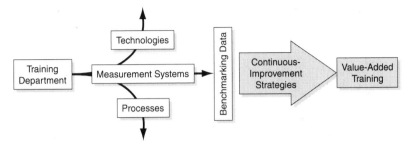

Figure 3.   A Strategic Training Audit Model

nologies used in the development and delivery of training. "Measurement systems" include assessing the return on investment (ROI) for all training activities as well as the other four levels of evaluation (Kirkpatrick, 1994). How the training is conducted is encompassed within the "processes" category. Audit data is compared with benchmarking data. Gaps between the training department and world-class systems are identified, and continuous-improvement strategies are formulated. This strategic audit cycle uses a proactive approach, allowing the training department to anticipate changing customer perceptions of value.

The formats of strategic training audits can vary; however, using a survey with a Likert scale is very effective. Organizational priorities and values, along with benchmarking data, should guide the creation of the survey statements. For example, if the organization places high priority on individual learning plans, then this criterion should appear in the audit survey. Similarly, if benchmarking data reveals that world-class training organizations typically utilize 20 percent online training, then this criterion should appear in the survey. Sample survey statements include the following:

Technologies

- Zero percent of training is delivered via online technologies.
- The training staff is aware of emerging training technologies.

Measurement Systems

- Training priorities are based on expected return on investment.
- Costs per student are tracked on a monthly basis.

Processes

- Training information is tracked on an easily accessed database.

- The training customer can go to a single source to find available training opportunities to meet his or her training needs.

In administering the audit survey, both training staff and nontraining staff should be asked to assess the effectiveness of training relative to the survey criteria. Multiple raters will increase the reliability of the results. Documentation or evidence of each criterion should be collected in an audit portfolio, to support the audit findings. When the audit survey is analyzed, the results should be compared to benchmark data.

ENSURING LEARNING AND A PERFORMANCE-DRIVEN PROCESS

The days of viewing the task of the training department in terms of just delivering training are over. Training-driven processes must give way to learning- and performance-driven processes. This requires a new framework for viewing how learning and performance can be maximized. Every aspect must be considered and analyzed. All structures, systems, processes, relationships, rules, procedures, and technologies must be examined. A very useful tool for doing this is the productivity audit. This provides big-picture analysis of the way the training department goes about its business.

The issue of priorities is critical. Priorities must be set so that learning and performance outcomes are impacting the organization in value-adding ways. What the training department decides to provide to its customers must take into account long-term and short-term needs, market-driven responses, and business imperatives. The training department must move beyond the old paradigms of cost center and profit center and become a value center. As a value center the training department provides products and services at any and all points in the value stream of the organization. Any product or service that does not help the organization enhance what the customer buys from the organization is not impacting the value stream. Such products and services should be eliminated.

ENHANCING LEARNING AND PERFORMANCE

If the training department is to demonstrate that it adds value by enhancing learning and performance, a thorough analysis of the methods used to deliver its products and services is essential. As with any department, the most important factor is costs versus results. One example of keeping costs under control is using technology properly and appropriately. The focus must be on learning and performance outcomes and the best methods for attaining them. Using computer and video technologies simply because they are available (i.e., the organization has already paid for them) is inconsistent with sound training practice.

Moving individuals and organizations to the desired levels of learning and performance outcomes, given the changing nature of organizations, is an enormous challenge for trainers. The requirements continually change and increase because of greater diversity, changing consumer desires, globalization, and many other factors. In the last few years, there has been a renewed interest in individual learning and self-directed learning packages as the best way to maximize the impact of training and take into account significant differences among learners.

Careful analysis of training methods and services does not mean that one cannot provide just-in-time training. It does mean, however, that such training may be delivered via new and nontraditional methods.

The training department often is required to customize its services. When there is little time to plan, it can be frustrating for everyone involved. Flexibility and multi-tasking are often necessary. Additionally, because the training department typically serves the whole organization, it may face conflicting demands and priorities. It is important that the department be able to set priorities to provide effective, value-adding services to all. If the training department is small or consists of only one person, multi-tasking can become critical.

Trainers may become so caught up in *doing* that they may take it for granted that their services have value. The tendency to skip several of the levels of evaluation is strong. However, if learning and performance outcomes are not tracked, it may turn out that there is no value—only outdated training. Trainers who find themselves overwhelmed with the amount of work to be done must become strong advocates for more resources to evaluate results.

MEASURING

If a training event or intervention does not add value, it is not worth investing in. Each time the organization invests in training, the question is: "Has individual or overall performance improved as a result of this training?" To answer this question, one must build performance models that show the logical steps and/or interactions in the organization's processes—how things are supposed to happen sequentially, reciprocally, or within a group.

Because value is based on the perceptions of internal customers, performance models are based on these customers' perceptions of how things should work. Trainers need to take an active role in helping to create these performance models.

Multiple models are needed because all areas of performance must be measured and because different groups see performance from different points of view. Most models can be built without much investment in technology. Once they have been built and verified, the interventions that are required become fairly obvious, especially if performance data is available. If performance data is not available, the trainer will have to help the customer design and build a system to capture it.

If there are intangibles that the customer believes are impossible to measure, the trainer also must help to find a way to measure them and to convince others in the organization that such measurement is possible. Measurement is necessary not only to prove the value of a proposed intervention, but for the sake of the customer, the trainer, and key corporate decision makers. Performance data is crucial in determining the appropriate intervention and even more crucial in measuring the effects of such interventions. The only way to show that value has been provided is by measuring the results against the bottom line, corporate strategy, long-term goals, and short-term objectives. Without measurement that proves its value, training often becomes a target for downsizing.

Creating performance models and measurement can be time-consuming and not as much fun as training delivery. However, the job of the training department is to help individuals and the organization to perform better. The days of "feel good" training are over. Every department must be able to show that it adds value to the organization, and the training department is no exception. Even if the corporate culture does not consider measurement to be important, trainers must take the initiative to prove their value.

Transfer of training—the improved performance on the job as a direct result of the training intervention—must be demonstrated conclusively. To facilitate this transfer, trainees often must receive support and coaching after the training. In some cases, remedial training may be required.

Performance can be measured in terms of quality, productivity, cost, and/or service. How the data are presented and to whom should also be considered carefully. Because increased competence builds an individual's self-esteem and motivation to perform at higher levels, the results must be reported back to trainees. Whether this is done via personal conference, e-mail, video, or some other way depends on the time available, the trainer's personal style, the geographic location of the trainees, and the corporate culture. The trainees' supervisors and key decision makers should also help to decide how the data is presented to achieve the desired effect. It may be necessary to use more than one approach. The key is to customize for each customer group.

PLANNING FOR CONTINUOUS VALUE IMPROVEMENT

Organizational improvement is no accident. It requires purposeful and conscious effort. To continue to add value to the organization, the training department itself must engage in ongoing self-improvement. High performance training departments consistently self-evaluate and they must change to meet changing demand for value.

It is fairly common practice these days for training departments to measure themselves against benchmark data from best-in-class companies in order to identify opportunities for improvement. However, it is just as valid to benchmark a department against itself. The training department, as well as all other departments, should continuously improve against its own performance.

To begin, a training department should do a *productivity* audit, collecting and analyzing data about its productivity, quality, costs, and services. This will help to determine which productivity standards are being met and which are not and also can be a starting point for enhanced development, design, delivery, and evaluation. It is also possible to conduct a *quality* audit of these areas and department leadership.

Cost-benefit and return on investment (ROI) analyses are also critical as tools for identifying opportunities to improve the financial management of training departments. So much has been written about how to do this, we will not repeat it here. Just get it done!

Conducting periodic customer service surveys also can help a training department to identify how to add value. A balanced analysis includes productivity, quality, and cost; it focuses on customer satisfaction with the how, when, where, and what of the delivery of training products and services.

The next set of variables to measure is based on Kirkpatrick's (1994) four levels of evaluation: (1) what they liked, (2) what they learned, (3) how they changed, and (4) how they performed. The results obtained can be used to develop an overall improvement strategy. Every product or service on the training department's menu should be evaluated at all four levels. When time is short or other resources are scarce, at a minimum Levels 1 and 4 must be used to receive feedback on the training itself and to identify how much performance has improved.

Using all four levels leads to improvement plans if comparative analysis is taking place from one time period to another. Again, the bottom line is the impact on the value stream. If no impact on the value stream can be identified, there is a problem somewhere. Attempts to solve the problem should probably begin at the beginning, with needs analysis.

Plans should be made to focus on all key areas in which opportunities for improvement are found. The first area to consider is any additional training skills required. The other areas are development, design, delivery, and evaluation of the training.

All appropriate persons should be included in planning an improvement initiative. Excluding appropriate people from planning limits the commitment and support that can be expected when the plans are implemented. An excellent rule of thumb is to include anyone who may be affected by the plan, whether line supervisors, managers, trainers, or vendors. The members of the training advisory council also should be included.

LOOKING OUTSIDE THE ORGANIZATION

Valuable ideas for improvement can also be obtained outside the organization. There are many possible sources, including the American Society for Training and Development, which has conducted benchmarking studies and made the results available. Because every organization is unique, a training department may choose to conduct its own benchmarking study. Every two years or so, new information should be made available for this kind of comparative analysis.

The benchmarking process begins with planning. It is important to identify which elements of the training effort you want to focus on. Develop a list of questions that will produce the needed information. Start with big-picture questions and cascade from there. Create a list of training departments outside your own organization that you can survey. Include only those you know are better and know in what ways they are better. Remember that you are looking for ways to impact the value stream.

Next, analyze the information that has been collected. Identify the gaps between your training department and the benchmarked training departments. Review both structures and processes. Identify practices that clearly contribute to the value stream. Avoid overanalyzing.

The final phase is integration. Determine the who and how of informing key people so that buy-in can be obtained. Determine how to eliminate gaps and develop an implementation plan. Implement the plan and adjust it as needed.

The most important thing to remember throughout the benchmarking process is to discover how the actions you find add value to the organization being studied. This is the true test of a trainer's contribution as an organizational leader. Is the trainer adding value? How is the training department impacting the value stream? Remember that positive answers are not always enough; marketing the products and services that are adding value is almost always necessary.

Marketing Performance-Improvement Services

A critical step in managing the customer's perception of value is to market the concept that value is being added by the training. Customers have specific needs and wants, and your products and services should aim to satisfy them. A marketing approach communicates to customers how their needs and wants can be satisfied by your products and services. The balance between customers' investment in time, effort, and money and the value they receive in return is depicted in Figure 4.

Figure 4. Role of Marketing in Balancing Customer Value and Investment

Marketing sometimes is erroneously thought to be synonymous with selling, which can connote pressure to buy an unneeded or unwanted product. Gilley and Eggland (1989) define marketing of human resource development as the offering of training programs and services that are designed to bring about voluntary exchanges of value with members of the organization. The operative words here are *voluntary exchanges of value*. Marketers do not create needs, needs exist first. Marketing your training function is communicating the value of your products and services to meet the needs and wants of your customers. Rather than focusing on the products and services that a performance improvement group produces, customer-driven marketing focuses on communicating the value of these products and services vis-a-vis the customer's needs and wants. Marketing helps to articulate the training department's value to the organization.

Strategic marketing incorporates seven key steps: (1) statement of mission and purpose, (2) situational analysis of the external and internal environments, (3) formulation of goals and objectives, (4) analysis of customers, (5) formulation of the marketing mix (product, price, place/distribution, promotion), (6) implementation of marketing strategies, and (7) evaluation of marketing efforts.

The training department's mission statement drives its marketing activity. The following questions should be answered by the mission statement: "What is the purpose of your department?" "Who are your customers?" "What do you do that is valuable for your customers?" "Is your mission reflective of the organization's overall mission and direction?" The mission statement is a starting point for further developing your marketing plan. Environmental analysis then follows: "What opportunities and barriers exist for your program?" For example, the organization may be facing a competitive issue such as a need for increased global business skills or local colleges may be competing with you. Find out what your department's internal strengths and weaknesses are in delivering your mission and whether your staff has the necessary skills and an adequate budget.

Environmental scanning and analysis will yield answers to these questions and move you to formulating specific goals and objectives. You may decide, for example, that your goal is to increase global business skills within your organization using online tools.

Customer analysis defines your target audience. Continuing with the global skills example, determine whether managers require international negotiation skills prior to expatriation. If so, your target audience may be this segment of managers.

Determining your marketing approach requires first defining your product and services, how and when they will be offered, at what price, and how to promote them. For example, you must decide whether your offering will be online, whether a secured password will be necessary, whether employees will have desktop access twenty-four hours per day, whether you will provide customized modules for different countries, and whether you will charge a fee. Many similar questions must be answered.

Your marketing strategy must also encompass an implementation plan, with specific actionable items, such as resources to obtain, desired return on investment, a timetable, milestones, and responsibility for each phase of implementation.

Finally, your overall strategic marketing plan should include a mechanism to evaluate the program's effectiveness. Decide whether, given your goals, objectives, and marketing plan, your strategy was effective. Find out whether the program met the value needs of your target customers and whether you were able to generate sufficient demand through your promotional efforts. Ask yourself whether one promotional effort was more successful than the others and whether the skills transfered to on-the-job behavior. Did your measurements indicate a positive return on investment? Does the program require revision? Does the program provide your target customers with value in exchange for their time, effort, and money?

References

Gilley, J.W., & Eggland, S.A. (1989). *Principles of human resource development*. Reading, MA: Addison-Wesley.

Kirkpatrick, D.L. (1994). *Evaluating training programs: The four levels*. San Francisco, CA: Berrett-Koehler.

Peters, T., & Austin, N. (1985). *A passion for excellence: The leadership difference*. New York: Random House.

Shandler, D. (1996). *Reengineering the training function: How to align training with the new corporate agenda*. Delray Beach, FL: St. Lucie Press.

Svenson, R., & Rinderer, M. (1992). *Training and development strategic plan worksheet*. Englewood Cliffs, NJ: Prentice Hall.

Rita S. Mehegan *is vice president of training and quality for First Data Merchant Services, Coral Springs, Florida. Dr. Mehegan has focused on value-driven training and development for over eighteen years in the finance, high tech, and travel* *industries. She holds a master's in business administration and a doctorate in adult education. She is an adjunct professor in the School of Business for Florida International University.*

Robert C. Preziosi, D.P.A., *is a professor of management education in the School of Business and Entrepreneurship at Nova Southeastern University in Fort Lauderdale, Florida. He is also the president of Management Associates, a consulting firm. He has worked as a human resources director, a line manager, and a leadership-training administrator and has consulted with all levels of management in many organizations, including American Express, the Department of Health and Human Services, Lennar, Motorola, and many hospitals and banks. Dr. Preziosi has been training trainers since the 1970s; his areas of interest include leadership, adult learning, and all aspects of management and executive development. In 1984 he was given the Outstanding Contribution to HRD Award by ASTD; in 1996 he received the Torch Award, the highest leadership award that ASTD gives, for the second time. He is the only person ever so honored. He is a frequent contributor to the Pfeiffer Annuals.*

FACILITATING EFFECTIVE DEBRIEFINGS

Joe Willmore

Abstract: The ultimate value of any experiential activity is determined by the debriefing and discussion that follow the activity. Without an effective debriefing, it is unlikely that participants will gain insight from the activity, and they will certainly not gain shared insights. Regardless of the nature of the experiential activity or the participant dynamics, certain types of questions consistently promote learning, and others do not. By understanding the progression of questions to ask, facilitators can improve the degree of participant learning that occurs in post-activity discussion sessions. This article describes this process, explains why the progression is important, and offers examples of appropriate and inappropriate questions to stimulate insight.

DEBRIEFING IS KEY

Experiential or activity-based delivery is a key component of all professional training because we know that adults are more likely to learn and retain by doing. Additionally, experiential activities are more likely to tap into a variety of learning modes. For instance, not everyone learns best through auditory sources. An experiential activity is likely to combine a variety of different learning methods.

Experiential activities also can consist of a variety of different approaches. Games, role plays, simulations, and challenge technology are just some examples. However, the key to the success of all experiential activities is the debriefing or discussion that follows. Yet consultants too often focus most of their preparation on the activity itself and treat the subsequent discussion as an afterthought. Regardless of the nature of the experience, the debriefing and discussion that follow determine just how much learning takes place. It is through the debriefing and discussion that lessons are shared and insights gained.

Even the worst game will lead to invaluable insights if the facilitator has good debriefing skills. In order to maximize the benefits from experiential training and activities, facilitators need to plan their debriefings well. This planning can include a range of techniques that encourage a "learning discussion" and promote appropriate participation. Good debriefing skills also involve asking the right questions and asking them at the right time.

WHAT NOT TO ASK

The worst initial question to ask is "Why?" (as in "Why did you decide to take that course of action?" "Why did your group choose green?" "Why does that approach make sense?" "Why do you feel that way?"). Asking "Why?" often puts people on the defensive. Facilitators are frequently tempted to ask "Why?" because participants may develop unique tactics or seemingly curious responses during the activity. Although you may be curious about their rationale, asking "Why?" implies they have to justify themselves, regardless of your intent. Making people defensive causes them to close down rather than open up, and you want people to open up during the debriefing stage.

Additionally, asking "Why?" tends to encourage participants to tell you what they think you want to hear rather than the truth. There are many ways to get at the issue of "why" without asking "Why?"

Another question many facilitators tend to ask is "What did you think of that activity?" Do not ask this type of question! As facilitators, we are eager to gauge the group's reaction and to determine whether the participants like the activity as much as we do. A desire for approval and validation may tempt us to ask participants what they thought of the activity. Do not clutter the training objectives with your personal objectives. Do not seek validation by asking participants to agree that your choice of activities was a wise one.

By asking people to offer opinions about the activity, you encourage them to put their biases out in front of the group before they have gained any insights. Initial comments such as, "I don't like touchy-feely stuff like that" or "I don't like role plays" can create an atmosphere that invalidates others' experiences and encourages self-censorship. Ask participants to evaluate the activity at the end of the debriefing, if you must. If some participants have major issues with the activity, those feelings will most likely come out without direct solicitation.

So, what are the *right* questions?

QUESTIONS TO ASK

Successful debriefings follow a consistent pattern, starting with participant emotions, moving on to events, followed by a focus on insights and learning, then concluding with speculation. Consistently sticking to this progression will generate rich discussions that promote learning and application—which should be what you used the experiential activity for in the first place.

Emotions: "Feeling" Questions

The first question to ask participants after an experiential activity is "How do you feel?" (Thiagarajan, 1994). If the training activity was ineffective, this question will reveal it immediately. Then you can quickly begin recovery efforts or transition into the next stage. Sometimes the activity shatters some expectations (perhaps the managers did not score as highly as they expected to, no one survived the disaster, the team's structure fell to pieces as they squabbled, or the result was counter to what was supposed to happen). By asking "How do you feel?" you allow participants to get their emotions out so you can move on to applications (Kroehnert, 1992).

Asking "How do you feel?" is different from "What do you think of this activity?" For starters, asking people to evaluate the activity is counter to the purpose of using an experiential piece. The purpose is to further learning, not as an end in itself (Scannell & Newstrom, 1996). Additionally, the trainer can gently refocus negative comments toward reactions that are more specific to the person or job ("What similar reactions might you have on the job?").

The challenge for the facilitator is to address the "feelings" issue without allowing it to become a venting session about the particular activity or that type of activity. Additionally, depending on the nature of the experience, participants may need a little time to come down from their experience (either because of surprise at the result, excitement from achievement, or frustration at unexpected problems) (Kroehnert, 1992). Asking participants "How do you feel?" provides a little depressurization time. If you do not address feelings first, they will continue to come up throughout the debriefing. Plus, the feelings issue may often point out some remarkable parallels to work situations ("If you felt pressured with observers watching, do you think new employees might feel the same way if you supervise them closely?").

Additionally, because everyone in the group will have some type of feelings about the activity, they can all contribute. Starting with a more task-focused question ("How does this apply to your job?") limits who can answer. Some participants will have a problem answering that type of analytical question at the start.

Events: "Observation" Questions

The next series of questions involves participant observations. These are questions such as "What happened?" or perhaps "What did you observe?" "What did you see?" "What did you notice?" (Thiagarajan, 1994). This is a good way to begin the analytical aspects of the activity. Most participants will ask themselves "What was happening?" and will mentally replay the activity. During this replay most participants begin to see some lessons from the experience. Also, the first initial participants' comments, such as "I saw other groups starting to develop strategies" will spur others by providing "aha" moments ("Wow, now that you mention it, that happened in our group too") and by encouraging them to share insights. Notice that as the facilitator you are still not asking participants to analyze what happened or why it happened, only to play back their memories of what they perceived. This simple question eventually creates a very rich area for discussion around differences in perceptions, why some events were unnoticed, commonalties among different groups or people, and individual differences.

The question ("What happened?") is also a good seed question. You can follow it with other questions about what they might have seen ("Did any of you see a pecking order start to emerge in your group?" "Did any group reach an agreement?" "Did you see the team leader check for consensus before you moved on?" "Did others encounter the same confusion that Maria shared with us?").

Finally, this question is open enough for people to feel safe giving a range of responses from basic, straightforward answers ("We managed to decide how to restructure the process") to answers that offer more insight or complexity ("I saw people starting to compete against each other because no one wanted to finish last" or "I saw our team falling into the same roles we have back at the office with the same problems we have there repeated here").

Insights: "Learning" Questions

The next questions revolve around what participants gained from the experience, for example: "What did you learn?" Do not ask *whether* they learned anything; ask *what* they learned and you'll force people to re-examine—to play back their mental tape of the activity. As one or two individuals publicly share their learning, everyone else is encouraged to search harder for meaning. Almost everyone will come up with insights they picked up from the activity. At this stage keep in mind that research on memory and recall from training sessions indicates that participants are more likely to remember what *they* said rather than what the *trainer* said. So, let the participants describe the lessons; they're more likely to retain them that way.

Sometimes participants may have trouble generating relevant insights from the activity. It may become necessary for you as the facilitator to point out the lessons. In this instance, after you have provided "the answers," then proceed to ask the participants for data to support or reject what you have said (Thiagarajan, 1994). They are more likely to retain the key learning principles this way.

An important follow-on question to "What did you learn?" is "How can you apply this to your work?" If you start out with this question, some participants will react with "I can't" or "Work isn't like this." Then you're forced into an adversarial position, trying to justify to some participants why the activity does provide a metaphor for their jobs. Once they have taken a position in opposition to you, they will even resist insights from peers about the value and possible application of the activity, because they need to defend and rationalize their initial positions. But if they can "discover" answers within themselves through the earlier questions ("How do you feel?" "What happened?"

"What did you learn?"), their confidence goes up and their enthusiasm and the perceived value for the training activity increase. They will be more likely to identify valuable ways to apply their own lessons to their jobs. This is especially important because, except for training of new hires, most participants will have job-specific or site-specific knowledge that the trainer cannot match. In other words, they can do a better job of explaining how this applies to their jobs than you can if you can release their ability to see those insights.

Speculation: "Meta" Activity Questions

There are three final questions a good facilitator can use to improve the value of the debriefing. These questions encourage the participants to speculate about issues brought out by the activity. By asking these questions, you press participants to look for truths about the system, the process, or the nature of particular behavior. These insights encourage participants to generalize from specific insights.

First, ask about hypothetical circumstances, such as "Would the results have changed if I had given you more time?" "Would it have been different if you were to receive a reward for finishing first?" "Would the presence of observers have changed anything?" Do not use this approach to debate with participants. Instead, use hypothetical options as a way of expanding their insights to see that the lessons they are learning are valid beyond the circumstances of the activity. When participants begin to see that the behavior or results from the activity are deep-rooted and systemic, then applications to work become obvious (Senge, 1990).

Second, ask the participants what, if anything, they would do differently. Questions of this vein are less effective early in the discussion because participants are likely to be defensive about any question implying there is a better tactical approach than the one they chose. Once they have spent time taking apart the events, replaying them, and looking for insights, it is much easier for them to critique their own approaches and develop alternatives. Ask them if they would change strategies or how they would apply the lessons they learned the first time around to a second version of this activity.

Third, question participants about the rules of the activity: "How could we change the rules of this game to make it more useful?" "What lessons did we learn from letting Jeff and his team break the rules?" "What rules would make this simulation more realistic?" These questions can generate insight into processes and relationships. Questions about the rules can also be effective ways of helping people to examine alternative strategies.

INSIGHTS FROM "MISTAKES"

Use confusion or disputes about the "rules" or directions for the activity to stimulate other insights (for example, about their jumping to conclusions, questioning assumptions, creative thinking, or competitiveness). The U.S. Army's National Training Center's facilitators use confusion and mistakes within combat simulations as a powerful discussion focus for learning insights (Pascale, 1996). Rather than just focusing on what was unclear, participants can examine why it was unclear or what could have made the instructions clearer. These kinds of discussions not only help improve the activity, but also force more self-examination about lessons learned and their application to work. Complaints that "We didn't have enough time" or "Our team was just thrown together" invite comparison with how work processes and procedures function within the organization.

If you have a need to receive feedback on the specific activity, this is also a good time to ask participants "What do you think of this activity?" This is also the time to find out what you as a facilitator might do differently the next time. Some participants may say they didn't like the nature of the activity (because they dislike role plays or assessments or challenge technology or competition). Ask if the perceived lack of value in the activity affected their performance or attitude toward participation. You can use their responses to make points about specific tasks at work (filling out time sheets, facilitating conference calls) that might be unpopular and how our attitude or the task's lack of perceived value determines our commitment to doing the task.

SUMMARY

The key to any experiential activity is the debriefing (Scannell & Newstrom, 1983). A good discussion can turn almost any experiential piece into one that generates rich and fertile learning. The results from the activity have much less to do with the activity itself and much more to do with the discussion that follows. The best way to promote a good post-activity discussion is through the questions you pose. Ask good questions that start with emotions and progress to evaluation, and you will facilitate powerful and thorough learning experiences for participants long after the activity is over.

References

Kroehnert, G. (1992). *One hundred training games.* New York: McGraw-Hill.

Pascale, R. (1996, August/September). Fight, learn, lead. *Fast Company,* p. 70.

Scannell, E., & Newstrom, J. (1983). *More games trainers play.* New York: McGraw-Hill.

Scannell, E., & Newstrom, J. (1996). *The big book of business games.* New York: McGraw-Hill.

Senge, P. (1990). *The fifth discipline.* New York: Doubleday.

Thiagarajan, S. (1994). *Teamwork and games.* Amherst, MA: HRD Press.

Joe Willmore is president of the Willmore Consulting Group, a human performance improvement firm located in Annandale, Virginia. He specializes in the areas of team building, facilitation, strategic planning, and creative problem solving. He is an adjunct faculty member of the University of Virginia and served as the 1997 president of the Metro DC Chapter of ASTD. He was a presenter at the 1998 and 1999 ASTD International Conferences and the 1999 ISPI International Conference.

IMPROVISATIONAL THEATER GAMES: A NEW TWIST FOR TRAINING

Cher Holton

Abstract: Trainers too often get into a rut with their training programs, doing the same old things for so long that even they are starting to yawn. Using improvisational theater games will set you apart from other trainers—making your presentations unique, generating audience participation, creating excitement and laughter, and emphasizing key points.

This article defines the concept of improvisational theater games, provides tips on using them effectively, and offers specific examples of games you can integrate into your programs immediately.

Improvisational Theater Games

We all have a little of the dramatist in us. Improvisational games let the actor inside each of us emerge, through techniques borrowed from the world of dramatic arts. They provide a semi-structured opportunity to let folks have some fun and play a part without feeling intimidated, and, in the process, drive home the key points of your training program.

You already know how to improvise. Consider what happens when you are asked—on the spot—to cut your program from an hour down to thirty-five minutes. Or what happens during a question-and-answer session when an audience member challenges one of your fundamental concepts. Or what you do when one of your clients telephones with a complaint about the program you just presented. How do you respond? You *improvise!* To improvise means to perform on the spur of the moment; handle something impromptu; talk off the top of one's head; ad-lib; extemporize. Improvisational theater games provide an opportunity for audience members to ad-lib, but in a semi-structured environment that allows them not only to have some fun, but also to practice techniques related to the program topic.

The Rules

For improvisational theater games to be most effective, follow these basic rules:

- *Do not explain the purpose of the activity until it is over.* The whole point is for participants to improvise without thinking about the reasons for doing it.

- *Build an environment of fun as you introduce the game.* People are naturally somewhat hesitant to participate in something new and different. It is your job to introduce it in such a way that is seems fun, risk-free, and exciting.

- *Interject the "towel foul."* At some times, participants can become a little too relaxed with their ad libs. To maintain the professional environment needed to make this technique work, bring along a brightly colored towel. (Try one imprinted with your company name and logo.) Explain to the group that if any comment is offensive or inappropriate for any reason you will call a "towel foul," at which point the participant who fouled must put the towel over his or her head for the remainder of that game. (*Note:* Towel fouls can be called on audience members as well as on participants in the activity.) Typically, the mention of a towel foul curbs the use of inappropriate comments or actions.

A Sampling of Games

Here is a selection of quick, no-props-needed improvisational theater games that can be used easily in a workshop setting:

Doctor Know-It-All

Select four to six volunteers, who collectively become Dr. Know-It-All. Seat them in a row at the front of the room. Solicit questions (one at a time) from the group. Repeat the questions for the Dr. Know-It-All team, who then work together to answer the questions one word at a time—with each person in turn saying one word. This technique can be used effectively to review material or to determine participants' level of knowledge at the beginning of a session.

Changing Emotions

Have the group brainstorm a list of words that describe emotions. Post these on flip-chart paper. Ask for two volunteers to be the "actors." Ask the group to generate a situation for the actors to role play. (Help the group to be specific when describing the situation.) Have audience members call out emotions for the actors to portray during the role play. The actors must switch to a new emotion without a break in the action. Several emotions can be called out during any scene. This technique can be used to practice new learning from a workshop or to plan how to use skills in the future.

A Hundred and One

This game uses a simple joke format: A hundred and one [fill in the blank] walk into a restaurant [or wherever] and the manager says, "I'm sorry, but we can't serve [fill in the blank] here." The hundred and one [blanks] say, "[punch line]." The group comes up with the "fill-in's," and a team of volunteers comes up with the "punch lines." It's good to throw out a few examples to get the group started:

- "A hundred and one football players walk into a restaurant and the manager says, 'I'm sorry, but we can't serve football players here.' The 101 football players say, 'You don't have to get *defensive!*' or they say, 'That's okay. We don't want to eat. Your jukebox is broken and we just want our *quarter back!*' "

- "A hundred and one pancakes walk into a restaurant and the manager says, 'I'm sorry, but we can't serve pancakes here.' The 101 pancakes say, 'Oh, how waffle!'"

Groaners are the best! This game is particularly useful when you are emphasizing the skill of flexibility and creative thinking. Once participants are familiar with the process, begin throwing in words related to your topic. For example, if your topic is customer service, you might want to focus on the need to be responsive to customers and search for creative solutions to problems. If you tossed out the word "complaint," a round of this game might look like this:

- "A hundred and one complaints walk into a restaurant and the manager says, 'I'm sorry, but we can't serve complaints here.' The 101 complaints say: 'Come on, all we want is a little cheese to go with our whine.'"

Others would follow with additional ideas. For the word "computer," a round might look like this:

- "A hundred and one computers walk into a restaurant and the manager says, 'I'm sorry, but we can't serve computers here.' The 101 computers say: 'No problem. We always have a back-up!'" or

- "A hundred and one computers walk into a restaurant and the manager says, 'I'm sorry, but we can't serve computers here.' The 101 computers say: 'We don't want to eat. We're just doing a cursor-y review of this place.'"

The goal of this game is to get people to think outside the box, stretching ideas around concepts in a new and different way. When participants appear to be a little hesitant to try this game, you can let them work in groups. Give each group a few key words and allow them fifteen minutes to come up with as many statements as they can for the key words. Then each group gets to present its concepts dramatically and enthusiastically to the rest of the groups. It's an excellent energy booster and adds a nice dose of humor to your program.

Once Upon a Time...

Select a group of four to six volunteers. Have the audience select a story that has never been written or told and that relates to the topic of your program. Inform the audience that when you, as storymaster, point to them, they are to shout out the story title. Explain to the volunteers that you will point to one of them, who will then begin to tell the story. The chosen person keeps talking until you move your finger toward another volunteer, who must then pick up the story without a break in continuity. The story continues with you pointing to different volunteers until someone falters. Then, after everyone laughs, you say, "Chapter Two of . . ." and point to the audience, who shouts out the title.

Play continues as long as you desire. Your job is to keep it moving, so no one person talks too long. This technique is effective for applications of what has been learned.

DEBRIEFING TECHNIQUES

Although improvisational theater games are fun and provide a great opportunity for audience involvement, they are useless unless they relate back to your topic. The secret to success in using these games is the debriefing—making sure that participants understand *how* the activity relates to the "real world." Here are a few tips to help you debrief effectively.

Know Your Goal

This sounds so obvious, and yet too often trainers use an activity because it is fun—with no idea *why* they are using it. The goal is to use an activity to illustrate a key point you are making in your training class. As you select an activity for your session, spend some time answering these questions: "What will the participants get from this activity?" "How, specifically, does this activity illustrate the point?" "How does it relate to the real world in terms of metaphors and actions?"

For example, if you are talking about communication, Dr. Know-It-All and Once Upon a Time both emphasize the value of listening without preconceived ideas. Teamwork is also a necessary component in both these activities.

Changing Emotions can be used to highlight the impact our attitudes have on the outcome of conversations and to show how our nonverbals and tone of voice affect the words we say. A Hundred and One is particularly useful when dealing with issues such as change, the need to think fast and outside the box, and flexibility. All of these activities are excellent to tie in with topics such as stress management, creative thinking, communication, and teamwork.

Develop Specific Debriefing Questions

Following the activity, list a few questions on a flip chart or overhead transparency or distribute questions as a handout. The questions should stimulate discussion around the purpose of the activity and how participants can transfer their learnings to their actual work environment. The questions will vary depending on the activity, but here are a few examples:

- "What helped make this activity successful?"
- "What got in the way or made success more difficult?"
- "How does this activity relate to the 'real world'?"
- "What things happened during this activity that could be a metaphor for the way things happen on the job?"

You could also use questions relating specifically to the point you are illustrating. For example:

- "What specific strategies did the group use to deal with the 'changing emotions' activity?"
- "When an emotion was changed while someone was talking, how did that person adapt to the change? What worked most effectively?"
- "When things became stressful, how did participants change?"
- "What impact did any changes in behavior have on the rest of the group?"

Guide, Rather than Tell

Let participants determine their own learnings (as much as possible). It is important that you have answers to the questions you present to the group. However, the impact is far greater if the participants themselves come up with their own learnings. Your role is to facilitate the discussion and gently lead them to their own discoveries. You may either form small groups to discuss the debriefing questions or lead a large-group discussion.

Examples are worth a thousand words. Encourage team members to give specific examples to illustrate their learnings and how they intend to apply the learnings back on the job. This forces them to go deeper than just a surface understanding of the activity and reinforces for them how practical the applications can be.

Let activities build on one another—and refer back to them. To build continuity into your session, refer back to activities and demonstrate how they are connected. For example, in a two-day team-building session, you may use Dr. Know-It-All early in the first day and use it throughout the rest of the session as a metaphor. You might say something like, "Tom, remember when you shared your need for control during Dr. Know-It-All? What impact did this have on how you acted during the negotiations of this activity?" or "You told me during Dr. Know-It-All that focused listening made things much easier. How well did you use that learning during this activity?"

Additionally, participants may pick up terminology from the activities and use it throughout the session. "Towel fouls," for example, may be used during other parts of the workshop and even be taken back to the office to use in staff meetings. Keep the list of tips for success below to remind yourself of what you need to do.

TIPS TO GUARANTEE SUCCESS

- Know the game well yourself. Be very clear about the rules and explain them well to the audience.

- Assess the size of your group and adapt the activity to fit it.

- Always ask yourself: "What specific point do I want to make with this game? How does it relate to my topic?" Know exactly what you want to achieve by using the game.

- Take sufficient time to debrief the game once it is over. Never assume the audience will "get it."

- Never embarrass an individual who is participating in a game. Use the "tag team" approach, in which a person can "tag" another to take over at any point, as a way for volunteers to avoid feeling stuck.

- Once you decide to use a game, do it with gusto! Act as if you could not fail! Your enthusiasm and confidence will sell it to the group.

CONCLUSION

Adult learning theory supports the fact that adults learn most effectively when they can be actively involved in the process—and improvisational theater games present an excellent opportunity to involve participants. But if a game does not actually relate to the goal of your training session, you may make things worse by using it than if you had no involvement at all. Adults *must* see the relationship between what they are doing in a training session and the real world; otherwise (no matter how much fun they seem to be having), the evaluations will show that the activity was a waste of time. Above all else, do not assume participants will "get it." Make the time to debrief every activity you include. The results will be phenomenal!

People are people, no matter how sophisticated their knowledge or skill may be. The secret is to select the appropriate activity for the audience, and then present it with confidence! If you believe it will work, you can pull it off. Just be sure you understand the activity and are comfortable with it; then have fun with the audience. William Shakespeare said, "All the world's a stage." This is your chance to let the audience members be the stars. Lights! Camera! Action!

Cher Holton, Ph.D., president of The Holton Consulting Group, Inc., is an impact consultant focusing on bringing harmony to life—with customers, among team members, and in life. She is one of fewer than two dozen professionals worldwide who have earned both the Certified Speaking Professional and Certified Management Consultant designations. Dr. Holton is the author of The Manager's Short Course to a Long Career *and* Living at the Speed of Life: Staying in Control in a World Gone Bonkers!

OBTAINING RESULTS
FROM TECHNICAL TRAINING

Brooke Broadbent

Abstract: Successful technical training stems from a systematically planned process that helps people to acquire new knowledge and learn how to use new tools and processes in the context of their day-to-day work. This article provides recommendations for how to design and conduct successful technical training. Through the example of an introduction to a training session on TRAC software, the author presents twelve key actions an instructor can take to introduce the training effectively. Twenty-two successful trainer behaviors are discussed, under the categories of personal habits, leadership, political savvy, and design skills. Rather than a prescription to fit all technical training, the author offers ideas that readers can adapt to their individual situations.

Employees of U.S. firms spend more time in job-specific technical training than in any other type of training. When combined with software training, another type of technical training, the time spent amounts to over 25 percent of the total time that employees spend in training, according to a recent survey (*Training & Development*, 1998). Obviously, technical training done right can have a huge impact on the bottom line. If you are an upwardly mobile employee, designing or delivering effective software training may give your career a boost. The discussion below covers the topics of (1) effective introductions to technical training sessions and (2) personal qualities the designer must have. Software training is used as an example of technical training for purposes of this discussion because it is currently such a popular area for workplace training.

THE INTRODUCTION

The opening words of a technical training session set the tone for the entire session. Instructors call this their two-minute commercial, motivation statement, or hook. The cliché "You don't get a second chance to make a first impression" says it all.

Let's look at two sample introductions to a training session:

The First Introduction

Here's the first example of an introduction to a training session on TRAC software:

> "Good morning. I'm Morris Richards. My friends call me 'The Rocket.' I've been working for Trainers R' Us for six years. I'm the most experienced trainer in our firm. I know TRAC inside out. I will show you things that nobody else knows about TRAC. It's terrific! I love it! You will too. I will be using presentation software. We have copies of the overheads for everyone. You can write your notes in the margins of the copies."

Imagine that you are a participant in Richards' class. You travel from time to time in your work. At the end of each trip, you complete paper-based travel forms. In your type of work, you juggle several projects at a time. You are required to keep track of all the hours you work on each project.

In the future, you will be expected to complete your expense reports electronically using TRAC. You have heard good things about TRAC, but that was from the bean counters and management. You remain skeptical about TRAC, and you are beginning to wonder what's in it for you. You are not particularly eager to learn new software. You don't see the benefits, and you are too busy to devote much time to learning new software and new work processes.

Now that you know your persona, let's look back at Morris Richards' introduction. Has he indicated any knowledge of your situation? Has he said anything that makes you want to stay for the rest of the session? Are you concerned that he is going to forget that you are new to this, take off at 90 miles an hour, and leave you in the dust? Are you concerned that Richards will drown you in details or bore you with a PowerPoint® presentation?

As you listen to Richards, chances are that your mind is beginning to lock onto your preoccupations. If you are a detail person you might wonder about all the detailed information you will need to input into TRAC. You might wonder how you will find and use project codes in the software. If you suffer from technophobia, you might be musing about your last disastrous encounter with a new electronic tool or a new software package. You realize that TRAC is going to upset the applecart of your present reporting system. You might wonder whether this new way of doing things will slow up reimbursement payments.

The Standish Group (1995) has reported that 70 percent of information-technology projects fail. Whoever you are and whatever technical training course you are attending, you will want to know how innovation will change the way you work. Will an introduction like Richards' put you at ease and encourage you to tune in? I think not.

The Second Introduction

This time the trainer's name is Rea Shuring. Rea starts to set up the training room at least an hour before the official opening of the session. She reviews the arrangement of everything, including the signs in the hall and in the seminar room, the flip-chart easels, wall charts, tables, chairs, handouts, and other course materials.

When participants start arriving, Rea greets them as they come in the door. She shakes their hands, asks their names, and engages in small talk that helps her to identify their interests and why they are taking the course. She has found that greeting people this way helps to create bonds between her and participants. These bonds help to ensure that people participate later, when Rea asks questions. They help to increase interaction and, most importantly, learning.

Rea starts the course on time, with the following introduction:

> "Hello, my name is Rea Shuring. I'm going to work *with* you today to help you learn to use TRAC. Have you heard of TRAC before? What have you heard about it? Do you know that TRAC stands for Total Records for Accounting? Are you using any other software now?"

Rea takes time for a short discussion in which the participants tell her what they know about TRAC. If the participants have not talked about what TRAC does during the initial discussion, Rea says something like the following:

> "TRAC is the software that you will be using to record the expenses you incur in your work and the hours you spend on different projects. It is a fine software program. However, it is new and it will change the way you do your work. We will look at how you record your expenses now. We will compare the way you do things now to the way you will do them in the future. We will review how you record the hours you work now and compare that to how you will record them electronically with TRAC in the future. We will explain all the procedures associated with recording your expenses and the allocation of your time to different projects."

As a review of the course plan, Rea goes over the session objectives, explaining that at the end of the session participants will be able to do the following:

1. Record expenses for mileage, accommodations, and meals in TRAC;

2. Associate expenses with the accurate project codes;

3. List the steps to follow in recording expenses in TRAC and having them approved;

4. Record hours worked; and

5. Allocate hours worked to specific project codes.

After reading through the objectives, Rea asks people whether there are any that she has missed. She asks which objectives are most important to people and why.

Rea then says that the participants will be exposed to a fair bit of information during the next few days and that the way to retain information is to use it. So the workshop will emphasize *using* the information. There will be plenty of hands-on activities in the course. Specifically, during the workshop, people will perform the same tasks they will do at work after the workshop. During the course, participants will complete mock-up reports. To help with the transition from the workshop to the workplace, Rea explains that participants will be provided with a manual containing detailed explanations of all steps to be taken and that they will become familiar with this manual by using it during the workshop.

She explains that people have different levels of knowledge and skills about software. As a result they will learn TRAC at different speeds. She promises to not leave anyone behind. She asks participants to speak up when they are having trouble so that she will be able to help. When teaching a class in which she anticipates that several people will have problems, Rea brings along coaches who can sit with participants and help them, one-on-one.

Rea adds that the course does not cover everything about TRAC. She says that she will explain key aspects of the software to ensure that people can use them and that the course will build fundamental skills and knowledge. With this strong foundation, participants will be able to increase their skills as required later on the job.

Next, Rea distributes copies of the participant manual and starts working through it page by page. She takes care to have everyone's undivided attention when she explains steps for using the software. She breaks down the content of the course into small groupings of steps. She demonstrates each step and ensures that the participants have time to practice after a few of the steps, using the manual as a reference.

Rea places every software feature and every exercise in the context of the learner. For example, when teaching people to locate project codes, she explains the importance of getting project codes right and illustrates this by giving an example of the problems that can be created if someone misallocates project codes.

We have gone much further with Rea's introduction than with Morris Richards.' In fact, Richards may know more about the software than Rea; however, he did not introduce his session as well. Rea's strategy was deliberate. She made the introduction relevant and nonthreatening to the participants. She established a learning climate. She related the course content to the work that the participants will perform on the job.

If you were asked to introduce a session about TRAC or any other technical training topic, how would you do it? Some of the more effective approaches to introducing technical training are described below.

Effective Approaches to Technical Training

If you would like to use some of Rea's techniques, here is a list. A few of her techniques are left out intentionally; you are invited to find them in Rea's introduction above.

1. Rea sets up the training room well in advance. As soon as participants arrive, she is ready to greet them and to engage in small talk that will elicit useful information. Her actions help to put people at ease and to create bonds between her and the participants. This helps to ensure participant involvement and participation during the course.

2. She explains in simple terms and is careful to avoid jargon. For example, she explains the acronym TRAC. She asks what people have heard about TRAC so that she can address any misconceptions they may have about it.

3. Rea articulates her commitment to working with participants to help them learn to use TRAC in their work. More importantly, she follows through on her commitment by placing the training in the context of how learners will use the software on the job.

4. Rea is realistic about her role as an instructor. She says that she will help the participants to learn, making it clear that participants are responsible for their own learning.

5. Rea creates a climate that is conducive to learning. She does this by explaining what she will do to help people to learn during the session. She acknowledges that they will forget some of what they hear, and she explains the role of the participant manual in helping them to refresh their memories of how to use TRAC after the training session.

6. By asking questions and listening intently, Rea establishes that the emphasis is on what participants say, think, and learn, not on what she says.

7. Rea is positive about the software and about its ability to help participants do specific tasks when they return to work after the training session. Her positive approach works wonders to gain credibility with participants. She calls TRAC a "fine" software program. She helps participants see "what's in it for them."

8. Rea acknowledges that it will take time for participants to learn to use TRAC. She promises to take the time needed to ensure that participants learn to use the software. This helps to put uptight participants at ease.

9. Rea has learned the business processes associated with TRAC. She integrates them into her training session. In talking about the procedures for approval of expenses and in helping people locate correct financial codes, Rea has moved into explaining work processes. This helps galvanize participants' interest. It also helps to ensure there is a smooth flow from classroom to workplace.

10. By placing exercises in the context of the work that will be performed, Rea makes it easier for participants to link what she is saying to what they do on the job. This links what they know now and what they will be learning. In addition, she helps learners to visualize when and how they will use the software. These images and subsequent practice with TRAC help to move information into the participants' long-term memories.

11. Rea helps people to see TRAC's relevance to their work. One way she does this is by reviewing the objectives and asking people to state what is most important for them, personally.

12. Rea does not try to tell people everything about TRAC. She sticks to the main points. Success with the main areas builds participants' competence and confidence. She knows that a confident learner succeeds. She knows that this confidence will continue after the classroom training. It will lead learners to think they can succeed—and to find ways to achieve the image they have of themselves as successful TRAC users.

Designing and Conducting Technical Training

Having stand-up delivery skills is critical, but it is only part of the package. Much of what Rea did to make her session successful was mapped out well in advance. A well-designed training program is the result of serious analysis (Broadbent & Froidevaux, 1998). Consideration of such things as the reasons for the training, participants' expectations, the work performed by participants, and approaches that have succeeded in the past anchors the training in the participants' reality. Technical training works when instructors leave their reality and walk in the participants' shoes—with people who have minimal knowledge of the topic being taught and do not have confidence about their ability to learn new knowledge, tools, and processes.

Qualities of Effective Training Designers

Designers of effective technical training have several winning attributes that can be classified as personal habits, leadership, political savvy, and design skills.

Personal Habits

The following are positive personal habits of successful technical training designers.

Patience. Listen intently and understand the positions of others. Understand that management and information technology (IT) specialists tend to become embroiled in animated discussions about budgets, timelines, and software functionality. When this happens, training may be placed on the back burner—at least for awhile.

Teamwork. Create synergy. Collaborate with all stakeholders. When management and IT folks seem to attach very little importance to training and you need to move ahead with your design, bite your tongue and offer to help them. For example, you might offer to analyze business processes. This will give you insight into design issues and make you a valuable member of the software development team.

Proactivity. Make things happen. When management and IT staff members are preoccupied with their own problems, maintain your design focus and momentum. Hold needs-assessment meetings, develop objectives, and do whatever else is required. Don't wait for others.

Critical Judgment. Don't assume anything. Check your information. Check your sources. When you are ready to interpret information you have received, consider alternative interpretations.

Leadership

Leadership is an especially important quality for designers of technical training. Here are some examples of ways to lead effectively:

Broadcast the Importance of Training. Make it clear that technical training is a key component in introducing new software successfully. Have training placed on the agenda of regular planning meetings. Integrate training into the project work plan.

Be Systematic. Use a training design system such as ADDIE (analysis, design, development, implementation, and evaluation). Information technology people understand a systematic approach to work. Explain your process to them and look for ways to integrate it with the software development processes.

Remain Task Oriented. Plan your work and work your plan. Conduct your needs analysis. Distribute your findings. Incorporate comments. Gain management sign-off. Move forward to the next phase, in a timely fashion, as planned.

Foster Clear Communication. Explain clearly, in writing and at meetings, your approach to designing the training. Explain the design process and its benefits to everyone who will listen. Prepare short "news releases" and presentations to convey your message.

Develop Project Guidelines. Capture and explain roles, relationships, and high-level layout issues in a clearly written work plan. Consult with stakeholders on the format of training materials, prepare an explanatory document, engage people in a dialogue about the guidelines, finalize the guidelines, and stick to the standards you have helped set. If you need to make revisions, do it in consultation with stakeholders.

Political Savvy

Effective technical training designers have political savvy and may demonstrate the following guidelines:

Don't Pre-Empt Management. Management is responsible for training. Although events may lead you to take command of training, always keep management closely involved. For example, when writing about training development, include other material written from a management perspective.

Analyze Needs Thoroughly. Gather data on such areas as the reasons for training, the backgrounds of the participants, the work they perform, the documents they use, standards for performance, and current levels of performance. Short, focused meetings with key people will reveal the information you require to analyze training needs.

Analyze Business Processes. Determine how the new knowledge, tools, processes, and software change the way people do their work. Work with decision makers to chart the flow of work before and after the software or other change is introduced. Map the work processes with flow-chart software.

Deal with Resistance. Identify reasons for resistance and deal with them during the training. In the training materials, explain very clearly the benefits of the new knowledge, tools, processes, and software. At the beginning of a course have participants identify their concerns, and address these concerns throughout the course.

Focus on Work Performed. Teach people how to use the new information to do their jobs. Stick to the essentials—what people need to learn to do their work. For example, explain how new software fits into the business process through flow charts.

Design Skills

Above all, effective technical trainers have finely honed design skills. Here are examples of some of the clever things they do:

Keep It Simple. Follow rules of clear writing. Keep sentences short. Use active verbs. Leave plenty of white space in printed materials so that they are easy to read and there is room for notes.

Use Features of Word Processing Software. Word processing templates, existing or custom-designed, will help you do your work consistently and quickly. Many of the most popular word processing programs include templates that you can use to guide you in preparing short, six-panel job aids, letters, brochures, and so forth.

Consider Electronic Tools. Electronic performance support systems (EPSSs) exist to help design training. Several firms have developed software tools to lead you through a systematic instructional design process to help you make good decisions and to save time.

Learn to Use the Software Yourself. If subject-matter experts are preoccupied with software development or other activities, don't wait for them to explain the new processes and software to you. Roll up your sleeves and teach yourself. If you rely on others to teach you, they might never get around to it. When teaching yourself the new processes and software, identify issues that new learners will face and address them in the instructional materials you design.

Use New Approaches to Instruction.   Check out mentoring, Web-based training (WBT), and technology-assisted instruction, for example. Depending on your budget and other factors such as learner preferences, you might find that the training program you are designing presents an opportunity to try something new. Technology-assisted instruction and mentoring might be particularly helpful in supporting classroom instruction.

Use Traditional Methods.   Don't rule out traditional instructional methods. Classroom instruction provides an opportunity to bring together managers, officers, and support staff and to give them the same message. You can combine new and traditional methods of instruction in one program.

Provide Training to All Who Need It.   Identify all parties who will use the new knowledge, tools, processes, and software and find out their particular training needs. Managers, officers, and support staff may perform different tasks and will therefore need different training.

Emphasize Skill Building.   Teach people how to fish, rather than giving them fish. For example, show the participants what is available in the software's "help" files and give them an opportunity to access and learn to use those files during the training session.

CONCLUSION

The best approach to technical training is a planned, analytical approach— one that emphasizes learning and frames the training in the context of new knowledge, tools, work processes, and software applications. The purpose of technical training must be to help the participants learn to use the new knowledge, tools, processes, and software so they will be capable of working more effectively. Technical training that simply explains how software functions has limited value. The emphasis should be on learning new work processes.

It also is important to engage managers and IT staff members in the training process. Business process experts, change management champions, software developers, testers, and managers all know that effective training is critical for implementing workplace innovations. Unfortunately, training often is organized at the last minute when harried software developers are asked to create software training sessions just when they are preoccupied with debugging the system. The best approach is for experienced training designers to work closely with software developers to design the training. Everyone involved benefits from close collaboration between developers and training professionals.

Delivery skills also are important for effective technical training. The session introduction sets the tone for the entire course. Software training is used as an example in this article; however, the approach presented here applies equally well to other technical training applications, such as safety training or labor relations training. These recommendations are not "one-size-fits-all." Tailor these ideas to your own situation. In doing so you will, no doubt, develop some new approaches.

In the end, successful technical training results from a systematically planned process that emphasizes helping people learn new knowledge, tools, processes, and software in the context of their day-to-day work.

References

Broadbent, B., & Froidevaux, L. (1998). Training-needs analysis: A broad view. In *The 1998 annual: Volume 1, training*. San Francisco, CA: Jossey-Bass/Pfeiffer.

The Standish Group. (1995). Chaos. *Standishgroup.com/chaos.html.*

Training & Development. (1998, January). State of the industry report. Author.

Brooke Broadbent *is an international management consultant with Pricewater-houseCoopers, specializing in crafting and conducting results-oriented innovative approaches to learning and managing. He has published over two dozen articles in the training field and is a contributing editor to ASTD's* Technical Training *magazine. He has a master's degree in adult education from the Université du Québec.*

CONTRIBUTORS

Erica Nagel Allgood
Enhanced Training & Development
6660 Delmonico Drive, Suite D111
Colorado Springs, CO 80919
(719) 577-6868
fax: (719) 579-9382
e-mail: etd@enhancedtngdev.com

Brooke Broadbent
PricewaterhouseCoopers
99 Bank Street, Suite 800
Ottawa, Ontario K1P 1E4
CANADA
(613) 237-3702
fax: (613) 237-3963
e-mail: brooke.broadbent@ca.
  pwcglobal.com
URL: www.brookebroadbent.
  mondenet.com

Heidi A. Campbell
University of Edinburgh
New College–Mound Place
Edinburgh EH1 2LX
SCOTLAND
011-44-131-650-8945
fax: 011-44-131-650-6579
e-mail: Heidi.Campbell@ed.ac.uk

Terry Carlyle
Enhanced Training & Development
6660 Delmonico Drive, Suite D111
Colorado Springs, CO 80919
(719) 577-6868
fax: (719) 579-9382
e-mail: etd@enhancedtngdev.com

Marlene Caroselli, Ed.D.
Center for Professional Development
324 Latona Road, Suite 6B
Rochester, NY 14626-2714
(716) 227-6512
(800) 876-4636 (for book orders)
fax: (716) 227-6191
e-mail: mccpd@aol.com

Sarah Bartholomew Ellerbee
Department of Political Science
Valdosta State University
Valdosta, GA 31698
(912) 245-2236

Judith A. Free
19012 Point Lookout Road
Lexington Park, MD 20653
(301) 862-3510
fax: (301) 757-1799
e-mail: ptbs@erols.com

Paul L. Garavaglia
57 Dennison Street
Oxford, MI 48371
(248) 969-4920
fax: (248) 969-2342
e-mail: ADDIEGroup@aol.com

Michael A. Gass
Professor and Browne Centre Director
University of New Hampshire
Durham, NH 03824
(603) 862-2024
e-mail: mgass@christa.unh.edu

Brian Gordon
6152 West Townley Road
Glendale, AZ 85302
(602) 792-3359
e-mail: briangordon@livetolearn.
com
URL: www.livetolearn.com

Brandon Hall
Multimedia & Internet Training
Newsletter
1623 Edmonton Avenue
Sunnyvale, CA 94087
(408) 736-2335
fax: (408) 736-9425
e-mail: Brandon@brandon-hall.com

Lois B. Hart, Ed.D.
President, Leadership Dynamics
10951 Isabelle Road
Lafayette, CO 80026
(303) 666-4046
fax: (303) 666-4074
e-mail: lhart@seqnet.net

Cher Holton, Ph.D.
The Holton Consulting Group, Inc.
4704 Little Falls Drive, Suite 300
Raleigh, NC 27609
(919) 783-7088
(800) 336-3940
fax: (919) 781-2218
e-mail: DrCher@aol.com

H.B. Karp
Personal Growth Systems
4932 Barn Swallow Drive
Chesapeake, VA 23321
(757) 488-3536
e-mail: pgshank@aol.com

Betty Jo Licata, Ph.D.
Dean and Professor of Management
Williamson College of Business
Administration
Youngstown State University
One University Plaza
Youngstown, OH 44555
(330) 742-2737
fax: (330) 742-1459
e-mail: bjlicata@cc.ysu.edu

Anne M. McMahon, Ph.D.
Professor of Management
Williamson College of Business
Administration
Youngstown State University
One University Plaza
Youngstown, OH 44555
(330) 742-3071
fax: (330) 742-1459
e-mail: ammcmaho@cc.ysu.edu

Rita S. Mehegan
Vice President, Training and Quality
First Data Merchant Services
4000 Coral Ridge Drive
Coral Springs, FL 33065
(954) 857-7524
fax: (954) 857-7317
e-mail: rita.mehegan@firstdata.com

Don Morrison
4009 Bridgeport Way West, Suite E
Tacoma, WA 98466
(253) 565-6253
fax: (253) 565-2575
e-mail: srm@lgi-srm.com; lgi@lgi.org

John E. Oliver, Ph.D.
Department of Management and
  Information Systems
Valdosta State University
Valdosta, GA 31698
  (912) 245-2236
  fax: (912) 245-6498
  e-mail: joliver@valdosta.edu

S. Andrew Ostapski, J.D.
Department of Management and
  Information Systems
Valdosta State University
Valdosta, GA 31698
  (912) 245-2236

Robert C. Preziosi
School of Business and
  Entrepreneurship
3100 S.W. 9th Avenue
Ft. Lauderdale, FL 33315
  (954) 262-5111
  fax: (954) 262-3965

Simon Priest, Ph.D.
Principle, eXperientia
P.O. Box 884
Lakebay, WA 98349
  (253) 884-6446
  e-mail: spriest@ups.edu

Debra Reed
President
D.K. Reed Consulting
7458 Granada Alcove
Cottage Grove, MN 55016
  (651) 458-8162
  fax: (651) 459-7062
  e-mail: debrareed@juno.com

A. Carol Rusaw
Assistant Professor, Department of
  Communications
University of Southwestern Louisiana
Lafayette, LA 70504
  (318) 482-6932
  fax: (318) 482-6104

C. Louise Sellaro, D.B.A.
Professor of Management
Williamson College of Business
  Administration
Youngstown State University
One University Plaza
Youngstown, OH 44555
  (330) 742-3071
  fax: (330) 742-1459
  e-mail: clsellar@cc.ysu.edu

Patti Shank, M.A. Ed.
Insight Ed
18698 East Berry Drive
Aurora, CO 80015-5136
  (303) 699-9377
  fax: (303) 699-9377
  e-mail: poshank@pobox.com
  URL: www.insighted.cnchost.com

Steve Sphar
2870 Third Avenue
Sacramento, CA 95818
  (916) 731-4851
  e-mail: sphar@pacbell.net

Elizabeth N. Treher, Ph.D.
The Learning Key, Inc.
58 West Bridge Street
New Hope, PA 18938
  (800) 465-7005
  e-mail: entreher@voicenet.com
  URL: www.thelearningkey.com

Augustus Walker
28 Tamanaco Drive
Charlestown, RI 02813
(401) 364-7177
e-mail: guswalk@netsense.net

Joe Willmore
President
Willmore Consulting Group
5007 Mignonette Court
Annandale, VA 22003-4050
(703) 855-4634
fax: (703) 323-5781
e-mail: Willmore@juno.com

Janet Winchester-Silbaugh
51 Pinon Heights
Sandia Park, NM 87047
(505) 286-2210
fax: (505) 286-2211
e-mail: silbaugh@ccvp.com

Robert Younglove
PATH Associates
8 Barranco Court
Towson, MD 21204
(410) 821-0538
fax: (410) 821-0538

Joanne R. Zukowski
The University of North Carolina
at Pembroke
Regional Center for Economic,
Community, & Professional
Development
P.O. Box 1510
Pembroke, NC 28372-1510
(910) 521-6198
fax: (910) 521-6550
e-mail: zukowski@nat.uncp.edu

Contents of the Companion Volume, The 2000 Annual: Volume 2, Consulting

---

*See Experiential Learning Activities Categories, p. 7, for an explanation of the numbering system.

**Topic is "cutting edge."

NOTES

NOTES

NOTES

NOTES

NOTES

NOTES

NOTES